Robert William Dale

The Jewish Temple and the Christian Church

A Series of Discourses on the Epistle to the Hebrews. Tenth Edition

Robert William Dale

The Jewish Temple and the Christian Church
A Series of Discourses on the Epistle to the Hebrews. Tenth Edition

ISBN/EAN: 9783337136291

Printed in Europe, USA, Canada, Australia, Japan

Cover: Foto ©Lupo / pixelio.de

More available books at **www.hansebooks.com**

THE JEWISH TEMPLE

AND

THE CHRISTIAN CHURCH

A Series of Discourses on the Epistle to the Hebrews

BY

R. W. DALE, LL.D.

Author of "The Epistle to the Ephesians," "Laws of Christ for Common Life,
"The Atonement," etc.

TENTH EDITION

London
HODDER AND STOUGHTON
27, PATERNOSTER ROW

MDCCCXCVI.

Printed by Hazell, Watson, & Viney, Ld., London and Aylesbury.

PREFACE TO SECOND EDITION.

These Discourses were delivered several years ago in the ordinary course of my ministry.

The Notes which I have added to this new Edition are intended, like the Discourses themselves, not for scholars, but for ordinary Christian people to whom learned commentaries are inaccessible or useless. I have not attempted either to correct every word or phrase which seemed to me inaccurately translated in our English Authorised Version, nor to discuss the conflicting interpretations which exegetical scholars have given of difficult passages.

R. W. D.

Christmas, 1870.

CONTENTS.

	PAGE
Introductory	1
The Son and the Prophets	11
The Son and the Angels	23
Drifting from Christ	34
The Dignity of Man	43
Christ Perfected through Sufferings	57
The Humanity of Christ	66
The Sin in the Wilderness	74
The Rest of God	81
The Sympathy of Christ	88
The Priesthood of Christ	97
Ignorance and Apostasy	109
Hopefulness	124
Melchizedek	136
What is a Type?	153
The New Covenant	163
The Old Sanctuary	172
Jewish Sacrifices	186
Access to God	205
The Testament	215

Contents.

	PAGE
Atonement	221
The Great Appeal	231
The Cloud of Witnesses	242
Chastisement	255
Mount Sinai and Mount Sion	264
Precepts	276
Conclusion	286
Notes	293

INTRODUCTORY.

The Epistle to the Hebrews is a letter with no Signature and with no Direction. The title, as it stands in our English Bible, is no part of the original document; and the two questions, By whom was it written? and To whom was it addressed? have given rise to intricate and protracted controversies.

One scholar maintains that it was written to the Churches of Galatia; another, that it was written to the Church at Thessalonica; another, that it was written to the Church at Corinth; another, that it was written to the Church at Rome; another, that it was written to a Church in Spain; another, that it was written to Jewish Christians scattered over Asia Minor; while the common, and, as I believe, the true opinion, the grounds of which I shall adduce presently, is that it was written to Jewish Christians living in Palestine.

The question of the authorship is more perplexing still. Did St. Paul write the Epistle as it stands, or did he write it in Hebrew and place it in the hands of one of his beloved companions for translation? Or did he supply the thoughts and leave his friend to cast them into what form he thought best? Or shall we believe, with Tertullian, that Barnabas was the author? Or, with some of the early Latin Churches, that the Epistle was written by Clement of Rome? Or, with Luther and a long line of German scholars, that it was written by Apollos? Or shall we concede the honour to Aquila, who taught Apollos himself the way of God more perfectly? Or to Silas, St. Paul's companion in work and suffering?

The discussion of the claims of all these various hypotheses could hardly be rendered intelligible to a popular audience. What I propose to do, before beginning to expound the contents of the Epistle, is to state as briefly and simply as possible, the evidence for and against the Pauline authorship, and then, the evidence, conclusive evidence, as I think, for believing that the Epistle was addressed to Christian Jews in Palestine.

I.

On the question of the Pauline authorship, I shall not quote the passages which preserve to us the testimonies and opinions of the ancient Fathers, but shall indicate how the evidence seems to lie.

(1.) *In the Church of Alexandria*, which was early famous for its scholars and grammarians, we have the express testimony of Pantænus, about the year 180, in favour of St. Paul. A few years later, we have the testimony of Clement to the same effect, though he believed that Paul wrote in Hebrew, and that Luke translated what he had written into Greek. A few years later still, Origen seems to say that the thoughts were St. Paul's, but that the form and language of the Epistle were from another hand: and he tells us that a tradition existed in the Alexandrian Church that Clement of Rome or Luke the Evangelist was the actual author.

(2.) *In the Eastern Church* we have no testimony to the authorship earlier than the middle of the third century. Paul of Samosata, Bishop of Antioch in 264; Methodius, Bishop of Olympus in Lycia, and afterwards Bishop of Tyre about 290; and Archelaus, Bishop of Mesopotamia a few years later, ascribe the Epistle to St. Paul. But the most important testimony is that of Eusebius, Bishop of Cæsarea at the commencement of the fourth century. From his writings it appears that in the East the all but universal opinion was in favour of the Pauline authorship, which he accepted himself, though he thought that St. Paul wrote in Hebrew and that probably Clement of Rome translated the Epistle into Greek.

In Alexandria, then, and throughout the East, St. Paul was regarded in the earliest times as the real author, although certain peculiarities in the style suggested to scholars and grammarians the hypothesis that some other hand composed the Epistle as it stands, translating it from Hebrew into Greek, or even expanding and modifying its original contents.

(3.) *In the Western Church* the evidence is of a very different complexion. Photius (A.D. 858) quotes the authority of Stephen Gobar, a writer belonging to the sixth century, to the effect that Irenæus, Bishop of Lyons, at the close of the second century, and Hippolytus, one of his pupils, did not acknowledge the Pauline authorship. In Carthage, Tertullian, at the beginning of the third century cites the Epistle as the work of Barnabas, and his manner proves that this was the common opinion.

Caius, a Roman presbyter belonging to the early part of the third century, did not include the Epistle to the Hebrews among the writings of St. Paul. Cyprian, Bishop of Carthage in the middle of the third century, appears to be fairly appealed to on the same side. The testimony of Jerome early in the fifth century, and the testimony of Augustine about the same time, indicate that even then the Epistle to the Hebrews had not, in the Latin Church, secured a firm place among St. Paul's acknowledged writings.

If, as I think is practically certain, the Epistle was addressed to Jewish Christians in Palestine, the Western Churches might very naturally be ill-informed concerning its authorship; and the testimony of Alexandria and of the East would, in my judgment, outweigh the testimony of Rome and Carthage. It is also, I think, very probable that the Roman Church, whose influence would determine the general opinion of the West, may have hesitated to acknowledge that the Epistle was written by St. Paul, on account of the striking contrast between its doctrinal teaching and the teaching of the Epistle to the Romans. In the eighth chapter of the Romans the power of Divine grace is maintained with a resoluteness of conviction and an exultation of feeling unparalleled in the New Testament Scriptures. The steadfastness of God's love, the immovableness of his purpose to save all that believe, the victorious energy of the Holy Ghost, are so exhibited, that to fall away from Christ seems impossible; it appears inconceivable that the links of the golden chain of divine calling, justification, and final glory should ever be broken. God's *idea* in relation to all that trust in Christ is presented in the simplest and most absolute form; life and death, angels, principalities, and powers, things present, things to come, height, depth, and the whole creation, are defied to separate the soul of the true Christian from the love of God in Christ Jesus our Lord. In the Epistle to the Hebrews the other and human side of the truth is presented. Tribulation, distress, persecution, had come upon the Jewish Churches, and courage was failing, faith was vacillating; they are warned of the possibility of drifting away from what they had heard and believed in former days, and are threatened with certain judgment and fiery indignation if they are guilty of apostasy. Nor, as far as I have noticed, is there any hint or trace throughout the Epistle of those exalted views of the constraining power of Divine grace which are so prominent in the acknowledged writings of St. Paul, and which were partly the result of the peculiarities of his own conversion and his sublimely vigorous spiritual life. There is no real contradiction between the two Epistles, but it was very natural for the Christians of Rome, if they were ill-informed about the authorship of the Epistle of the Hebrews, to hesitate in believing that it was written by the Apostle who had written to themselves.

These two considerations—the distance of Rome from Palestine, and the doctrinal contents of the Epistle—would lead me to estimate very lightly the testimony of the Roman Church against the Pauline authorship, and to accept the favourable testimony of Alexandria and the East, *but for one remarkable fact.* Clement of Rome, at the close of the first century, in his well-known Epistle to the Church at Corinth, quotes repeatedly from this Epistle to the Hebrews, though without naming the author; it seems to me extremely improbable that if St. Paul really wrote it, Clement should have been ignorant of the fact; and if Clement believed it to be St. Paul's, it is difficult to understand how the adverse opinion rose up and became so strong in the Church of which he was the bishop. The external evidence, therefore, leaves the whole question of the authorship in doubt.

The evidence arising from the style and from peculiarities of expression is equally inconclusive. One of the opponents of the Pauline authorship has diligently collected between one hundred and ten and one hundred and twenty words which occur in this Epistle, and are not found in any of St. Paul's acknowledged writings. A scholar on the other side, to cancel the force of this argument, has, with equal diligence, collected from the first Epistle to the Corinthians, which everybody acknowledges to be St. Paul's, two hundred and thirty words which are not found in any other of his epistles. A list of words is given on the one side, which are used in this Epistle in a sense in which Paul never uses them: another list is given on the other side, of words which occur nowhere in the New Testament except in this Epistle and in the acknowledged writings of St. Paul, or which, if used by other New Testament writers, are used in a different sense. The internal evidence of this kind is as unsatisfactory as the evidence derived from external sources.

I believe that the only conclusion possible is, that the materials for determining the question have disappeared, and that the authorship of the Epistle to the Hebrews must remain uncertain. There is no adequate evidence that St. Paul wrote it, and the evidence for any other name is still less satisfactory. The claim on behalf of Apollos, was never made, I think, till it was suggested by Luther; and the arguments by which it is supported seem to me of the flimsiest character.

II.

That the Epistle was addressed to the Christians of a particular church, or at least to those living in a particular country, and not to Christians generally, is proved by the solitary passage in xiii. 23: "Know ye that our brother Timothy is set at liberty; with whom, if he come shortly, I will see you." That it was addressed to Jewish converts only, is proved by the general contents of the Epistle. That it was addressed to Jewish converts in Palestine is proved by the fact implied throughout, that the persons for whom it was intended were under the immediate and powerful influence of the ritual worship still maintained in the Temple. St. Paul was engaged in incessant controversies with Jewish teachers scattered over the Roman world. But with them, whether we derive our information from the Acts of the Apostles, or from his Epistles to the Romans, Corinthians, Galatians, or Colossians, the subjects of dispute were the permanence and universal obligation of circumcision and of the laws relating to food and the like : not a word is ever said about the priesthood or the sacrifices. The Jewish converts in distant countries, who were seldom able to be present at the Temple, were in no danger of having their imagination fired, and their sympathies entangled, by the pomp and mystery of the ceremonial worship. But the persons to whom this Epistle was written were evidently in a very different position : the ancient system of worship retained a powerful hold upon them ; and this can be accounted for only by supposing that they were actually living in Palestine, and were the constant or frequent witnesses of the ancient rites. Nor is there any reason to believe that the Jewish element so predominated in any church out of Palestine as to account for an Epistle like this being addressed to it.

The only other hypothesis which has any show of probability is that the Epistle was addressed to the Church at Alexandria. In that city there had existed for three centuries a powerful Jewish colony; and a Jewish temple was built at Leontopolis (B.C. 161). It is alleged on behalf of the claims of Alexandria as against those of Palestine—

(1) That the arguments of the Epistle pre-suppose a power in its readers to appreciate the spiritualising and allegorical method of interpreting the Old Testament which distinguished the Alexandrian school of Jewish theologians.

To this it may be replied that no such peculiarity in the method of treating the Old Testament can be pointed out in this Epistle as to render it necessary to suppose that its original readers had received Alexandrian culture. There is less of "allegory" in the Epistle to the Hebrews than in the Epistle to the Galatians.

(2) That, had it been written to Jews in Palestine (*a*) the Old Testament quotations would have been made from the Hebrew text, not from the Septuagint; and (*b*) the Epistle itself would not have been written in Greek.

But in reply to (*b*), it may be urged that Hellenistic Greek was commonly understood in Palestine itself and throughout Western Asia; and that—as the Epistle was no doubt intended for the instruction of the Jews generally, though addressed in the first instance to the Jewish Christians of a particular city or country—Hellenistic Greek was the fittest language to write it in. The other argument (*a*) is of no weight, inasmuch as the Palestinian Jews themselves admitted the divine authority of the Septuagint version.

If the Epistle was addressed to one of the churches of Palestine, the troubles which came upon that country at the close of the first century, quite account for the fact that the tradition of the authorship has been lost, and that we have to determine who its original readers were, mainly by internal evidence; but had it been addressed to the Church at Alexandria, it is hard to understand how any uncertainty could have arisen on either of these points. Surely, if it had been sent originally to their own church, the Alexandrian fathers would have found some trace of the fact, but they make no claim. The opinion that the Epistle was written for the special benefit of Jewish Christians in Palestine was "held," says Dr. Davidson, "by most of the fathers, as far as we have the means of enabling us to form a judgment respecting their views of the point; by the *Alexandrian* theologians, by Eusebius, Jerome, Chrysostom, Theodoret, Theophylact, and others." *

III.

On the question whether the Epistle has a right to a place among our canonical Scriptures it is unnecessary to say much. It is quoted by Clement of Rome at the close of the first century, just as he quotes the other canonical writings—by Justin Martyr in the middle of the second century—and by the theologians of the Alexandrian Church:—it has a place in the ancient Latin and Syriac versions of the New Testament, made at the close of the second century; by the Churches of the East it was regarded not only as authoritative, but as written

---

* Davidson's Introduction to the New Testament, Vol. iii., 267.

by St. Paul. Whether an Apostle was the author of it or not, it can hardly be supposed that it would have attained this wide and early recognition, had there not been sufficient reason for believing that it was sanctioned by Apostolic authority.

Erasmus, Luther, Calvin, denied the Pauline authorship, and for a time some Lutheran divines placed this Epistle with other books about whose authority there has been controversy, by themselves at the close of the New Testament; but the distinction soon disappeared, and the Lutheran and Reformed Churches, as well as the Church of Rome, unite in acknowledging its canonicity.

That it was written in Greek, not Hebrew, hardly admits of dispute.

Try now to blot out from your memory the last eighteen hundred years of Christian and general history. Nero is Emperor of Rome, and the hatred of the Jewish nation for their foreign rulers is becoming every day more intense. Already there are signs of a fierce and bloody revolt. The magnificent prophecies of ancient days, the history of the splendid miracles which had been wrought for the deliverance of the people from their wretched and shameful bondage in Egypt, the thrilling and heroic war songs of David, and the story of the patriotic achievements of the Maccabees, are kindling to a furious and fanatical heat the passion for independence. Priests and politicians are plotting against the Roman government; and the dark, turbulent life of the whole people is sweeping forward with fierce impatience to the final tragedy of tears and blood, baffled rage and ghastly horrors, demoniacal courage and demoniacal sufferings—in which the crimes and chastisements of this wonderful race closed and culminated. At such a time the Nazarene heresy is an offence not only against the religion but against the patriotism of the nation. It divides the national strength. The Christian teachers hold back their followers from the current of revolution, and have told them to resort to flight whenever the armies of the heathen threaten the holy city. This intolerable treachery to the national cause has deepened the abhorrence with which the whole sect is regarded. Many who have been baptized into the name of Christ and have taken joyfully the spoiling of their goods for his sake, are beginning to falter They have continued to unite in the worship of the Temple and cannot endure to think of its ancient ritual being overthrown; they exult in the memory of the brief bursts of glory which have shed a transient brightness on their national history, and their hearts burn to unite with their fellow-countrymen in one last and desperate struggle against the heathen oppressor.

Imagine yourselves, if you can, agitated by these passions. Let us suppose that we are a church of Jewish believers, assembled in Jerusalem or in Cæsarea, between twenty-five and thirty years after the crucifixion of the Lord Jesus Christ. The meeting is unusually large: some are present who have almost forsaken the assemblies of the Church;—for it is known that a letter to the Christian Jews on their present dangers and duties was received by one of the elders of the Church a few days ago, and something will be said about it to-night. We have celebrated, as is our custom whenever we meet for worship, the Supper of the Lord. One of the elders rises—and I can imagine him speaking in such words as these:—

"My beloved brethren, children of Abraham, Isaac, and Jacob, and disciples of our Lord Jesus,—During the past week a brother, who has come from one of the countries of the Gentiles to visit the land which God gave to our fathers, brought to me this letter, written by one whom we know well and hold in honour for his faith, and suffering and labour—a man full of the Holy Ghost, and enriched with all knowledge and wisdom. The letter is meant for us—who are of the seed of Jacob, but who have believed that Jesus of Nazareth is the true Messiah, the Son of God, and the King of Israel. Our brother who writes it, has been sorely troubled by what he has heard of the Churches of Christ in this land. He writes to warn us of the guilt and peril of permitting ourselves to be carried back to the bondage of our old law, and he explains with wonderful depth the true purpose of the ordinances which God gave to our fathers.

"The letter is too long, my brethren, to be read through to-night; but I will tell you the substance of what it says, and will read a few passages, that you may be able to see with what anxiety and with what wisdom our holy brother, who, like ourselves, is of the stock of Abraham, pleads with us and with all our brethren. Already, some of our best scribes have begun to copy it, and in a few days we shall be able to send copies to all the churches of the saints in Galilee, Samaria, and Judea. We ourselves shall retain the handwriting of our brother, and in future meetings of the Church we shall carefully read the Epistle, and confer with each other about it. But we shall be able to understand it better if I tell you now what are the chief subjects of which it treats, and the manner in which they are treated."

If we begin our study of the Epistle by constructing for ourselves such an outline of its contents as might have followed this introduction, and imagining the impression produced by one argument and appeal after another, upon the Jewish believers who listened to them for the first time, we shall be far more likely to arrive at the true meaning of the inspired writer, than if we satisfy ourselves with reading isolated passages—no matter how carefully—in the light of the circumstances and experiences of modern times. In the Sermons on the Epistle which I am about to deliver, it will be my endeavour, first of all, to assist you to place yourselves in the actual position of the persons to whom the Epistle was originally addressed; and then to point out and illustrate the relation of what was said to them, to the temptations and controversies by which christian people are being tried and disciplined in our own days.

THE SON AND THE PROPHETS.

"God who at sundry times and in divers manners spake in time past unto the fathers by the prophets, hath in these last days spoken to us by His Son," &c.—HEBREWS i, 1-3.

IN entering upon the study of this Epistle, it is necessary to remember that the position of a Christian Jew in Apostolic times was very different from that of a Christian Gentile. If, on the one hand, the Jewish Christian derived great advantages from his possession of the ancient revelation, and from the discipline he had received under the Mosaic Law, on the other, he had difficulties of which the Gentile knew nothing. The converted heathen was never likely to sink back into heathenism. He might find it hard to overcome his old habits of falsehood, dishonesty, violence, and impurity, and might sometimes be almost ready to abandon the struggle from mere weariness and exhaustion; but he had discovered, once for all, that the popular mythology was a collection of wild and wicked fancies, that the gods he used to worship were idols, that their priests had no divine consecration, and that their temples were the homes of imposture, covetousness, and vice. Nothing but cowardice, moral weakness, or a longing for the sensual excitement of heathenism could ever make him a heathen again.

It was not so with the Christian Jew. The NEW FAITH did not contradict, but developed and perfected the OLD. He had not to separate himself from the religious observances of his countrymen, or to renounce his former religious convictions as monstrous delusions. He continued to worship in the temple and to listen to the law and the prophets in the synagogue. He still believed that the sons of Aaron were priests by divine appointment, and that the sacrifices they offered had been instituted by divine command. The Jewish sabbath was still honoured as a memorial of the rest of God after the creation of the world. Jewish feasts perpetuated the remembrance of wonderful deeds which God had wrought in the old times. Prophets and Psalmists were still acknowledged to have been divinely inspired men, and for many years their writings were the only Scriptures the church possessed. Christ Himself was a descendant of Abraham; He had been circumcised; had kept the Sabbath; had come to Jerusalem to celebrate the feasts; some of the very men to whom this Epistle was written could remember His form among the crowds of worshippers in the temple; He had eaten the Passover with His disciples immediately before the crucifixion. The Holy Spirit had descended on the Church during a great Jewish Festival. Nor had any command been given by Christ, nor any revelation made by the Holy Spirit, that the Mosaic institutions were to be abandoned. Why *should* they be abandoned? A system of religious observances, instituted by God, which had lasted for sixteen centuries, and had ministered to the holiness, and had expressed the devotion of David, and Samuel, and Elijah, and Isaiah, and Daniel, was surely intrinsically good and noble.

It was not wonderful, therefore, that as the enthusiastic patriotism of the Jewish nation increased in violence, and the growing hatred of their heathen rulers came to be associated with a growing hatred of the followers of Jesus of Nazareth, who divided and diminished the national strength,—it was not wonderful, I say, that the Jewish Christians were dismayed at the prospect of being excluded by their unconverted countrymen from the temple they so dearly loved, that they gradually began to drift back to Judaism, that their passionate love of their country and of its magnificent traditions, began to overpower their loyalty to their crucified King. It was to tell them of these dangers, to show them that they were on the very edge of apostasy, to warn them of the dreadful penalties they would incur by renouncing their faith in the Lord Jesus, that this Epistle was written.

There was another object which the Epistle was intended to accomplish. The final overthrow of the civil and ecclesiastical polity of Judaism was fast approaching, and the Jewish Christians who clung to it as a divine institution—which it was,—and who thought it was intended to be permanent—which it was not,—were likely to be perplexed and confounded by the great catastrophe. They are here instructed in the imperfect character and transitory purpose of the whole system, and are prepared for the shock of seeing all their ancient institutions overthrown. The Epistle is a doctrinal exposition, written not for a scientific but for a practical purpose, of the relations between the Old Faith and the New, between THE JEWISH TEMPLE AND THE CHRISTIAN CHURCH.

We may be strengthened in our own fidelity to the Lord Jesus by the exhortations contained in this Epistle to patient continuance in well-doing; and the study of the relations between Christianity and Judaism may increase our knowledge of both.

I

Both Jew and Christian acknowledged that *God spake in time past to the fathers by—or in—the prophets;* but the writer, without developing a formal contrast, suggests several important points of difference between the earlier revelation of God and that which had been made when the old dispensation was coming to a close.

(1) The earlier revelation was given in "fragments," the expression "*sundry times*" referring not to the successive ages over which the ancient revelation was spread, but to the numerous portions into which it was broken up. Moses, David, Isaiah, received only partial and imperfect disclosures of the divine will; one aspect of truth was made known through one prophet, another through another. But in Christ dwelt all the fulness of the Godhead bodily. He was God manifest in the flesh. In Him are hid all the treasures of wisdom and knowledge. The teaching of the Apostles does but illustrate the glory of Christ's character, the dignity of His person, the purpose and the results of His mission. He that hath seen Christ hath seen the Father.

2) The variety of the forms by which God had made

Himself known in past times indicated that by none of them could He fully reveal Himself. He spake to the fathers "*in divers manners*"—to Samuel in a voice which came to him while he slept; to Elijah by a strong wind which rent the mountains, and brake in pieces the rocks before the Lord, by an earthquake, by fire, by a still small voice; to Isaiah by a glorious vision, in which the prophet saw the Seraphim bowing before the Throne, and heard them crying, "Holy, Holy, Holy, Lord God of Hosts." These voices, symbols, visions, were transient. They revealed God imperfectly. Now He has spoken to us by His Son—a Living Person—"the brightness of His glory and the express image of His Person."

II.

The remaining verses speak of the original and essential glory of Christ, of His creation and preservation of the universe, of the atonement He effected for human sin, of the new greatness He has acquired by His sufferings and death.

(1) Human language is baffled in the attempt to express, human thought in the attempt to conceive, the interior life and relations of the blessed Trinity. The metaphors employed in Holy Scripture can only be most inadequate representations of the actual truth. Their variety warns us that the mystery remains unrevealed. But, though various, they are harmonious and consistent, and one idea runs through them all,—*God is made known to His creatures through the Son*. The secret thoughts and passions and purposes of our souls assume a definite form, and are revealed to our fellow men in our words; and the Son is "the WORD" of God. A luminous body is perceived by the splendour which streams forth from it, and the Son is the ray or "*brightness of* the Father's *glory*."

But lest it should be supposed that the Son is a merely transitory effulgence of the divine glory, constantly originating and constantly perishing, (although the form of the Greek word corresponding to "brightness" in our version is itself a protection against that error), the writer goes on to say that He is the "*express image of* the Father's *Person*." The substantial being which the Father has, the Son has also; He is Light of Light, but also very God of very God; a divine Person, not merely a divine Power; possessing in Himself the attributes of the Father, and not merely manifesting those attributes; by Him God is known to us, and He is Himself God over all, blessed for evermore.

(2) It is affirmed that *by Him " God made the worlds."* This is not the only place in the New Testament in which creation is ascribed to Christ. St. John declares that " all things were made by Him, and without Him was nothing made that was made ;"* St. Paul, that " by Him were all things created, that are in heaven and that are in earth, visible and invisible, whether they be thrones, or dominions, or principalities, or powers; all things were created by Him and for Him."† And *" He upholds all things by the word of His power."*

. (3) He *effected a cleansing from sin.* Remember that this writer was not addressing philosophers of the nineteenth century, and that he was not using their language. He was addressing Jews. He used Jewish words, and, of course, in the sense in which Jews used them, for he intended to be understood. He knew how they would understand this word which we have translated " purged ;" that they would think at once of the sacrifices of the Jewish law and of the cleansing from impurity which those sacrifices effected. How impossible it is that he should have been thinking merely of the purification of the soul of man by instruction, by example, by spiritual influences, will become clearer as we continue our study of the Epistle.

Consider now what has been said concerning the greatness and glory of Christ. It has been declared that the Lord Jesus, in whom God has spoken to us, and whose sufferings atoned for our sins, created the heavens and the earth. His history did not commence when He was born in Bethlehem. He made every shining planet and every burning sun—this world of ours and the world in which the angels dwell, with its stainless purity and unfading splendour. And but for Him all

* John i, 3.   † Col. i, 10.

things would sink back into chaos and night. The burden of the creation rests on Him from age to age. He upholds the material universe, upholds the universe of holy creatures, upholds *all things*, not by laborious effort, not by the strength of His right arm, but "*by the word of His power.*" "The heavens declare *His* glory and the firmament showeth his handiwork." "Every creature which is in heaven, and on the earth and under the earth, and such as are in the sea, and all that are in them," may be heard saying, not in Apocalyptic vision merely, but day by day, through all the ages of their existence, "Blessing, and honour, and glory, and power, be unto Him that sitteth on the throne, and unto the Lamb for ever and ever," for "by Him were all things created," "and by Him all things consist."

When we are oppressed by the sense of guilt, and our faith in God's willingness to forgive falters, we should not expect peace from thinking merely of the physical tortures or the mental anguish of the Great Sacrifice for the sins of the world, as if mere suffering could be set over against sin; but should remember that He who atoned for human transgressions is the brightness of the Father's glory, and the express image of His person, made the worlds at first, and upholds them still. The Jewish worshipper was not concerned about the keenness of the pain endured by the victim he brought to the altar; his only anxiety was that the victim should be of the right kind, free from imperfection, and that it should be offered according to the divinely appointed ritual. And our consciences will find little rest while we think only of the agony of Christ; what we need to remember is, that He who stoops to atone for our sins is the Creator and Moral Ruler of the Universe.

(4) Christ is made "*heir of all things,*" and is seated on "*the right hand of* God;"—Christ who stood in the judgment-hall of Pilate, and whose body lay in Joseph's tomb. He did not cast aside the vesture of humanity when the day of His coronation came, but he stands among the hosts of heaven in His complex nature, man as well as God. With His human body, transfigured and glorified, He ascended into heaven. Nor did that intellect perish which was first instructed by the teaching

of His mother, a Jewish peasant—which had to learn, as you and I learnt, first the wisdom of childhood and then the wisdom of youth—which once employed itself in teaching a few peasants and fishermen the simplest religious truths;—that very intellect, expanded, strengthened, He has now. The heart which was once open to the assaults of the devil, and had to struggle against temptation in the wilderness—which was worn out, crushed, and broken by His earthly disappointments, labours, and sufferings—still beats in His breast. In the very centre and fount of all the glories of heaven, compassed about by the burning splendours of the divine throne, one with the eternal God in majesty and bliss as He was one with man in weakness, sorrow, and shame, Christ reigns King of kings and Lord of lords.

And his honours are not mere personal decorations and ornaments. The government is upon His shoulder. All races of men, all angelic ranks and orders, are subjected to His control. He is *heir of all things;* needing no fiery terrors to maintain His sovereignty over the armies of heaven, but ruling them by the majesty of His holiness and the golden influences of His love; winning to himself the hearts of the sorrowful and the penitent of all nations by His yearning compassion for their sufferings and their sins. He is *heir of all things;* every region of the universe is at His disposal; all material forces are at His command; the love and the homage of holy angels and of the innumerable multitude of the redeemed are His for ever; and it will be His lofty prerogative, His everlasting joy, to augment and to perpetuate the bliss of all who bow before His sceptre and obey His laws.

I need hardly remind you that this passage, this whole Epistle indeed, has a very important relation to questions which have long been the subject of keen and strenuous controversy among theological scholars, but which now, in every country in Christendom where there is intellectual life and freedom, are agitating the minds of ordinary christian people. Does the Old Testament contain the record of a Divine revelation, or is it a badly edited, ill-digested collection of the untrustworthy traditions of an illiterate and superstitious people? I hardly know to what extent recent discussions have disturbed the faith of our own congregations, but I am inclined to think that there is an uneasy feeling in the minds of many who never utter their disquietude; and the mere existence of the controversy may shake the religious confidence of some who have no opportunity for mastering even the outlines of the arguments of the opposing disputants. I feel that the subject is almost too complex and too intricate to be dealt with at all, except in a formal treatise; and it certainly cannot be fully dealt with in mere incidental notices in sermons on other subjects. But there are two or three thoughts which I cannot but express.

(1) It is a logical mistake to abandon faith in the Lord Jesus, because of difficulties, insoluble perhaps to us, which occur in the books of the Old Testament. There are two great divisions of divine revelation: God spake in old times to the fathers by the prophets; God spake to us by His Son. The earlier revelation was fragmentary; it was given in various and imperfect forms, and by inferior agents. The later revelation is complete; it was given once for all, it was given in the noblest form,—in the form of a human life and death and resurrection; in the form of human speech from the lips of One who was filled with the Spirit;—in the form of biography and doctrine, written by those who were specially and supernaturally qualified to record the actions and discourses of Jesus, and to interpret the purpose of His mission. Difficulties of many kinds are inseparable from the conditions under which the earlier revelation was made, but surely it is unreasonable on this account to reject the later. You may doubt whether you can recognise the Divine hand in the elementary structure of patriarchal and Jewish faith; but this is no reason for refusing confidence to the open vision of God in the face of His only begotten Son. Look at the block of marble which has only just begun to feel the formative hand of the sculptor, and you may be uncertain whether or no the great master has really had anything to do with the rough hewing of the still unshapely mass; but because of this you will not hesitate when the idea of th artist is perfected, when

the marble has been inspired with beauty, majesty, and strength, and seems to have caught an immortal life from the imagination of genius. And so, whatever difficulty any of you may have for a time—and I believe it will only be for a time—in discovering the presence of God in His primitive revelations to the human race, this should be no reason for regarding with diminished faith the full revelation He has made of Himself in the Son.

(2) We need feel no surprise that particular books of the Old Testament have lost the independent evidence of their authority and inspiration, and depend for their acceptance on the fact that they are found among others which are unquestionably the works of inspired men. In those ancient Scriptures we have the record of what God spake to the fathers; it is in the New Testament that we find what God has spoken directly to us. To the fathers, the authority of particular prophets was demonstrated by evidence which has now disappeared. That the evidence, whatever it may have been, was to them irresistible, is surely almost proved by the solitary consideration that the books of the prophets are filled with denunciations of national and individual sin; there is hardly any praise—there is no flattery at all; every form of crime against God and against man is charged upon the Jewish people, and dreadful penalties are threatened. If the books were mere legends embodying the wonderful history of the nation, or mere speculations on the character and nature of the invisible powers which rule the destiny of man, they might have been originally accepted as from God without consideration and upon inadequate evidence. But they are filled from end to end with the crimes of the people, the crimes of the priesthood, the crimes of the kings; and yet, people, priests, and kings received them as bearing a divine signature, and transmitted them as a most precious inheritance to subsequent generations. We may surely believe that "the fathers" saw very ample reason to acknowledge that God was speaking in the men by whom such books as these were written. But the point I wish to urge is this, that the clearest, fullest, and most direct evidence of prophetic inspiration would be given to those to whom the prophets spake; and that it is very possible that people living in remote lands and

remote ages, may be unable either to recover the external evidence of their divine commission, or to solve many questions which the contents of their books suggest. It is enough for us if the revelation given more directly to ourselves is sustained by evidence which commands our belief.

(3) This text raises the inquiry, To what extent is the New Testament responsible for the Old? I have already maintained that our first duty is to satisfy ourselves that God has spoken to us by His Son: if we see reason for believing *that*,—for believing that Jesus of Nazareth was indeed the brightness of the Father's glory, the express image of His person, that He is the Creator of all things, the Upholder of all, the Sacrifice for the world's guilt, the Heir and the Ruler of heaven and earth,—we ought to rest with perfect confidence in Him, although we may be disturbed by controversies about preceding revelations. But still the question, To what extent is the New Testament responsible for the Old? is of great interest, and cannot be evaded. I believe that its responsibility amounts to this:— Throughout the New Testament, in the discourses of Christ contained in the Four Gospels, in the teaching of the Apostles contained in the Epistles, the authority of the line of Jewish prophets is clearly recognised, the divine sanction of the Jewish institutions is clearly acknowledged. Not in incidental allusions, not in isolated passages merely, but in the whole structure and spirit of the new religious faith, the divine origin of the old is implied and taken for granted. "God spake in times past to the fathers by the prophets;" this occurs and re-occurs in ever-varying forms in the history of our Lord and in the teaching of His inspired representatives. The divine commission of Jewish prophets, the divine sanction of Jewish institutions—the New Testament is responsible for these. But many of the questions which have been discussed so vehemently of late, concerning the perfect accuracy of the historical parts of the Old Testament must be determined on other grounds. The Jewish institutions may have been divinely sanctioned, the Jewish prophets may have been divinely inspired, yet the books which describe the institutions and record the history of the people, may not have been kept free, even in their original and

uncorrupted form, from all mistake. What ill success recent critics of the earlier documents have had in attempting to expose their errors some of you know; and I do not think it likely, that after the Jewish Scriptures have stood for so many centuries against the keenest adverse criticism, they are likely to fail now; but it is of some importance to maintain, that even if it were demonstrated, which it has not been,* that mistakes existed in the Pentateuch when it came from the hand of its author or editor, the authority of the Lord Jesus Christ and of His apostles is not thereby overthrown. They are directly responsible only for the Divine authority of the Jewish system, and the Divine commission of the men by whom it was founded and maintained. To determine the questions agitated in many modern controversies, we must carefully examine the ancient books themselves.

I can only anticipate one result of that examination. Search the literature of the world, and where, except in the Gospels of the New Testament, will you find narratives so radiant with a divine beauty as those contained in the very earliest books of the Old?—narratives which bear their own evidence that they were written under divine guidance,—narratives which touch the heart, and the conscience, and the spiritual life, with a

---

* I do not refer, of course, to those unscientific references to the material universe which occur in the Holy Scriptures, as in all other ancient books. A revelation *must* be given in the forms of thought common among the people to whom it is made. Had the incidental references of Moses to the celestial bodies, and the form of the earth, been in perfect harmony with modern science, the Pentateuch would have been not more Divine but less natural; it would have been a prodigy to be wondered at, but not a whit more precious as the record of a Divine revelation. Human forms of thought and human conceptions of material things, were the necessary vesture of Divine revelation, as truly as human language, which is indeed nothing but a brief summary of what man has come to think about himself and the world. It would be as reasonable to complain that Moses has not written in the style of Addison or of Pascal, as to complain that he did not think of the material world like Sir John Herschel or Arago. Moreover, a distinction must be drawn between a Divine revelation and the human record of it. What God revealed to Moses is one thing; the account which Moses gives of that revelation is a very different thing. In what Moses writes we may expect to find many things which did not come to him direct from Heaven, and we shall certainly find that the form in which he has communicated even what he had heard and seen in supernatural vision was determined by the laws and culture of his own intellectual and moral life.

power which none who have felt it can ever ascribe to any inferior origin. Wonderful histories! fascinating the imagination of childhood, consoling the sorrows of old age, the charm of the illiterate, the marvel of the learned; receiving through century after century the homage not only of hostile races, but of men of hostile religious faiths—of men hating each other with fanatical hatred, but forgetting their animosity in the presence of these venerable records—Christian and Jew bowing together over the same pages, regarding Abraham, and Isaac, and Jacob with the same reverential love. I can trust to the authority of Christ and His apostles for the divine authority of Jewish institutions; I can trust to the simple and irrepressible instincts of the human heart, the wide world over, for a recognition of the divine origin of Jewish books. We needed perhaps these controversies to try our faith of what sort it is. God grant that we may all have that direct and personal knowledge of the Lord Jesus which will enable us to say to honest doubters and flippant sceptics—Herein is a marvellous thing, that ye know not from whence He is, and yet He hath opened our eyes; we have heard Him ourselves, and know that this is indeed the Christ, the Saviour of the world.

THE SON AND THE ANGELS.

"Being made so much better than the Angels, as He hath by inheritance obtained a more excellent name than they," &c.—HEBREWS i, 4-14.

EVEN if there were no hint in the Holy Scriptures of the existence of angelic beings, it would have been very natural and very reasonable to suppose that man was not the only creature capable of knowing and loving God, and of rendering Him voluntary obedience.

In the visible universe, the Divine wisdom and power are revealed in an infinite variety of forms. God has manifested in His works the inexhaustible fulness of His own nature. In the heavens there is the sun with his robe of burning light, and the moon with her meek and quiet splendour; there are shining planets moving in silence and majesty along their appointed paths; glittering stars, themselves the centres of other systems of glory; and comets plunging fiercely and passionately through the depths of space. And, without looking away from the earth which is our own home, we see the ocean and the dry land, flowers and trees, the fish of the sea and the birds of the air, animals of prodigious size and enormous strength, and insects so minute that myriads of them dwell together on a leaf.

It would, therefore, have been very natural and reasonable to suppose, even apart from Revelation, that there was variety in God's spiritual universe. We could hardly have believed that there was only a single race of creatures that could adore the perfections of the Creator, and offer Him thanksgivings for His infinite love. We know that He delights in holiness and should have thought it altogether improbable that He would have created only one order of beings capable of doing homage to His righteous Law. This improbability would have been increased by human sin. Our holiness, even when consummated in heaven, will be a holiness that has had its origin in penitence and been disciplined by chastisement, a holiness perfected indeed by our earthly experiences of sin and suffering, but for that very reason different from the innocence of unfallen beings. And we should have argued that surely in some region near or remote, there were creatures on whose purity no stain had ever rested.

But we are not left to such speculations as these. In the Old Testament and the New, there are many references to a glorious kingdom of spiritual beings, mighty in power, and perfect in happiness, who serve God day and night without ceasing, and who, from the moment of their creation, have never grieved His heart nor broken the least of His commandments. Angelic messengers conversed with Abraham, and led Lot out of Sodom. Jacob saw in a dream angels ascending and descending on a path of light between the heavens and the earth. When man was driven out of Eden, the flaming sword of the cherubim guarded the tree of life. When the law was given on Sinai, and Jehovah revealed His presence in lightnings and thunders, thousands of angels were round about Him. It was an angel of the Lord that told Mary of the honour that was coming to her of being the mother of Jesus; an angel appeared in a dream to speak of His birth to Joseph; an angel announced to the shepherds that there was born in the city of David a Saviour, Christ the Lord; and as soon as the announcement was made, a multitude of the heavenly host sang "Glory to God in the highest, and on earth peace and good-will towards men." An angel strengthened Christ in Gethsemane. Angels watched in His deserted tomb. Angels spoke words of comfort to the disciples when he had ascended into heaven. When the apostles were put in prison, the angel of the Lord opened the prison doors and brought them forth. When, somewhat later, Peter alone was imprisoned, it was an angel who touched him while he slept, loosened his chains, and led him away from the sleeping guards, and through the opened doors, and so delivered him from the hand of Herod. When Paul was in danger of shipwreck, an angel appeared to him and assured him of safety. "The angel of the Lord encampeth round about those that fear Him:" and God has given "His angels charge over" His people, "to keep them in all their ways." They shouted for joy, they sang together when the foundations of the earth were laid; and still "there is joy among the angels of God when a sinner is brought to repentance." The magnificent hymn of St. Ambrose, the common inheritance of all the churches of Christendom, has nobly described their blessed occupation. "To Thee all angels cry aloud—the heavens and all the powers therein—to Thee cherubim and seraphim continually do cry, 'Holy, holy, holy, Lord God of Hosts!'"

Now the writer of this Epistle places the Lord Jesus Christ in contrast with these glorious beings, and claims for Him a higher and more honourable rank: *He is made so much better than the angels, as He hath by inheritance obtained a more excellent name than they.*

Those of you who are acquainted with any of the learned commentaries on this Epistle will understand how impossible it is to discuss in a sermon the intricate questions which are raised by the chain of quotations from the Old Testament, by which the writer maintains or illustrates this position. Having carefully endeavoured to satisfy my own mind on the principal questions requiring solution, I shall give the results, without attempting either to show the grounds on which they rest, or to state my reasons for rejecting other interpretations.

I take this section of the Epistle, then, and suppose that I am explaining to a Christian Jew the line of the writer's thought. This is the point at which he starts—that Christ is greater than the angels. He is greater, because in those ancient scriptures on which you Jews rest your hopes of a Messiah, and in which the spirit of prophecy gradually revealed the glories of His person and of His kingdom, a "*more distinguished name*" is given to Him than is ever given to them, and that name with all the dignity it implies, Jesus—who is the Christ—has "*inherited;*"—it comes down to Him from psalmists and from prophets who spake ages ago of His coming. The holy and happy creatures who are the invisible agents of the Divine will, are spoken of in scripture by an honourable name; they are the "*angels,*" that is, the messengers of God; but the name by which the Christ is spoken of is more honourable still.

For look into the second Psalm. There David, who had received through the lips of Nathan a clearer and fuller prophecy of the Messiah than had ever been delivered before, is giving utterance to his vision of the greatness and glory of the future King. Just as our own poets sometimes take their flight across all the generations of mankind that intervene between ourselves and the final restoration of the world to God, and sing rapturous songs of victory over the disappearance of the sin and wretchedness which it will take centuries yet to banish from the earth, and over the holiness and joy for which age after age must continue to labour, and to pray, and to wait,—so this inspired poet sees the Messiah already placed on His throne—sees the hostility which will rise against His sceptre—sees the manifestation of the Messiah's victorious energy—and puts in the Messiah's lips a declaration of the Divine decree which is the foundation of His authority and dignity. "The Lord hath said to me, *Thou art My Son, this day have I begotten Thee.*" To which of the angels has He ever said that?

Turn again to that prophecy of Nathan's which is the foundation of so many of the later prophetic declarations. "When thy days be fulfilled," said Nathan to the king, "and thou shalt sleep with thy fathers, I will set up thy seed after thee, which shall proceed out of thy bowels, and I will establish his kingdom. He shall build a house for my name and I will establish the throne of his kingdom for ever. *I will be his father, and he shall be my son.*"*

This was the relation in which all the kings of the house of David were to stand to God—and this relation, in its highest and most perfect form, belongs to that king of whose royal authority the kingship of Jewish sovereigns was but the dim and

---

* 2 Samuel vii, 12.

mperfect symbol. "I will be his father, and he shall be my son,"—was the promise given to David concerning his children; this promise the Christ who is David's great descendant has inherited, and it confers on Him a more honourable name than the angels have ever received. They are called God's messengers: He is called God's Son.

Nor is this all. So superior is Christ to the angels that, as every Christian knew, a company of the heavenly host did homage to Him at His birth, came from the skies that men might hear their adoring songs; so that if the evangelist Luke, instead of telling us what the angels sang on earth, had opened the gates of heaven and permitted us to listen to the divine command which bade them come down to the plain of Bethlehem, he might have given that command in the very words which occur in the Old Testament Scriptures—words which are quoted from the ninety-seventh Psalm, which is a prophecy of the Messiah's kingdom, or from the thirty-second chapter of Deuteronomy, where the words in this exact form are preserved in the Septuagint though they have disappeared from the Hebrew: "*And let all the angels of God worship Him.*"

It was thus that in old time the Messiah was described: this is the name He "inherits." He is "Son of God;" and if any one suggests that the angels too are called the sons of God in the Old Testament, it may be answered that a Jew who had read the Old Testament aright, would see that there was the same distinction between the manner in which the ancient inspired writers speak of the Messiah as Son of God, and the manner in which they speak of the angels as sons of God—that every orthodox Christian recognises in the New Testament between the application "Son of God" to Christ, and "sons of God" to those that believe on Him. In the one case it is a title shared by a multitude of individuals; in the other it is so employed as to denote a solitary, unique, and unapproachable dignity.

And now, how are the angels spoken of? Why, in the hundred-and-fourth Psalm the very name assigned to these glorious spirits, their characteristic designation, "messengers" of God, is given to the powers of the material world. "O

Lord, my God, Thou art very great, Thou art clothed with honour and majesty, who maketh the clouds His chariot—who walketh upon the wings of the wind—*who maketh the winds His messengers*, or, His angels—a *flame of fire* (the lightning) *His servants.*" The title given to the angels, honourable as it is, is one which they share with the unconscious energies of God's creation: the winds and the lightnings are His angels too.

In contrast with this, look to another Psalm in which the Psalmist is speaking again of the glory of the King; and, as the contents of the Psalm show, is speaking of that King whose greatness could not be possessed by any of His predecessors on David's throne. He is speaking of the King of inspired prophecy—the King of Jewish hope—he sees Him already, though afar off, fairer than the children of men, grace is poured into His lips and he exclaims, "Gird Thy sword upon Thy thigh, O most Mighty, with Thy glory and Thy majesty. *Thy throne, O God, is for ever and ever, a sceptre of righteousness is the sceptre of Thy kingdom: Thou hast loved righteousness, and hated iniquity; therefore God, even Thy God, hath anointed Thee with the oil of gladness above Thy fellows.*" Kindling with the vision of Christ's glory the writer then quotes a passage from the hundred-and-second Psalm, which is directly addressed to God Himself. Christ was acknowledged by the Jewish Christians to be Creator of all things, though their hearts were losing the vivid perception and profound impression of His greatness; the words he quotes, whether addressed originally to the Messiah or not, only express more fully what the faith of the Jewish believers confessed:—"*Thou, Lord, in the beginning hast laid the foundation of the earth; and the heavens are the works of Thine hands: they shall perish; but Thou remainest; and they all shall wax old, as doth a garment; and as a vesture shalt Thou fold them up, and they shall be changed: but Thou art the same, and Thy years shall not fail.*"

Again, "*To which of the angels said He at any time*" what He says in another Psalm, (the hundred-and-tenth), which plainly relates to the Messiah—"*Sit Thou at My right hand*" —share My authority—share My glory—"*until I make Thine enemies Thy footstool?"* The Messiah is to sit on the throne of God, but the angels are *"ministering spirits sent forth to minister to them who are about to inherit salvation."*

Concerning this series of quotations generally, I wish to say before passing on, that we shall misapprehend the spirit and structure of the whole passage, if we suppose that these texts from the Old Testament were intended to form such a demonstration of the divinity of the Lord Jesus as should convince those who theoretically denied the doctrine. The writer of this Epistle is not arguing with unbelievers, and therefore his argument is not shaped with any reference to their intellectual position. He is addressing those who acknowledged the Messiahship of Christ, who confessed that He was God manifest in the flesh, but in whom this faith was becoming practically ineffectual through the returning power of their old religious life. He therefore takes their ancient Scriptures, and points to passage after passage in which the Messiah's glory is predicted, not to demonstrate that glory as an abstract truth—they believed the doctrine already—but to give depth and vividness to their conceptions of it, just as a Christian preacher addressing a Christian congregation, is constantly reviewing and reiterating the Scripture teaching on important Christian doctrines, not with the idea of convincing those who intellectually reject the doctrines, but to intensify the influence of a true Christian faith which he supposes his audience already to possess. If he were reasoning with unbelievers his argument would rest on other premises, or, at least, be conducted in another method. It is necessary, of course, that his reasoning should be sound in itself, but it is not necessary that it should be of the same kind that he would adopt if he were maintaining a controversy with men of another creed.

Let us review for a moment these sublime representations of the Lord Jesus Christ. They may strengthen our faith, they may animate our courage, in these days of conflict and of doubt, even as they were intended to confirm the fidelity of Christian people who were living in a still more tempestuous age.

Christendom is agitated by a thousand controversies—on some of the principal of them we can look this morning, while under the shelter of this inspired teaching, with untroubled calmness, and can anticipate their final issue with exulting hope. Scholars and philosophers are engaged in discussions concerning the claims of Jesus of Nazareth, His character, and the value of His teaching. They begin by placing Him among the merely human founders of great religious systems, and it is no wonder that they are baffled in attempting to construct a satisfactory theory of His history, and to account for the success of His mission. They analyze the records of His wonderful life, and every quarter of a century some new theory is found necessary to get rid of the supernatural element in the records of the four evangelists. There is confusion, perplexity, darkness, among the disputants, and they seem still far off from the only solution of their difficulties which is likely to give them lasting satisfaction and rest. But, rising above the clamour of this loud debate, we hear a voice which quiets all our anxiety. We have satisfied ourselves that the voice is Divine, and its utterances are too plain to be misunderstood—"'Thou art my Son," "Let all the angels of God worship Him." Thankfully escaping from the transient controversies of our time, we too bow before him whom the angels are commanded to adore, and we exclaim "Thou art the King of Glory, O Christ: Thou art the everlasting Son of the Father: we pray Thee help Thy servants whom Thou hast redeemed with Thy precious blood; make them to be numbered with Thy saints in glory everlasting."

Again, we are told by some who have thoughtfully considered the history of the human race, and have constructed a theory of the secret laws which regulate the gradual civilization of barbarous tribes, the growth and the decline of empires, the development and the vicissitudes of philosophical systems, the origination, diffusion and decay of various forms of religious faith, that Christianity, like other systems of belief and worship, has sprung from the instincts, and experiences, and hopes of mankind; that it is no Divine gift, but the representation of the degree of growth to which the religious life of a remarkable people had attained eighteen centuries ago; that already it is giving place to other and higher conceptions of the Divine nature and will, and must in a few generations altogether disappear. We have heard prophecies of that kind too often to be greatly troubled by them; but if for a moment we begin to tremble, and to be saddened by the thought of the possibility of the Christian faith becoming some day a mere memory of the past, like the religious systems which flourished in the nations and empires of ancient times, our hearts are thrilled with delight and confidence as we listen to the song of ancient prophecy, a song addressed to the Christ whom we serve— "Thy throne, O God, is for ever and ever:"—"therefore will not we fear though the earth be removed, and though the mountains be carried into the midst of the sea."

But again it is urged, that the progress of natural science is sapping the foundations of the Christian faith, that every year the battle between the ancient books and the demonstrated results of modern discovery is becoming more fierce, and that the conflict can only terminate in the complete overthrow of the fancies which have ruled for so many centuries the intellect and the heart of Christendom. We are not afraid of the results of patient and fearless inquiry into the structure of the material universe; that, too, is a divine revelation; and in explaining the meaning of its phenomena, we are interpreting the very handwriting of God. No doubt some things may be found there (in that inspired book of nature I mean) "hard to be understood, which they that are unlearned and unstable wrest, as they do *the other Scriptures*, to their own destruction," but that is no reason for closing the book or for quarrelling with those who are honestly endeavouring to understand it, or for apprehending that a fuller knowledge of the heavens or the earth will destroy our faith in Christ, or cause our worship of Him to cease. Destroy our faith in Him! cause our worship of Him to cease! Impossible—why it was He who "in the beginning laid the foundations of the earth, and the heavens are the work of His hand: THEY shall perish, but Thou, O Christ, remainest; and they all shall wax old as doth a garment, and as a vesture shalt Thou fold them up, and they shall be changed, but Thou art the same, and Thy years shall not fail."

Yes—He will reign for ever and ever. Not in the heavens alone, but also upon earth. He is King of mankind, and all men shall bow before His throne. The honest doubts and difficulties of the good He will dissipate and dispel, and over all the hostility of His foes He will win a complete and an immortal victory. His enemies—the crime, the vice, the sin, the ignorance, the wretchedness of individual men; His enemies—the unjust laws of nations, the gigantic systems of oppression and wrong which have broken the spirit, darkened the intellect, corrupted the heart, wasted the happiness of whole races of mankind; His enemies—all the ruinous falsehoods, all the cruel and polluting superstitions which have afflicted and cursed the human family,—they are all destined to destruction, for the Most High hath said to Him, "Sit Thou on My right hand, till I make Thine enemies Thy footstool."

Meantime, while we are struggling, in His name and relying on His help, against all kinds of misery, of error, and of sin—we are surrounded by invisible forms that watch our labour with delight; and are near in our times of peril, of weakness, and of doubt, to shield us from danger, to strengthen and support. He who sitteth at the right hand of God is served by all the hosts of heaven, and they have learnt long ago that the brightest crown which glitters on the head of their King, was won by His work for us sinners, that His greatest joy is in our salvation. And so they, too, are eager to be the ministers of His mercy in assisting to accomplish the redemption of the human race. They esteem it the most honourable of employments. They watch with more than fraternal love over the destinies of those whom Christ calls His brethren. They know that by and by their songs will welcome us into everlasting bliss, and they want to be able to tell us when we meet them in heaven of kindly services they rendered to us before we had been permitted to gaze on their glory, and when we knew not they were near. They are "*ministering spirits sent forth to minister,*" not to the kings and princes and great men of the world—but to little children, to solitary, aged men and women, to the desolate whom human sympathy seems to have forsaken—to the poor—to those that love Christ everywhere; they are sent forth "*to minister to them about to inherit salvation.*" And that which makes their service most grateful to our hearts is the thought that they render this service, not merely because they are commanded to do it, but because they know that Christ's love for us is so great that by helping us they win His highest approbation.

DRIFTING FROM CHRIST.

"Therefore we ought to give more earnest heed," &c.—HEBREWS ii, 1-4.

THERE are three principal thoughts in this passage, and these will form the three principal divisions of this morning's sermon. The persons to whom this Epistle was written are warned against neglecting the great salvation; they are charged to give earnest heed to the things which they have heard, that is, to the facts and promises and laws which form the substance of Christian teaching; and there are several reasons given why they should fulfil the duty.

I.

Let us consider what is meant by *neglecting the great salvation*. It is indispensable to a right understanding of every argument and every exhortation in this Epistle that we should constantly recall the character and circumstances of those to whom it was written. They were not irreligious people. They were not people who rejected the mercy and resisted the authority of the Lord Jesus Christ. They were Jewish Christians, some of whom had believed in Christ for many years. Their faith had been severely tested; they had endured, as they are reminded afterwards, a great fight of afflictions; they had been subjected to public shame and reproach themselves, and they had been the companions of those who had been thus persecuted; they had taken joyfully the spoiling of their goods, knowing that they had in heaven a better and an enduring substance. But they were getting weary of the protracted struggle. Some of them were forsaking the Christian assemblies. To their intellect and heart the glory of the Christian faith was gradually becoming dim. The excitement they had felt in the earlier years of the conflict had gone off, and through sheer exhaustion they were giving way. The influence of their earlier Jewish habits and passions was silently but rapidly recovering strength; and they were in danger of "letting slip" or being "*drifted from*" the things they had heard.

The image wrapped in the word which the writer uses is a very impressive and instructive one. The idea is, that these Jewish Christians were in danger of being carried away from the gospel of Christ just as a vessel will be drifted down the stream unless it is held firmly to its anchorage, or unless there is constant exertion on the part of those who are on board to resist the current. There was a strong tide running, and unless they gave earnest heed to the gospel they would be swept away from the side of Christ back into their old Jewish life.

It is against this that they are warned. This is the kind of "neglect" of which they were likely to be guilty. It was the neglect, not of those who are openly irreligious, not of those who positively reject the gospel, but of those who have become weary of struggling against powerful influences adverse to their Christian fidelity, and who are gradually, and perhaps almost unconsciously yielding; whose reverence for Christ is gradually diminishing, whose zeal for His honour is gradually cooling, whose resistance to what is anti-Christian is gradually becoming less resolute; of men who are gradually being carried away from the great objects of Christian faith and hope—like a boat whose head has been kept against the stream hour after hour, but in which the rowers are almost exhausted, and which has now begun to drift back again.

Is there not something like this in very many of us? The influences adverse to a pure, and healthy, and vigorous religious life among ourselves, are indeed very different from those by which these Jewish Christians were nearly overcome. We are in danger of being carried by the current, not into another religion, but into what is surely much worse—into mere worldliness, and neglect of God altogether. We too may be "diverted" from the things which we have heard, by the constant stress of thoughts and occupations from which we can hardly escape, but which it is our duty to master. The mind and the heart may be gradually filled with inferior interests until the love of Christ seems wholly quenched, and we become as completely secular in thought and feeling, as though we had never believed at all. It may be continuous trouble, it may be quiet and uninterrupted happiness, it may be eager devotion to business, it may be a fierce struggle against poverty and misfortune, it may be sudden, and unexpected, and intoxicating commercial success, it may be intellectual activity and excitement, it may be absorption in public affairs, nay, it may be incessant activity in religious work; anything, everything, that so occupies the mind as to leave little time, or little strength, or little inclination, for giving "earnest heed" to the things which we have heard, places us in the same danger as that of which the writer of this Epistle warns the Christian Hebrews of his own time. We are likely to drift away from the highest objects of faith and love, and then to us the startling question is addressed—"How shall we escape if we neglect so great salvation?"

II.

Consider the duty which is inculcated. We must "*give earnest heed*" to the things we have heard, we must not neglect, —*we*, who are Christians already—must not neglect "the great salvation." I believe it is impossible to exaggerate the absolute importance of the first act of the soul in forsaking sin, choosing God's service, and trusting to the atonement and grace of the Lord Jesus Christ for forgiveness and for eternal life. But I cannot conceal from myself, I ought not to conceal from you, the tremendous importance which is also assigned in the New Testament, to persevering fidelity to the Lord Jesus Christ. It is a happy time, no doubt, when the good seed which has been sown in the heart, instead of being carried away by the birds of the air, begins to germinate, and when the green shaft begins to appears above the dark soil—but we are told that after it has sprung up it sometimes withers away on the rock, because it has not much earth; and that sometimes the cares of this world choke the word so that it becometh unfruitful.

It is a happy time, no doubt, when a man first ceases to do evil and learns to do well, but it is only by patient continuance in well-doing, that he can hope to obtain glory, honour, and immortality. It is a happy moment when those who have lived in sin escape the pollutions of the world through the knowledge of the Lord and Saviour Jesus Christ, but if after this, they are again entangled therein and overcome, "the latter end is worse with them than the beginning. For it had been better for them never to have known the way of righteousness than after they have known it to turn from the holy commandment delivered unto them." *

It is, therefore, a mistake to suppose that by the solitary act of faith and self-consecration to God's service, which stands at the beginning of the religious life, we release ourselves from the necessity of subsequent exertion. That act marks, indeed, the transition of the soul from a condition of danger to a condition of security; from a condition of hostility to God to a condition of friendship; but not a transition from a condition in which energetic exertion is necessary to a condition of indolence and inactivity. To preserve and maintain what is then acquired, demands incessant and vigorous effort. At once, God listens to our cry for mercy, asking no service from us to induce Him to forgive; but when we are pardoned He does require us to be most diligent and painstaking in keeping His commandments. At once, God listens to our prayer that He will permit us to become His servants; but to do His will and to please Him perfectly, demands the crucifixion of the flesh and a perpetual struggle with temptation. It is necessary, if we would be saved, not merely to repent once, to believe once, to stand face to face with God once, but to "give earnest heed" till the very end of our life, to the things we have heard. It is on Christian men who have been persecuted for Christ's sake, that the inspired writer presses the momentous question, "How shall we escape if we neglect so great salvation?"

Nor is there any difficulty in understanding what is meant by our *giving earnest heed*. It means, that we should perpetuate

---

* 2 Peter ii, 20-21.

and increase the earnest devotion to Christ, and to all that Christ has said and done, which marked the commencement of our Christian life. Take, for instance, the sense of danger, associated with the sense of unforgiven sin. It was true then, that only by Jesus Christ could we be delivered from everlasting destruction—it is just as true now. It was true then that by the life and death of the Lord Jesus our sins were atoned for; and all the wonder, and thankfulness, and joy, with which we then thought of His sacrifice, are as appropriate now as they were then. It is still true that we need the power of the Holy Ghost to sanctify our hearts. The work of Christ has not become less important to us; His love is not less amazing; the necessity of trusting in Him is not diminished. It is by permanent faith that we have permanent justification—by permanent unity with Christ that we have permanent spiritual life. Cease to believe, and again you are "condemned already." Cease to abide in Him, and you are "cast forth as a branch;" you are "withered;" you are "burned." To every one of you, no matter though you are in Church membership, no matter though your repentance of sin, years ago, was deep and genuine, no matter though your faith in Christ was firm and strong, your love for Him fervent, your devotion to Him apostolic—to every one of you, I say, that it is still necessary to "give earnest heed to the things you have heard," for "how shall we escape if we neglect so great salvation?"

III.

Consider now *the motives for giving this earnest heed*.

(1) This salvation has been proclaimed to us by the Lord Himself, and the *greatness of His dignity* is a motive for giving "earnest heed" to it. In the previous chapter, the writer appeals to the long series of divine revelations which had covered many previous centuries, in order to exalt and to illustrate the glory of the Lord Jesus Christ. Prophets were but the servants of God, and brought to men only fragmentary intimations of His will. Angels themselves, like the wind and the lightning, are but His messengers. He has spoken to us

now by One whom even the angels are commanded to worship, who is the brightness of His glory, the express image of His person; by One who created all things, and upholds them still by the word of His power; by One, who having purged our sins, is made Heir of all things, and is seated at the right hand of the Majesty on High. Yes, it is *He*—God manifest in the flesh, who speaks; who speaks to *us*, as he spake to the men that lived in Judea and Galilee eighteen hundred years ago. We still read His very words; we see Him still revealing the Father,—in His gentleness to human sorrow, in His pity for human weakness, in the welcome He gives to the most wretched and profligate that repent of sin and appeal to Him for help, in the agony of Gethsemane, and the sufferings of the cross, in which divine love plunges into the depths of human misery that sin may be atoned for and the human soul be restored to God. It is *He*—who speaks to us; to *us* who have believed for years, as well as to those who have never believed at all; to us, this morning, after years of religious profession, as He spake to us years ago, warning us of our danger, reproving us for our sin, and imploring, commanding us to receive forgiveness and eternal life. We, above all men—we, His servants, are bound to listen.

And it is the living Christ that speaks to us. I cannot but feel that the religious life of Christendom has suffered grievous harm from the constant representation of the Lord Jesus by artists, poets, and preachers, in the weakness and humiliation of His death on the cross. In the Romish Church, the heart is scarcely ever permitted to escape from His dying agonies. Day after day, generation after generation, He is crucified afresh, and His shame is perpetuated. Men look upon Him in those dreadful hours when He was crowned only with thorns, when His sceptre was a reed, when an imperial robe was thrown upon Him in mockery, when He stood as a criminal before an earthly ruler, when the cruel instruments of ecclesiastical tyranny were permitted to heap upon Him insult and scorn, when the rabble of a degraded nation triumphed over His apparent discomfiture, when He was deserted by His friends, when even the Divine glory was unable to penetrate the dense clouds of suffering and disaster into which He entered for the salvation of mankind. We hear Him asking for vinegar to relieve His burning thirst; crying out, in the bitterness of His soul, because the light of God's countenance is hidden from Him. God forbid that we should ever cease to speak of having redemption in His blood. We are not ashamed of the cross; to us it is the symbol of triumph and the memorial of salvation ; but it is not fitting that we should forget the glory which preceded, or the glory which was to follow. He is no longer in Gethsemane, no longer on the cross, no longer in Joseph's sepulchre. We are adoring, not a living Being, but a creation of our own fancy, when we pray to a Christ crowned with thorns. He has resumed His former glory. He reigns at the right hand of God. He wears the signs of the most awful and august authority. "How shall we escape," if, when He speaks, we refuse to listen ?

(2) There is another reason for "giving earnest heed to the things we have heard"—the *greatness of the salvation* of which Christ has spoken to us, and *speaks* still.

Every time we invoke the Divine mercy, our impressions of the wonderfulness of the redemption accomplished for us by Christ, must surely be intensified and deepened. Violated vows, broken purposes, relapses into sins we have again and again renounced, and for which we have again and again sought forgiveness, do not render our condition hopeless. They may, and they should, fill us with shame and bitter self-reproach ; we may find it hard to look God in the face and tell Him of our wickedness; we may be ready to think it impossible that He should still be willing to pardon ; but as soon as we appeal to His mercy, our sins, which are "as scarlet," become "white as snow."

Nor are we merely tolerated in God's presence, permitted to look upon His glory from afar, appointed to obscure duties, and called by an inferior name. The open vision of God's face, the royal priesthood, the Divine sonship, are ours still, after repeated, aggravated, and inexcusable offences.

We may have resisted, grieved, quenched the Holy Ghost, but the grace which cancels our guilt grants us again "the baptism of fire." Yes, though after we believed, we were sealed with the Holy Spirit of promise, and though through our folly and weakness we have almost banished Him from our hearts, there is still possible to us, not only ultimate escape from the perdition of ungodly men, but the recovery in this world of the image of God, perfect union with Christ, the fulness of life and power and joy.

It is a "great salvation" which we are charged not to neglect. We know it. Already we have trembled at the prospect of the final judgment and the terrors which lie beyond; we were once among "the wicked," "reserved unto the day of destruction;" we were in fear of "the outer darkness," "the terrible tempest," "the indignation and wrath, tribulation and anguish," "the vengeance of eternal fire;" and we can recall the blessed rest which we found in the Divine mercy, "the peace passing all understanding," our triumphant hope of everlasting glory. We were guilty, and God freely pardoned us. We were His enemies, and He gave us "power to become the sons of God." We were corrupt and impure, and He gave us "a new heart" and "a right spirit." We received "the spirit of wisdom and revelation." We rejoiced "in hope of the glory of God." Heaven was not afar off. We saw "the holy city, the new Jerusalem, coming down from God out of heaven;" we passed through its gates; we were conscious that already we had come to "the festal assembly of angels," and "to the spirits of just men made perfect," and that we were "blessed with all spiritual blessings in heavenly places in Christ."

After such experiences as these, with the unseen world revealed to us, the blessedness of heaven already ours, what plea can be urged, what palliation, what excuse, for drifting back to our old life? The thanksgivings of earlier days, our unforgotten joys, our testimony to others concerning "the fulness of the blessing of the gospel of Christ," condemn us. We are neglecting a *"great salvation."*

(3) Finally, if we continue to "neglect," there can be *no escape for us from an intolerable doom.* This is the "great salvation;" there is no other. We have not to speculate this

morning on the future condition of those who have never heard of the Lord Jesus Christ, or to whom the gospel has been presented under such a dark disguise that it is not wonderful they refuse to give any heed to it, or whose intellectual idiosyncrasies have made it almost impossible for them to receive the theory of the Christian faith, or who, from the miserable influences under which they have lived from their childhood, have lost nearly every moral element to which the gospel appeals. Nor are we considering how those can "escape" who, with no such reasons for unbelief as these, have uniformly and persistently rejected the grace of our Lord Jesus Christ.

But "how shall *we* escape,"—*we* who once believed; *we* who were once forgiven; *we* who were once renewed; *we* who have seen the face of Christ and heard his welcome into the household of faith; *we* who, in addition to all the external proofs of the divine commission of the Lord, have had the consciousness of the power He exerts over the soul in awakening a new life, giving strength to overcome the world, and to do the will of God? "How shall *we* escape, if we neglect so great salvation?" Can we hope that God will pardon our sin? It is God's pardon to which we are becoming indifferent. Or can we hope that He will give us a better mind? He has already renewed us, but we are actually resisting His grace, and sinking into "the second death." "How shall we escape?" A law transgressed, still leaves an appeal to mercy; but for those who have received mercy and who now reject it, there is nothing but "a certain fearful looking for of judgment and fiery indignation."

THE DIGNITY OF MAN.

"For unto the angels hath He not put in subjection the world to come whereof we speak," &c.—HEBREWS ii, 5-9.

How difficult it is to unite in one firm and harmonious conception, the true divinity and the true humanity of the Lord Jesus Christ, is felt by all thoughtful Christians. But the difficulty must have pressed with unparalleled force upon those Jewish believers to whom this Epistle was written. For the apostles themselves, however, who had known Christ, as well as for their Gentile converts in lands remote from Judea, the task was far easier.

Of what the Lord Jesus Christ was in His human nature, Peter, and James, and John, and the rest of the original apostles, could not fail to have a very definite conception. The features of His countenance, His height, His dress, His voice, His gestures, were perfectly familiar to them. To the end of their life they would remember when they first heard of Him as a new teacher who had risen up in Nazareth; and how, before they saw Him, they talked to their friends about the reports of His goodness and wisdom which were creating excitement all through Galilee. They would remember, with imperishable distinctness, the place and the day they met Him for the first time and all the circumstances of their meeting; they would remember His appearance as He sat with them in their boats, as He walked with them on the shore of the Lake, as He spoke to them and to the people on the hill-side, as He went with them up to the annual feasts; they would remember eating and drinking with Him, sitting with Him in the house of Lazarus at Bethany, and in the upper chamber at Jerusalem; they would have engraven on their very hearts His looks, His tones, when Judas kissed Him in the garden, and when He was taken to be crucified on Calvary. Every recollection of His human nature and life must have been intensely and vividly instinct.

On the other hand, He had produced upon them, from the first, the impression of a mysterious dignity, which prepared them for the subsequent discovery of His true greatness. His miracles were wrought with an authority which filled them with awe. He taught as one in whom God was speaking. Again and again He had forgiven sins. He had claimed unity with the Father, and they had felt that in this there was nothing to shock or to startle them, for the claim was in perfect harmony with His bearing and character. Some of them had seen His person radiant with glory on the Mount of Transfiguration. All of them had seen Him after His resurrection, and had gazed on Him with reverence and wonder as He ascended into heaven. His humanity was most real to every one of them; and every one of them had been in direct contact with those indefinable personal influences, as well as witnessed those irresistible supernatural proofs, which constrained them to believe that He was also Divine. They surrendered neither side of the truth; they not only *believed* both with a stedfast and immoveable confidence—they were under the power of both.

The Gentile converts in Rome and Corinth and Galatia, would also be able to hold firmly both the humanity and the Divinity of the Lord Jesus Christ. Their conceptions of His human life, which was passed in a land few of them had ever seen, were not much more vivid than our own; and their idea of God, in consequence of their heathen education, was not very lofty: moreover, it was no new thing to them to think of a Divine person as living a human life and performing human actions: their very heathenism had prepared them for this article of the Christian faith.

But the Jewish converts in Palestine, who had not known Christ, were in a different position. *Their* conceptions of His humanity were extremely vivid. He had lived in their own country, in the very towns in which they lived themselves.

There were houses standing in which He had eaten and in which He had slept. Some of them, no doubt, had seen Him, though they had not known Him intimately enough to receive the same mysterious impression of His dignity which had been given to the apostles. They knew people who had talked with Him, and who remained unbelievers. His relatives were living among them still. The judgment-hall, in which their worst criminals were still condemned, was the place where He had been tried for sedition. Their own priests had clamoured for His blood. Their own governors had condemned Him to die. They *believed* He was Divine; overwhelming evidence had brought them to that conviction; but they were surrounded every day and all the year through with what reminded them of the darkest circumstances of His humiliation. His humanity, in its poverty and suffering and shame, was most real to them; and their thoughts of this were not modified by those manifestations of His Divinity which were interwoven with all that the apostles remembered of His earthly history. His Godhead they *believed;* His humanity they *felt*, in all its saddest, weakest, most humiliating attributes and manifestations.

It is not surprising, therefore, that to them the Divine glory was obscured by the human weakness and sorrow. In their creed they acknowledged both, but their hearts, like our own, were more powerfully moved by what they saw than by what they believed; and all that they saw gave a cruel and discouraging emphasis and prominence and reality to Christ's humiliation. With their recollections of the glorious angelic appearances in connection with the earlier revelations of God to the Jewish race, it was harder for them than we can imagine, to escape a feeling of dissatisfaction with the Christian truth, though they believed it, that God had been manifest in the flesh.

How does the writer of this Epistle deal with their difficulty? We have seen already that, in the first chapter, he recalls to their minds the Divine sonship and regal dignity of the Lord Jesus, which conferred on Him a glory infinitely transcending that of the angels of God; and now He turns to His human nature, and shows that man, according to the Divine idea of humanity, is not to be thought of as placed at an immeasurable distance below angelic dignity. *His endeavour is to rescue human nature from that dishonour which made the Jewish Christians feel it so much harder to recognize Divinity when revealed in the man Christ Jesus, than when revealed in angelic forms.*

He begins this new process of thought, by affirming that under the new constitution of things of which he is speaking—and which had been spoken of in former times as " the kingdom of heaven "—" the last days "—"*the world to come*"—angels had not been appointed to authority and dominion. In the material universe, according to the belief of the Jews—a belief deriving some slight sanction from certain passages in the Old Testament Scriptures—angels had been invested with great and honourable functions. They controlled or superintended the action both of the kindly and terrible powers of nature. They smote nations with pestilence. They governed the motions of the winds. They had charge of individual men. Empires were under their rule.

The incidental and sometimes obviously metaphorical language of the Holy Scriptures, was so strained by rabbinical interpreters, that a mighty host of spiritual beings were formally enthroned, with distinct and separate powers over the visible world, and over the life of man. Without pausing to distinguish how much truth and how much superstition co-existed in this belief, the writer simply declares that " the world to come," by which—as I intimated just now—he means the new order of things since the establishment of the Messiah's kingdom, is not subjected to angelic government. Throughout God's previous revelations, alike in the definite prophecies of Holy Scripture, and in the institutions which God established for the religious discipline and education of man, no hint had been given that angels were to be supreme when the divine purposes were consummated in the kingdom of the Messiah. "*Unto the angels hath He not put in subjection the world to come of which we speak.*"

He then proceeds to shew that in the ancient Scriptures a lofty dignity had been claimed for man; he also affirms that this dignity had not been actually and perfectly realized; and he points to Jesus Christ, as the Man in whom all that had ever been asserted concerning the honourableness of human nature was gloriously fulfilled.

I.

He shows that in the ancient Scriptures a lofty dignity had been claimed for man. "*One in a certain place testifieth,*" (the quotation is from the 8th Psalm), "*What is man that* THOU *art mindful of him, or the son of man that* THOU *visitest him?*" Human weakness, ignorance, and sin, made it appear to David most wonderful that the Great and the Holy God should manifest so profound an interest in our race; that we should be, as we evidently are, the constant objects of the Divine thought, solicitude, and care; that we should receive direct communications from heaven; that God should be troubled by our sin and rejoice over our right-doing; should care for our love, and confidence, and obedience. The Jewish Scriptures taught that the most magnificent and splendid objects in the universe were created by the Divine power; that the Divine perfections are infinite; and the Divine blessedness complete; —What then is man, that God, who is so great, should have any thought or care for him?

We ought to lay a firmer hold than ever on the truth which occasioned this exclamation. The whole current of modern thought runs against it. Men are thinking so much of the laws of nature, which are only God's settled modes of blessing and caring for His creatures, that the idea of His free and personal love for every human soul, and of His interest in the separate and individual history of every man, is being lost; and we are gradually coming to think of ourselves as surrounded only by a complicated and tremendous system of material forces, which work on grimly, relentlessly, unpityingly, from eternity to eternity, taking no knowledge of the effect of their vast and ceaseless activity, blessing men without joy, cursing them without sorrow. The Jew had a deeper wisdom, and a wisdom which, if it be lost, is ill-exchanged for all that natural science can tell us of the construction of the material universe. The

Jew would have been shocked if he had been told that the God of Abraham and Isaac and Jacob had constructed a huge machine and simply left it to work; and that there was no room for His own direct interference to relieve the sorrows, to strengthen the weakness, to guide the conduct of man. Those lines of the representative poet of an artificial and unbelieving age, which teach the doctrine of the calm indifference of the Most High, and affirm that

> "He sees with equal eye, as God of all,
> A hero perish, or a sparrow fall:
> Atoms or systems into ruin hurled—
> And now a bubble burst, and now a world,—"

those lines, I say, have no parallel in the inspired songs of the Jewish people; their poets held a loftier and a nobler creed:—

"The Lord is my Shepherd, I shall not want. He maketh me to lie down in green pastures: He leadeth me beside the still waters." "Yea, though I walk through the valley of the shadow of death, I will fear no evil: for Thou art with me; Thy rod and Thy staff they comfort me." "In the time of trouble He shall hide me in His pavilion." "He bindeth up the broken in heart." "He is the husband of the widow, and the Father of the fatherless." "The steps of a good man are ordered by the Lord, and He delighteth in his way." "Like as a father pitieth his children, so the Lord pitieth them that fear Him."

Nor is this Divine interest in human affairs all. In that same Psalm from which the writer of the Epistle has already quoted, it is also declared, "*Thou madest him*"—that is, man—"*but a little lower than the angels. Thou crownedst him with glory and honour; and didst set him over the works of Thine hands. Thou hast put all things in subjection under his feet.*" And this is not a doctrine peculiar to the Psalmist; it is not merely the excitement and rapture of genius which affirm it. Read the earliest pages of the Jewish Scriptures, and you will discover that in the record of creation it is said that man was made in the image of God, was appointed to have dominion over the fish of the sea, and over the fowl of the air, and over the cattle, and over all the earth; and he was charged by God to subdue the earth, which had been made his kingdom.

The dignity originally conferred upon human nature may be illustrated in several particulars.

(1) According to the Jewish faith, this material universe, whatever other purposes were to be answered by it, was made for *man*; to be his home, to develope his physical powers, to stimulate his intellectual faculties, to be a test and discipline of his moral character. This was the old faith of Jewish patriarchs, and prophers, and psalmists; and it is mine. I refuse to be reduced to the same rank, to be placed in the same order, as the cattle that browse on the hills, or the fish that people the sea. I assert my supremacy. I believe that I have received from the hand of God crown and sceptre, and that although other designs may be accomplished by the existence of the material and living things around me, they are intended to serve *me*. The sun shines, that I may see the mountains and the woods and the flashing streams, and that I may do the work by which I live. For me, the rain falls, and the dews silently distil,—to cherish the corn which grows for my food, to soften the air I breathe, and to keep the beauty of the world fresh and bright on which I rejoice to look. The music of the birds is for me, and the perfume of flowers. For me it was, that forests grew in ancient times and have since been hardened into coal; for me, there are veins of iron and of silver penetrating the solid earth; and for me, there are rivers whose sands are gold. The beasts of the earth were meant to do my work; sheep and oxen are given me for food. Fire and hail and the stormy wind were meant to serve me. I have authority to compel the lightning to be the messenger of my thought, and the servant of my will. Man is placed over the works of God's hands; for those works were meant to minister to man's life, man's culture, and man's happiness.

(2) Man can understand God's works. He can trace the paths of the planets and calculate the rapidity of their motions. He studies the structure of animals; knows the place and the uses of bone, and muscle, and nerve; perceives the purposes to which beast, and bird, and fish are unconsciously led, by the

guidance of instinct; discovers the mutual relations and interdependence of all the multifarious races of living things. Manifestly, this intelligence confers on man a great superiority over all the unintelligent works of the Divine power. To him, not to them, are revealed the secrets of their nature, and the end of their existence.

(3) But he has a third and still higher claim to supremacy. Man was made in " the image of God." In the creation which surrounds us, there are marvellous manifestations of the Divine attributes. A power to which we can give no other name than Omnipotence, a knowledge which we cannot but call infinite, a wisdom whose depths are unfathomable, and an inexhaustible goodness, are revealed in the heavens above, and in the earth beneath. But in man, God has given existence to a creature in whom we recognise not merely the operations of the Divine attributes, but *the attributes themselves*, though in a less noble form and an inferior degree. There is the manifestation of wisdom, of power, and of love, in the other works of God; but in man there is wisdom itself, power itself, love itself.

(4) Again, the sun and moon and all the stars are bound by laws of which they are unconscious, and which they cannot transgress; and the movements of the lower animals are guided by impulses and instincts over which they have no reasonable and moral control. But man is like God in this,—that he possesses freedom to choose the objects of his life, and the means by which he will secure them. Let the iron hand of Necessity control all things besides—the eagle in her daring flight, the tumult of the ocean, the dance of the spray, the rush of the winds, the fury of the storm,—the will of man stands erect, confronting and defying all authority and all power. No outward force can compel it; no inward necessity bind it. The foundations of that throne on which the human will has been placed by the hand of the Creator, cannot be shaken by the tremendous energies which rend asunder the everlasting hills. A solitary man can stand against a million; they may torture his physical frame till he cries aloud in his agony, but the whole force of a great empire has been met and mastered by the will of a quiet scholar and of a feeble woman. God has given to the human

will the power of refusing to bow before His own greatness, and of disobeying His own commands.

This imperial faculty it is, beyond all others, which stamps man as the rightful master of the world. He alone has this indispensable attribute of sovereignty. All creatures besides are in bondage to irresistible law; he alone has received the gift of freedom. "Thou crownedst him with glory and honour, and didst set him over the works of Thy hands; Thou has put all things in subjection under his feet."

This was God's idea of human nature; and hence, the possibility and reasonableness of the Incarnation. It is true that man is lower than the angels by the limitation of some of his faculties; but he was made in the image of God; his moral attributes corresponded to the Divine perfections, he had the gift of moral freedom, he was made supreme over that order of things to which he belongs, even as God is supreme over all

II.

This is the first thought; the second is, that "*we see not yet all things put under him.*" Man's sovereignty, conferred on him originally by the appointment of his Creator, has not been fully realized. How miserably he has come short of it, has been shown by the condition of all nations and of all ages. His freedom has been manifested in his violation of the most solemn and imperative obligations. The image of God has been so defaced that it has almost disappeared. The intellect of man has sunk into a chaos of ignorance and error, and instead of rightly understanding the universe, he has constructed a thousand monstrous theories concerning its origin, concerning the very structure of material things, concerning his own nature and destiny. The commonest laws of the external world remained hidden from him for thousands of years, and remain hidden even now from the immense majority of his race. Instead of being the master of the inferior creation, he has been —and to a large extent, continues still—its unhappy victim. His life is destroyed by the poison of reptiles, and by the brute strength of beasts of prey. The vineyards he has laboriously cultivated he cannot protect from blight. The harvests he is ready to reap are wasted by destructive rains. On the land, his cities perish by earthquakes: on the sea, his ships go down in the storm. His health is ruined and his moral nature corrupted by the strong temptations of the outward world, which betray him into sensual excesses. He has come to be so humiliated and degraded, that he has looked up to the moon and stars which were made to serve him, and has called them his gods; he has placed four-footed beasts and creeping things in the shrine of his temples, and has implored them to avert the calamities he dreaded, and to bestow on him the blessings for which he longed. The traces of his kingship have not disappeared; slowly and painfully in one province of his dominions after another, especially since Christ came, and in the lands of Christendom, he has been winning back the authority he had lost; but his hand is too feeble to hold the sceptre, and on all sides the subject creation is in open revolt—revolt which he seems often unable even to check, and is quite unable to subdue. "*We see not yet all things put under him.*"

III.

It might be said, that the acknowledged ruin of human nature cancels all that can be affirmed concerning man's original and native dignity. Though free from sin Himself, Christ was subject to the infirmities and sufferings which had come upon men in consequence of sin. He appeared on the earth, not in the glorious form to which alone the description of the Psalmist can fully apply, but oppressed with the heavy and degrading burden of human woe. Man's nature, as it came from God at first, might have been a noble thing, and his position, a position of splendid supremacy; but the nature had been injured, and the position lost. It was still hard to think of humanity as a fitting and honourable medium for the revelation of God.

This brings in the third thought. It is acknowledged that man's dominion over the world had not been maintained; it is impossible to avoid seeing the signs and proofs of man's weakness and disgrace; but we turn our eyes to Jesus, and what do we behold? He is truly man; He was made inferior to angels; but because He hath suffered death He is crowned with glory and honour, and His exaltation to the right hand of God was intended to redeem and rescue the whole race from its ruin, and to make His death minister to the immortal life and blessedness of every man.

In other words, we are bound, when thinking of the incarnation of the Divine Word in the Lord Jesus Christ, to consider not merely the brief history of the thirty years between Bethlehem and the cross. A believing Jew might say, I am sorely troubled, spite of my faith, while I see the Lord Jesus in the home of Joseph and Mary at Nazareth; while I see Him living in poverty among the villages of Galilee, without a place where to lay His head; while I see Him hungering when He has fasted; sitting in weariness by the well of Samaria, because His journey has been long; sleeping in the ship, because He is exhausted by His public labours; while I see him agonising in Gethsemane; standing at the judgment seat of Pilate; enduring the mockery of the soldiers of Herod; hanging on the cross; lying in Joseph's sepulchre:—spite of my faith in His Divinity, there are times when I cannot feel that He is God manifest in the flesh; the interior glory is obscured and eclipsed by the visible humiliation: He has been loaded with all, and more than all, the common shame and suffering of humanity.

True, replies the inspired writer, this human life on earth is far from being the royal thing it was meant to be; and Christ came and lived it; but remember what man was according to God's original idea: see Christ crowned, as the reward of His suffering, with glory and honour, then tell me whether, after all, human nature may not be wonderful and sublime.

If it be urged that though in His own person He may have risen to a splendid height, the dishonour of universal humanity still clings to Him, and He has become the brother of a degraded race, still it is answered No; He has received His greatness not for Himself merely, but for us; He has become the glorified head of mankind; so that His death might be the fountain of redemption for every man.

This, I believe, is the pith of the thought in these remarkable verses; and, as I need hardly remind you, the full developement of their meaning would require not a single sermon, but a complete theological system; a full account of the Divine idea of human nature, of the results of human sin, of the temporary humiliation of Christ, of His present glory, of the relation of His death and enthronement at God's right hand to the whole human race, of the restoration to man, in consequence of the sufferings and victory of Christ, of all his original prerogatives in a higher form, and with securities of permanence which they did not possess before.

In conclusion, I have only to say, that in every controversy in which the Church of Christ has been engaged from the earliest days of her history, until now, she has been contending for the honour of human nature as well as for the glory of God; and even in the struggles which the purer Churches of Christendom have maintained with the more corrupt, the two have always been indissolubly associated. Looking only at the more formidable foes which we have had to encounter, whose enmity has been directed against the essential elements of our faith, this is most manifestly true.

In vindicating, for example, the Divinity of the Lord Jesus, we are not only claiming for Him the honour which is His righteous due, but we are claiming for the human race the most exalted distinction,—for we are maintaining that whatever ruin may have come upon our nature, it is capable of being the very home of the Godhead; and that whatever may be our sins, God Himself in the person of Christ, has become the brother of us all.

Heresy within the Church and a false philosophy without it, have denied the corruption of humanity. While we have been asserting the honour of God by contending that only His power can redeem us from our degradation, we have been asserting at the same time the honour of man;—declaring our conviction that according to his true nature,—the nature God gave him at first,—he holds a more exalted rank than his present condition intimates. *They* would have us believe that we see in man as he now is, what God made him that he has not sunk beneath his original estate, has not lost his proper dignity; we contend that however great man may be now, whatever may be the lustre of his genius, whatever may be the nobility of his moral impulses, he is far beneath the true ideal which the race was created to fulfil—that he has lost his ancient glory, but through God's grace may win it again.

When we go to the heathen we have still this double commission. While we charge them, in the name of the Most High, no longer to withhold their adoration from the true God, but to love and serve and honour Him in whom they live and move and have their being, we are also telling them that the heroes of their ancient story, whose high achievements have won for them Divine honours, were men of like passions with themselves, and that with the greatest of them they may assert equality of birth and name; that the powers of nature which they reverence and dread, and the birds and beasts and creeping things they have made their gods, have been placed under their feet, to be ruled over, instead of worshipped, and that man is greater than them all.

Here at home, in all the multifarious debates with which our country is ringing, we are still fighting the battle at once of God and of humanity. Men begin discussions on the claims of Christ by telling us that miracles are impossible, that the common laws of the universe cannot be superseded or interrupted. While demonstrating the reality of Christ's wonderful works and maintaining that they are adequate proofs of His Divine commission, we have also to assert that the moral culture and discipline of the human race are in God's judgment of higher significance than the steadfastness of natural laws. It was for our sakes, to minister to our life and happiness and to our moral discipline, that the laws of nature were established, that nature itself was created; and if by the interruption of those laws God can come nearer to man and man be brought nearer to God, *they shall be interrupted.*

Now, at last, the trustworthiness of Divine revelation is impeached by hasty conclusions from newly-discovered facts, some of which, at least, have been most imperfectly verified, and which, if they are all true, admit of another interpretation—

conclusions which would make us of one blood with the ape and the gorilla—and assign a common origin to man, the divinely-anointed sovereign of the world, and to the beasts which were made to drag his burdens and to furnish him with food. In resisting this ignoble theory, we are the champions of the dignity of mankind. We appeal against it in the name of humanity. We say, that while, on the one hand, the apostles of error are excluding the presence and activity of God from His own creation,—on the other, they are covering man with dishonour, and renouncing the dignity and supremacy which belong to our race. They will be met with a learning and a science equal to their own, governed by sounder principles and applied with more reverence and caution. But we also appeal to the instincts of our common nature to resent and repel the outrage. We appeal to man's self-respect, to his indestructible consciousness of his superior origin and characteristic attributes. We invoke the noblest principles and passions of humanity. Nor are we doubtful of the issue. The last conclusion of science will be one with the instinctive faith of the soul. God has made of one blood all nations of men to dwell upon the face of the earth; but between man and the inferior creation a great gulf is fixed. "THOU crownedst him with glory and honour"—who shall impeach his supremacy? "Thou didst set him over the works of thy hands: Thou hast put all things in subjection under his feet."

CHRIST PERFECTED THROUGH SUFFERINGS.

"For it became Him, for whom are all things, and by whom are all things, in bringing many sons unto glory, to make the captain of their salvation perfect through sufferings."—HEBREWS ii. 10.

IN the second half of this chapter, the connexion between the sufferings of the Lord Jesus and His eternal priesthood is very fully unfolded; and most of us have had trouble enough, to be thankful that the Lord Jesus Christ whom we worship as God over all, blessed for evermore, and on whom our faith rests for strength to bear sorrow with patience, as well as for the forgiveness of sin and everlasting life, was once tried as we are. The reality of His sufferings is of infinite importance, not only in relation to the atonement He made for the sin of the world, and as a test and proof of the energy of His love for man and zeal for God, but as establishing between ourselves and Him an immortal sympathy. We can speak to Him of our sorrows with greater freedom, remembering His own; we can invoke His aid with greater confidence, remembering His strong cries and tears; we feel the surer of His pity and merciful help, because by personal experience, and not merely as our Creator, "He knoweth our frame, and remembereth that we are dust."

Perhaps some of us have been accustomed to quote the words of the text as though they were intended to express this most precious truth, and meant that the human excellencies of Christ, and especially His capacity of sympathising with us in our trouble, were perfected by suffering.

The being "made perfect" in this verse has been often regarded as equivalent to His becoming "a merciful and faithful High Priest," which is spoken of a few verses further on. But this is not exactly what the writer of the Epistle intended. The word "to be made perfect" occurs in four or five places in this Epistle,—sometimes in reference to ourselves, sometimes in reference to the Lord Jesus Christ; and I think it is intended, in every case, to describe the attainment of a final, permanent, and fully developed strength and glory. It is substantially the same thing as that which is spoken of in the preceding verse, where Christ is said to be "crowned with glory and honour." The Old Testament saints, without us, were not to be "made perfect." The spirits of the just are "made perfect." Christ when He was "made perfect" became the author of eternal salvation to all them that obey Him. "The law maketh men high priests who have infirmity, but the word of the oath, which was since the law, maketh the *Son*, who is consecrated—or *perfected*—for evermore."

You will not forget that the inspired writer, in that part of the Epistle which we have already examined, has been striving to prevent the gradual drifting back to Judaism of the Hebrew Christians, by recalling to their minds the Divine dignity and supreme glory of the Lord Jesus Christ. In the first chapter he shows how much greater He is than the angels; in the second, he protests against the supposition that the nature of man is so far inferior to the nature of angels, that the incarnation is to be thought of with revulsion of feeling, though the manifestation of God in angelic forms was to be exulted in, as conferring singular honour upon the old Jewish dispensation. Man, according to God's idea of him, is "but a little lower than the angels," and he has been appointed to supreme authority in that order of creation to which he belongs. It is true, that he has sunk below his original dignity, and that weakness, suffering, and shame, have come upon him; but in the midst of the general misery and ruin of the race, we see the Man Christ Jesus—crowned with glory and honour, because He has suffered death—fulfilling in His own person all the lofty descriptions in the ancient Scriptures, of the true power and greatness belonging to mankind;—"*For it became Him, for whom are all things, and by whom are all things, in bringing many sons unto glory, to make the Captain of their salvation perfect through sufferings.*"

The sufferings of Christ were grievous. To the minds of the

believing Jews, the depth and darkness of Christ's humiliation obscured both His original glory and the glory which had followed His death. The reasons why it was necessary for Christ to suffer, the writer speaks of afterwards, but *here*, the emphasis of the thought is this—that it did not become God to leave Him under the power of those sufferings, or unrewarded for them. It was a fact, that Christ had been crowned with glory and honour; and it was fitting that He should be crowned.

I.

It "*became*" God so to exalt the Lord Jesus, because Jesus, in His sufferings, was accomplishing the Divine will, fulfilling a Divine commission. It is a frequent argument with the inspired writers that no act of obedience to God, no act of self-sacrifice, prompted by love to Him, will pass unrewarded. "He is not unrighteous to forget your work and labour of love." The duties He imposes on us, seem to have this for one of their purposes, that God's blessings may come to us, not as the mere gifts of His infinite bounty, but as the recompense of our service. The poorest, slightest proofs of our devotion to Him, are carefully treasured up in His memory, and are to receive public honour. It does not become Him, "for whom are all things, and by whom are all things," to permit any who endure hardship or toil in His service, to remain without reward.

The life, and sufferings, and death, of the Lord Jesus, emphatically required a splendid recompense. To these Jewish Christians who felt, as we cannot feel, how ignoble His life was according to all the common rules of human judgment, how bitter were His sufferings, how shameful His death, this appeal had peculiar force. Let it be granted, that there was a dark contrast between the angelic messengers of the earlier faith and the Son of God by whom the new faith was founded; let it be granted, that He lived in poverty and affected no outward greatness; that even His miracles were quiet and unostentatious; that hunger, and thirst, and weariness, and all the common infirmities of human nature were His inheritance; that

He was a man of sorrows, and acquainted with grief; that His death was the death of a criminal;—what then? Why, He was doing God's work in it all, and it is certain that the depth of His temporary humiliation only increases the height of His everlasting glory. Had He come into the world as a prince, with crown and sceptre, and a bright and splendid army of angels to accomplish His will, there would have been far less in His work for God to honour and reward. But as it is, every sorrow of His earthly life must be recompensed with an infinite joy; His weakness with immortal strength; His human shame with Divine honour; the mockeries and insults of wicked men with the songs of holy angels. Mysterious, and awful, and protracted as were His sufferings, He too, can say when comparing them with their boundless and everlasting recompense, that those "light afflictions" which were "but for a moment," have wrought out for Him "a far more exceeding and eternal weight of glory." "*It became Him, for whom are all things, and by whom are all things,*" to confer on Him, who being His Son, had taken on Him the form of a servant, the highest and most illustrious reward.

II.

It "*became*" God so to exalt the Lord Jesus, because God is "*bringing many sons to glory,*" and it is impossible that He who, in the highest meaning of the term, is the "Son of God" should remain unglorified.

These Jewish Christians were themselves hoping for a blessed immortality. Their fathers had received dim revelations of the future life; but to themselves a clearer and fuller revelation had been made of the glory of heaven than patriarchs or prophets or psalmists had possessed. All who are accustomed to read the Psalms will remember many striking illustrations of the obscurity and imperfection of the knowledge and faith of good men in Jewish times, concerning everlasting blessedness. David, in the greatness of his trouble, cries to God, "O save me, for Thy mercies' sake: for in death there is no remembrance of Thee: in the grave who shall give thee thanks?"

We are not to suppose that he had no knowledge of a future life; elsewhere, there are the clearest proofs that he had. He knew that God would shew to him the path of life—that when heart and flesh failed God would be the strength of his heart and his portion for ever. But his knowledge was very indistinct; his hope of future glory was very cloudy; and just as we find, that in times of darkness and despair we lose sight of nearly all the inferior objects of faith, and only one or two of the greatest sources of consolation remain, so it was with him; and when his trouble was upon him, one of the first truths to disappear was the truth, that even if death came there was a life beyond death, and a life in which God would be better known and worshipped more worthily. But to these Jewish Christians life and immortality had been brought to light through the gospel. They believed that they were the sons of God, and that God intended to confer on them an inheritance of glory. Yes, they too, as the writer intimates in the following verses, were the sons of God. He by whom they had been "*consecrated*" to God, and they who had "*been consecrated*" were "*all of one;*" they had a common father and a common title; for which reason Christ was "*not ashamed to call them brethren.*" With the Psalmist, He could say, I will declare Thy name unto my brethren: with the prophet He could say, I, like those whom I have to teach, will put my trust in Him; and again, Behold I and the children that God hath given me.

They were the sons of God, and God was bringing them to glory. Their own hopes of everlasting blessedness should have reminded them of the greater blessedness which God must already have conferred upon the Lord Jesus. They were being led by the Divine hand to immortal honours in the world to come. How marvellous it was they should need to be told that honours far more exalted must already have been conferred on Christ! If *their* sins were to be forgiven, how certain it was that Christ's holiness had received a glorious reward; if *they* were mercifully to be restored to the Divine favour, how certain it was that Christ had received the very highest proofs of the Divine approbation; if they, who had deserved shame and death, were being brought to the thrones of heaven, how certain it was that Christ had been crowned with glory and honour. If they were to become the companions of angels, Christ must surely have been exalted above all principalities and powers. "*It became Him for whom are all things and by whom are all things, in bringing many sons unto glory, to make the Captain of their salvation perfect through sufferings.*"

III.

It "*became*" God so to exalt the Lord Jesus, because it was by Him that the glory of all the saved was rendered possible. He is "*the* Captain *of their salvation.*" The sons of God derive their sonship from Him; and if they are the heirs of a bright inheritance it is because they are joint heirs with Him. It was the most shameful ingratitude, it was the most ignoble meanness, for Christians to shrink from their profession of fidelity to Christ because of the sorrows and sufferings and contempt which He had endured in His earthly history. His temporary humiliation was the means of securing their deliverance from everlasting ruin; His shame, the means of securing their everlasting honour. If He was poor, it was in order that they might be made rich. If He was put to a cruel and shameful death, it was that they might live a happy and glorious life. And the argument of the inspired writer is this, that it became God to raise to the highest dignity Him whose sufferings were the means of bringing many to glory. It was impossible that He should remain unhonoured, who had rescued many from the deepest degradation and disgrace. The Captain of salvation must receive, in a larger measure and a nobler form, what those who are saved are hoping for.

IV.

The particular term "*make perfect*" which the writer uses in order to describe the exaltation of Christ—while it means substantially the same as "crowning Him with glory and honour"—seems to have been chosen to indicate that as Christ had voluntarily assumed the infirmities of human nature, had voluntarily endured human woe in its most grievous forms, had voluntarily submitted not only to become man, but to be oppressed with burdens and troubles which man, according to God's original idea of man's condition and rank, was never to know, it "*became*" God to *realise in Christ all the possibilities of power and joy which were implanted in man's nature.* What man was meant to be, the writer has already described; and since Christ, to rescue man from ruin, exhausted all the possibilities of suffering which can belong to sinless humanity, it "*became Him*"—from whom man's nature came at first—to develop in Christ all the possibilities of *glory* which belong to sinless humanity. The Divine idea of man must be perfected in Him who became man to save men from eternal destruction. It became the Creator of all things to let the universe see, in the glorified human nature of Christ, the accomplishment of a conception which human sin had prevented being realised before.

V.

But the greatness of Christ's reward is measured not only by the greatness of His service to God and the greatness of His service to man, it is measured also by the infinite resources of the Almighty Creator and Universal Sovereign. It is not accidentally or without a definite purpose, that the inspired writer speaks of God as Him "*for whom are all things and by whom are all things.*" The intention is to suggest how vast, how boundless, are the means which God has for conferring honour on Christ. The recompense is to come from One who has absolute control not merely over the wealth and greatness of this world, but over all created things.

Every region of the universe is under God's command. All the magnificence of the heavens is His; and the glory of angels and archangels and principalities and powers. There is no throne so exalted that He may not give it to Christ—there is no sceptre so mighty that He may not place it in Christ's hand—there are no creatures so illustrious that He may not make them Christ's servants. "*For Him are all things,*" and therefore it "*became*" Him to confer on service such as Christ has rendered, the most magnificent reward.

Nor is this all. God is not merely the Sovereign of the Universe; He is its Origin and Creator too; "*by Him are all things.*" If this universe is not great enough to constitute an adequate reward of Christ's obedience and death, He who created it can create another. He who filled the sun with light can enthrone in the sky a still more splendid orb: He who commanded the stars to glitter in the darkness can multiply their numbers and make them shine with a clearer and intenser brightness. On earth, He can lay the foundations of more majestic mountains, He can hold vaster oceans in the hollow of His hand. In heaven, He can build palaces of light of nobler dimensions and more dazzling splendour than the present mansions of the glorified, and people them with occupants whose powers and blessedness shall exalt them into a rank far transcending that of the most princely of His angels. He is able to reward the service of the Lord Jesus; for all things that exist, exist for Him, and if He pleases, He may lay aside the pomp of the universe as a worn and faded garment, and create new heavens and a new earth, and place them under the feet of Christ. It "*became*" Him, therefore, to perfect the Captain of our salvation.

If it thus "*became*" God Himself to honour Christ—if Omnipotence is worthily exercised in establishing and defending His throne—how does it "become" us to think and to act? Does it "become" any of us, to withhold from Him our supreme affection, our perfect trust, our devoted obedience? Does it "become" any of us, to refuse, as long as we dare, to yield our heart and life to Him; does it "become" any of us, to resolve to bow before Him in penitence and prayer only when it is too late to find any joy away from His presence—only when His outraged mercy alone can save us from swift and irretrievable destruction? Does it "become" any of us, to postpone honouring Christ until we have exhausted forbidden pleasures, or until we have accumulated a fortune, or wrought out any of the schemes of a laudable but secular ambition? It "*became*" GOD, whose merciful purposes Christ came to accomplish, to crown Him with glory and honour: does it "become" us, whom He came to save, to be indifferent, disobedient, or ungrateful?

And let those who trust they have attained the forgiveness of sins through Christ's sufferings and death, ask themselves whether it "becomes" them, to be satisfied with securing their eternal salvation, and to be careless about augmenting the honour of their Lord. If it "*became*" the everlasting Father to glorify Him in heaven, does it "become" us, whom He has condescended to call and to constitute His brethren, to neglect the service by which He may be glorified on earth? Does it "become" us, ever to be indifferent to His worship when we have the opportunity of worshipping Him? Does it "become us, to leave multitudes of our race, who might be doing Him homage, ignorant of His authority and love, when, if we tried to instruct and reclaim them, they might join the angels in offering Him perpetual adoration?

Does it "become" us, by coldness of sympathy, to discourage those who are trying to honour Him? Does it "become" us, by neglecting intercession as well as work, to delay the final subjection of the world to Christ? Does it "become" us, by careless living, by inconsistencies of conduct, by an unchristian temper, to dishonour His name, instead of enriching it with ever-increasing glory, by a holiness originating in love for Him, and sustained by the power of His Spirit and the influence of His example? If it "became" God to exalt the Captain of our Salvation, it "becomes" us to enthrone Him over all the affections and faculties of our nature—over all our earthly possessions—over all the activities of our life: and while angels and archangels serve Him in heaven, and God Himself crowns Him with glory and honour, we ought to try by fervent thanksgiving, by reverential worship, by holy living, by generous gifts, by earnest Christian toil, to fill up the measure of His everlasting joy, and to let Him see of the travail of His soul and be satisfied.

THE HUMANITY OF CHRIST.

"Forasmuch then as the children are partakers of flesh and blood, He also Himself likewise took part of the same," &c.—HEBREWS ii, 14-18.

So far as we know, the Incarnation is unparalleled in the history of the universe. Never, before the Eternal Word became man, did God stand among His creatures as one of themselves, walk along the paths by which they travel, and bear the necessary limitations of a created nature.

I.

It is not surprising that this great mystery should have given rise to many philosophical and theological theories, evading or denying its reality; it is, however, important to remember that the earliest heretics disputed, not the super-human dignity of Christ, but His true humanity. And though the wild and fanciful speculations which troubled the early ages of the church, have long ago disappeared, the errors to which they gave a definite and scientific form may still linger among us.

The great controversy of the English Evangelical Churches of the last generation, was on behalf of the Divinity of the Lord Jesus; perhaps our impression of His humanity is less strong and vivid than it should be. And yet the evidence of Holy Scripture on this point is abundant and most conclusive. The *body* of the Lord Jesus was not a mere phantom. He was born "in the city of David;" His mother "wrapped Him in swaddling clothes, and laid Him in a manger." "The child grew," like other children, "in stature," as well as in wisdom. He needed food and rest, was liable to hunger, thirst, and weariness; and in His agony He "sweat great drops of blood." He was nailed to the cross and laid in the sepulchre; and even after His resurrection He could say, "Behold my hands and my feet, that it is I myself; handle me and see; for a spirit hath not flesh and bones, as ye see me have."

A far more subtle heresy than that which denied the reality of the physical nature of the Lord Jesus, was that which denied that He had a *human soul.* There were some who, while believing that He had a body like ours, and, that what they called the animal soul or life, which renders us capable, like the lower creatures, of physical pleasure and pain, dwelt in Him, supposed that His Divine nature took the place of that higher element of humanity to which belong the affections and the intellectual faculties. The sect of Apollinaris has perished and his name is almost forgotten; but I have known intelligent Christian people who, through never having had their attention specially directed to the truth, have thought that what we mean by the Humanity of Christ is, that He had a human body, and that what we mean by His Divinity, is that His soul was Divine.

But human nature does not consist of a body merely; and it is as certain that the Lord Jesus "humbled Himself" to the limitations of our intellectual nature, as that He assumed an external form. "He increased in wisdom;" He declared that His knowledge was limited. "Of that day and that hour knoweth no man, no, not the angels which are in heaven, *neither the Son*, but the Father."* If it be asked how it was possible for One who, being Divine, was omniscient, to lay aside His glory, and to stoop to the conditions of our own intellectual life, I cannot profess to be able to reply. The fact is inexplicable, but this is no reason for denying it.†

---

* Mark xiii, 32.

† There are some physiological facts which may, perhaps, help to alleviate to some minds the speculative difficulty which the orthodox doctrine involves, It is well known, for instance, that a man who has mastered a foreign language,

That the Lord Jesus had the ordinary *affections* of humanity is not less certain. There was an unearthly sanctity about Him, but the unique impression produced by His character did not result from the absence of those gentle sympathies and varying emotions, which give a colour and a charm to human nature. If holiness consist in the expulsion from the heart, of hope, and fear, and love, and sorrow, the Lord Jesus was not a saint. He "loved Martha, and her sister, and Lazarus." Among His apostles there was one who was the object of His special affection, and who spoke of himself as "the disciple whom Jesus loved." Of His love for His mother we have a most touching proof; when the agonies of His last hour were upon Him, and the sins of the world were being atoned for by His solitary sufferings, He looked down from the cross on Mary, and, remembering her desolate condition, committed her to the care and shelter of His dearest earthly friend, saying to His mother, "Woman, behold thy Son," and to John, "Behold thy mother." His sympathies were quick to respond to any appeal that touched them. When the young man who was rich came to Christ, asking what he must do to inherit eternal life, there was something in the simplicity of his character, his frankness, his very unconsciousness of how seriously he fell

---

and can speak and read it with perfect ease, may have all the treasures of his memory suddenly locked up and completely closed against him, by an injury inflicted on the brain. The orations of Demothenes, the plays of Terence, which he read a week ago without the slightest difficulty, are now as unmeaning to him as to a child who has yet to begin the Latin and Greek declensions. His memory may be unimpaired in every other direction, and yet his classics have clean gone. That the knowledge, though not present to consciousness, and, for the time, beyond the reach of recollection, is not lost, is clear from this, that in some cases of this kind a change has suddenly taken place in the condition of the brain, and the missing language has immediately come back. But, for the time, he was learned, and yet ignorant; he knew, and yet he knew not. I am quite aware of the points in which this illustration fails to touch the mystery of the assumption by an omniscient person of the limitations of a human intellect, and yet it may not be without service to the faith of some. It shows the possibility of the removal beyond the limits of consciousness, of knowledge which the mind still retains.

Since writing this note I have met with the following passage in Ebrard's "Gospel History," which although not intended to illustrate the exact point

short of the highest goodness, which affected the heart of the Lord; "looking on the young man, He loved him;" He felt that sudden outflow of affection towards him which most of us have often felt towards a stranger after hearing only a few words from his lips. The innocence and helplessness of childhood awakened in Him, as in every kindly heart, a yearning tenderness. "Suffer the little children to come to Me, and forbid them not—and *He took them up in His arms, and put His hands upon them, and blessed them.*" Seeing the leper, He was "moved with compassion." When He looked down on Jerusalem from the Mount of Olives, and anticipated its doom, He "wept over it." At the grave of Lazarus He "groaned in spirit, and was troubled;" and though He was about to restore the dead man to life again, "Jesus wept" in sympathy with the mourners, and, perhaps, at the thought of the millions who carry their dearest to the grave, knowing nothing of Him who is the Resurrection and the Life.

When the Jews watched Him, whether He would heal the man with the withered hand on the Sabbath day, He "looked round about on them with anger, being grieved for the hardness of their hearts." When Peter denied Him, that look which made the strong man turn aside and weep, was surely the expression not so much of Divine rebuke, as of human love, wounded and cut to the heart by the temporary failure of the disciple's affection. Finally, before His agony came He had

---

under consideration, touches one of the difficulties which the great mystery involves. Speaking of the Baptism of Jesus, Ebrard says, "In substance, Jesus was the Eternal Son of God ; but through the simple act of His incarnation, He had, by voluntary self-limitation, made the human form of existence, both in time and space, entirely His own, and, therefore, reduced His conscious life within the limits of a human sphere. In the development of His *consciousness*, He had just reached that point in which He clearly apprehended the vocation given to Him by the Father, &c." In a note Ebrard adds, "No man is conscious here on earth, at one and the same moment, of all that he *is* or of all that he possesses, as the *substance* of pneumatico-psychical being. A somnambulist, when waking up from magnetic sleep, will continue the clause which was broken off (sometimes in the middle of a word) as he fell asleep. Consciousness was suspended, the substance remained unchanged. A man who has been insane or delirious with fever, knows, when he recovers, all that he knew before ; though during his illness it has all been withdrawn from his *consciousness*."—Ebrard's Gospel History (Clark's translation), p. 199.

the same longing and yearning for it to be accomplished, that we have to get through some great and painful crisis of our history,—" I have a baptism to be baptised with, and how am I straitened till it be accomplished ; " and when it came, there was human shrinking and fear,—" My soul is exceeding sorrowful, even unto death. Father, if it be Thy will, let this cup pass from Me."

Christ has vindicated the affections of our nature from foolish and wicked reproach. Protestants as we are, I fear that some of us still feel the attraction of that unreal and ascetic virtue which has been canonized through century after century by the Romish Church. The voluntary desertion of society, the renunciation of the joys and duties and solicitudes of friendship and love, the crucifixion and murder of many of the harmless instincts and passions of the heart, that the soul may dwell for ever in the mysterious stillness or ecstatic raptures of a solitary devotion, appear to us to constitute a higher and purer type of perfection than can be attained amidst the ordinary cares and pleasures of men. The legends of Rome, her wondrous stories of saintly hermits, monks, and martyrs, have won her more converts than all the logic of her illustrious theologians. The true missionaries and apostles of that Church are not her accomplished divines, but her ascetics, worn out with fastings and prayers.

The best corrective of the morbid condition of the imagination which renders us susceptible to these perilous fascinations, is to turn to the pages of the four Gospels. How tame are the inspired representations of the Lord Jesus, after the stimulating histories of the saints of the middle ages! How cold His devotion, compared with their vehemence and fervour ! What self-indulgence was there in Him, when we think of their self-mortification ! As soon as we find that, without saying it, we feel all this, it is time to conclude that we are in great danger. There must be something false and meretricious in that saintly aureola which makes the glory of the Lord Jesus appear dim. Our vision needs purging. Our taste has been fatally corrupted.

It is one of the most successful frauds of the devil, to divert our strength from the struggle with real sins, by causing us to feel scruples about what is harmless, and to condemn what is positively good. A conscience morbidly acute in one direction, will be insensible and powerless in another; or, after protracted irritation and distress, will sink into permanent and universal inactivity. The endeavour to attain an unreal virtue often ends in a hard indifference to the plainest and simplest duties.

"*Forasmuch, then, as the children*—(we have been told, in a preceding verse, that God is 'bringing many *sons* unto glory') —*are partakers of flesh and blood, He also Himself likewise took part of the same.* * * * *In all things it behoved Him to be made like unto His brethren.*" This relationship resting on a participation of our "flesh and blood," and a sharing of our "infirmities," must render possible a nearer and more blessed communion with Him than even His angels or archangels can ever know. His humanity was sanctified by the same Spirit that sanctifies us. He was tempted by the same evil power that tempts us. His religious life was cherished and developed by the same ancient Scriptures which are our consolation and strength. He sang with a loftier rapture and a keener sorrow the very Psalms in which we utter our joy and grief. He travelled to the throne of God by the same rugged and weary path by which we are now travelling. Our final blessedness will be a rest from toil, and He is resting from His labours. Those who, like Himself, have reached "perfection" through suffering, must be nearer to Him for ever, than those bright and happy spirits on whose joy the shadow of grief has never fallen.

II.

Christ came to save a race over which "death reigned;" "*it is not angels* that He helpeth, but the seed of Abraham:" hence it was necessary that He should destroy "*him that hath the power of death, that is, the devil.*" This description of the

Wicked One is remarkable, and there is considerable difficulty in apprehending its exact meaning.

Holy Scripture teaches us that death, the death of the body, is the penalty of sin. Had man not transgressed the Divine law, he would never have died at all. Perhaps it was in anticipation of man's disobedience, that the living creatures which inhabited the world in ages long before the creation of our race were subjected to the law of mortality.* Explain it how we will, there is a dread of dying which cannot be wholly traced to an instinctive shrinking from the breaking up of our physical organisation, nor to an unwillingness to be separated from the scenes and society with which our hearts have grown familiar. Death has always looked like a terrible proof that God is against us; like the execution of a sentence pronounced against us by the Supreme Power. At its approach the heart is agitated by moral alarms; slumbering consciences are startled into wild activity; the soul is haunted by its sins.

And if death is the punishment of sin, it is the visible sign that we have yielded ourselves to the malignant power of the devil. It is a proof that we have become his. He reigns in dark supremacy over all who are cast away from God's presence. They are his victims. The regions of condemnation are in some sense under his control.

But when the mercy of God rested the moral constitution of the world on the atonement of the Lord Jesus Christ, death ceased to be the expulsion of the soul from the Divine love. Christ, by His own death, rescued the human race from condemnation, and so "destroyed" him whose "power" extends only to those who have been abandoned by God to the just consequences of their wrong-doing.

We *"fear"* death no longer. The *"bondage"* which the fear produced is broken. Death, which was once the sign of God's anger, has been made the most glorious proof and illustration of God's love; He "commendeth His love toward us, in that,

---

* See a remarkable chapter (cap. vii.) in Dr. Bushnell's "Nature and the Supernatural."

while we were yet sinners, Christ died for us." Life and immortality are brought to light through the gospel. In thousands of instances the instinctive fear of death has been mastered by the "desire to depart and to be with Christ."

The consideration of the sympathies of the Lord Jesus for mankind, arising out of His personal experience of temptation and sorrow (vv. 17, 18), may be postponed till we reach the close of the fourth chapter, where the writer recurs to this consolatory subject, and treats it more fully.

THE SIN IN THE WILDERNESS.

"Wherefore, holy brethren, partakers of the heavenly calling," &c.—
HEBREWS iii, 1—19.

I PROPOSE, this morning, to place before you the impressive and startling series of thoughts contained in this chapter. The strain of warning commencing in the seventh verse is, indeed, continued through the next chapter, but it would not be possible to illustrate and enforce the whole passage in a single sermon.

As the writer has just spoken of Christ as a merciful and trustworthy High Priest, it would have been very natural had he immediately proceeded to describe the perfection and glory of His priesthood; but he pauses, that he may show Christ's superiority to Moses—the supreme object, under God, of Jewish veneration—and that he may avail himself of the most awful argument afforded by Old Testament history for strengthening the fidelity of Jewish believers who were in danger of drifting back into Judaism.

In introducing this new line of thought, he addresses his readers as "*holy brethren.*" The pathos of this honourable title is best understood by recalling what has been said already about the ultimate purpose of God in the mission of the Lord Jesus. Through Him God is "bringing many *sons*," not servants, "unto glory." There is a brotherhood between Christ and all believers. They are "partakers of flesh and blood;" "He also Himself took part of the same." He has been "crowned with glory and honour," and they are predestinated to be conformed to His image, for "He tasted death for every man." "He is not ashamed to call them brethren." The readers of the Epistle are reminded, by the title by which they are addressed, of their brotherhood with each other and with Christ.

Having been called to heavenly dignity and blessedness, they are also *"partakers of the heavenly calling."*

They are exhorted to *"contemplate earnestly"* Christ Jesus, *"the Apostle and High Priest"* of the Christian faith; the *"Apostle,"* for it was He who brought from heaven the messages of mercy which are the heart and life of the new revelation; the *"High Priest,"* for He stands before God to make reconciliation for human sin.

The special reason alleged in this place for so contemplating Christ, is that He has received an honour and a reward far more illustrious than had been conferred on the founder of the Jewish faith and polity: *"He has been judged worthy of more glory than Moses."*

The writer might have proceeded to expatiate on Christ's exaltation to the right hand of God, but he is writing to those who had often heard the story of His ascension into heaven from the lips of the very men who saw Him ascend; to those who knew that the crucified Jesus had been made Prince as well as Saviour; and in this very Epistle it had been said that the angels of God worshipped Him. All that the writer does here, therefore, is to point out the reason, or one of the reasons, why the Lord Jesus has been exalted to greater glory than Moses.

I.

I shall state the separate thoughts which are interwoven in his contrast between Moses and Christ.

(1) The community of God's servants which has existed in the world from the earliest ages is called God's *"house,"* or *"household."* Between Him and them there has been a holy intimacy. He has given them moral laws, promises, religious ceremonies, institutions of worship. They have been under His special protection. He has revealed to them His character. He has dwelt among them. The true house of God in this world is not in material temples, but among those who love Him and keep His commandments. In the old time the

Jewish nation was God's visible dwelling-place. St. Paul, in his first Epistle to Timothy, speaks of the Christian Church as being "the house of the living God," for in the church the Divine presence dwells and the Divine glory is revealed.

Now of Moses it is said, in Numbers xii. 7, he "is faithful in all My house;" words which are quoted in the second verse of this chapter, and which show that by *"His house"* is meant, not the house of Moses, but the house of God.

(2) In God's house Moses was faithful as a *"servant."* This is all that even the Old Testament claims for him. In the passage in Numbers, just quoted, it is declared that Moses had nearer intercourse with God than others who had received Divine revelations: to them God spake in a vision or a dream, but "My servant Moses is not so, who is faithful in all Mine house. With him I will speak mouth to mouth, even apparently, and not in dark speeches; and the similitude of the Lord shall he behold." When God is asserting for Moses a higher rank than belonged to other inspired prophets, he is described as a "servant" still.

(3) Lofty as were the functions of the Jewish legislator, it is affirmed that in faithfully discharging his duties as a servant, he was bearing *"testimony of things which were to be afterwards spoken."* He prophesied of one who was to come in after ages; the priesthood that he consecrated, the altars he built, the whole structure of the Jewish system, was but a temporary provision for the religious necessities of mankind; and the hearts of devout Jews were always longing for the full revelation and perfect accomplishment of God's thoughts and purposes concerning our race.

(4) Christ is more than a servant. *"Every house,"* or *"household,"*—for the word includes not merely the material edifice, but all the appointments and offices that minister to the life and comfort of the family,—must be *"founded by some one, and God is the founder of all things."* The Jewish Church was not founded by Moses but by God himself, and Christ, as His Son, shares with Him His superior honour. He does not belong, as Moses did, to the house; He is the Son of God by whom the house was established: and as God the founder has

more honour than the household He has founded, in which Moses was a servant,—Christ, the Son of God, has more honour than Moses.

It is not possible for us to imagine the enthusiasm, the almost idolatrous veneration, with which Moses was regarded by the Jewish people; a veneration which was deepened, an enthusiasm which was intensified, as the final struggle for national existence drew near. All the ordinary elements of human greatness culminated in his history, and to these were added the mystery and glory of supernatural endowments and of a Divine commission. There was romance even in the story of his infancy. He was born when his race was enduring cruel persecution; but his mother's instinct, quickened by his personal beauty, and guided by the hand of God, led her to make a desperate effort to preserve him from the destruction to which he was doomed by the bloody decree of the king. He was found on the waters of the Nile by a princess, adopted by her, and educated in all the accomplishments and learning of a great and splendid court. Arrived at manhood, his heart was fired with a patriotic love for his own people, and having slain an Egyptian who was treating a Hebrew with violence, he was obliged to flee into the desert for safety. For forty years he lived in the solitude and wild freedom of a pastoral life; and then it was Divinely revealed to him that he was to be the deliverer of his countrymen. His struggle with the Egyptian king was fierce and protracted. At his word, terrible plagues came upon Pharaoh and his subjects; and at his word, the plagues departed. The great river was turned into blood; foul diseases affected cattle and men; showers of hail, thunder and lightning destroyed the crops; and, finally, in one dreadful night all the firstborn of Egypt perished. The oppressed race marched out of the land of bondage by thousands and tens of thousands' and at the word of Moses the sea divided, that the vast host might pass over; the pomp and power of Pharaoh and his armies perished in the returning waves. For forty years the great Jewish chief governed his restless countrymen in the wilderness · he gave them bread from heaven to eat, and water from the rock to drink; he brought them face to face with God, at whose voice and glory they trembled. And, at last, lest his mortal remains should be the object of superstitious worship, he went up alone into a mountain to die, and no man ever knew of his sepulchre.

He was a patriot, and punished the enemies of his race with tremendous chastisement; he was a legislator, and his laws had retained their authority for more than sixteen hundred years; he founded a national literature, and his writings had been the daily reading of the kings and priests and commonalty of the Jewish people throughout their subsequent history, and no doubt was ever urged, no appeal was ever made against a solitary sentence that had come from his pen; he established religious institutions, and through generation after generation inspired men had been commissioned to defend their sanctity; and the fortunes of the nation proved that no commandment of Moses could be forgotten or violated without provoking the vengeance of heaven. No other name in the history of the world has ever had the power to stir the heart of a nation like his. More than Luther is to Germany, more than Napoleon is to France, more than Alfred, or Elizabeth, or Cromwell, or William III. is to England, Moses was to the Jewish people—prophet, patriot, warrior, lawgiver, all in one.

How strange a contrast between this romantic, brilliant, and splendid history, and the life of the Lord Jesus! He was called a Nazarene; He was despised and calumniated by the rulers of His nation; His religious claims were branded by the priesthood as blasphemous, and He was crucified by the civil power as a turbulent political criminal. And yet Moses was only God's servant—Christ was God's Son. "Consider the Apostle and High Priest of our profession," "for He has been held worthy of more honour than Moses."

II.

This exhortation is driven home to the heart and conscience of the vacillating Jewish believers, by an appeal to the miserable end of the generation which came out of Egypt.

Never did a nation occupy a grander position than the ancient Jews, when they stood on the eastern shore of the Red Sea. The wonderful procession of miracles which had terrified and yet hardened the heart of Pharaoh, broken but not subdued his haughty and imperious will, was sublimely closed. The security of the fugitive race was now complete; their wrongs were terribly avenged. The armies of Egypt, her chariots and horsemen, her princes and her warriors, were cast into the sea; "they sank to the bottom as a stone, they sank like lead in the mighty waters." For their leader they had a chief who fought against their enemies with storm and tempest, pestilence and famine, with the waves of the sea, and with the invisible swords of supernatural ministers of vengeance. They had with them the pillar of cloud and of fire, the visible symbol of the Divine presence and the visible pledge of the Divine favour. Very soon they were to enter into a fertile and beautiful land which God had promised to their ancestors, and they were to dwell for ever under the Divine protection. Bright visions of wealth and splendour, mighty cities, noble palaces, glittering armies, military renown, were floating before the imagination of many a man in that vast encampment,— visions, however, which fell far short of the glory which the nation had actually within its reach.

But it soon became evident that the triumphant race was doomed to disappointment, disaster, and shame. Hardly any of that generation reached the land of promise. They perished miserably. The "mighty wonders" which God had wrought to break the power of their oppressors effected nothing for them except to give them a grave in the wilderness.

And you, my brethren, the writer seems to say, are exposed to a like danger. In the terrible punishments which came upon your fathers, you may see dimly foreshadowed the curse which must come upon all apostates. You have obeyed the voice of God till now. Divine acts far more sublime than those your fathers witnessed have separated you from your old life, and brought everlasting glory near to you. From a worse bondage you have been emancipated by more wonderful miracles, and you have been made heirs of a more blessed inheritance. But your confidence is faltering. You are beginning to distrust God, as your fathers distrusted Him; His anger is rising, and in His wrath He may swear that you shall not enter into His rest.

Nor is it for Jewish Christians alone that this warning is charged with awful solemnity. It sternly rebukes the folly of supposing that because God has delivered us from our former slavery to sin, we need have no anxiety about our ultimate salvation. The writer of this Epistle plainly requires that faith should continue to the end, and would refuse to listen to any appeal to past religious experiences, if intended to diminish alarm occasioned by the present consciousness of sin. Had you told him that you were hoping to be safe at last, because of the remarkable manifestations of the Divine mercy which accompanied the commencement of your religious life, he would have asked whether or not you had now "an evil heart of unbelief." If you had pleaded that, after God had done so much for you, it was impossible you should ultimately perish, he would have answered that by amazing miracles the people of Israel were delivered from Egypt, and yet "their carcases fell in the wilderness." We are to escape from final ruin, not by the memory of former supernatural experiences, but by cleaving still to the living God, and watching earnestly and prayerfully against the great danger of being "hardened through the deceitfulness of sin."

THE REST OF GOD.

"Let us therefore fear, lest a promise being left us of entering into His rest, any of you should seem to come short of it," &c.—HEBREWS iv, 1-13.

IN this passage, as in so many other parts of the New Testament, argument and exhortation are closely interwoven; a truth is established by reasoning, and an appeal is made to the conscience and the heart.

In the preceding chapter the writer has warned the Hebrew Christians of their danger, if their faith in the Lord Jesus Christ is overborne or destroyed; He has reminded them that their fathers perished in the wilderness through loss of courageous trust in the Divine goodness and power. "*Let us therefore fear, lest a promise still remaining of entering into the rest of God, any should appear*—at the great judgment—*to have come short of it.*"

In the following verses, the writer appeals to the Old Testament to show that the peaceful possession of Canaan did not exhaust all that God meant by the rest to which He had destined His people. There is another rest of a higher and nobler kind still "remaining" for the descendants of Abraham, —for all who listen to and obey the word of God. "A promise is left unto *us*."

The passage he appeals to, is that in the ninety-fifth Psalm, which he has already quoted in the preceding chapter.

(1) In that Psalm an inspired writer speaks of the Divine rest, and declares that God had sworn that those who had been guilty of unbelief in the wilderness should not enter into it. And this reference to the sin of the generation that left Egypt, derives all its practical power from the truth that the generation to which the Psalmist was speaking,

might be guilty of the same sin of unbelief, and through it, might incur the same penalty of exclusion from the rest of God.

(2) It is added that this rest, though the object of hope to God's people, had already begun for Himself: "*His works were finished from the foundation of the world;*" in the earliest pages of Divine revelation it is said that "God rested on the seventh day." But, in the Psalm, though written so many centuries after the entrance into Canaan, the contemporaries of the Psalmist are clearly addressed, "To-day *if ye will hear His voice, harden not your hearts.*" "*If Joshua had given the people rest,*" God would not afterward have spoken in a manner that implied the possibility of the people of David's time being subjected to a punishment like that which came upon their fathers. And, therefore, "*there still remains for us a rest,*"—a glorious Sabbath,—a fellowship with the peace of God. "*He that hath entered into rest*" has escaped from all the labours and conflicts of his life. "*He hath ceased from* his own *works, as God ceased from* His." "*Let us labour, therefore, to enter into that rest, lest any man fail after the same example of unbelief.*"

And now let us consider separately the principal thoughts contained in this passage.

I.

The foundation of the whole, is the rest of God after the creation of the world. In the first chapter of the book of Genesis, we have the story of the creation of all things, presented in a form intelligible to the minds of untaught men of every country and every age, and intended, not to anticipate the results of scientific investigation, but to convey important religious truths. A description, however brief, of the actual processes by which the Divine wisdom and power gradually brought into existence this material universe, with all the living things which have their home in it, would have occupied, not a single page of an inspired book, but many volumes. And, in the earlier days of human history, no language existed in which that description could have been given. Just as the writers of the New Testament are obliged to represent the glories of the world to come, by employing the most brilliant and gorgeous imagery with which we are familiar in this life, and tell us that the streets of the city of God are gold, its gates pearls, its walls jasper, and its foundations precious stones, so the writer of the first chapter of Genesis was obliged in describing the history of creation, to employ language and forms of thought derived from actual human experience. That mysterious and blessed existence which lies beyond the close of human life on earth, is so exhibited to us that we long to enter into its glory and peace; but we are sure that, when we reach heaven, we shall discover that the brightest and fairest things of this world were but a dim and imperfect parable of the splendour and joy of the world to come. And so, the wonderful series of Divine acts which preceded human life on earth, is exhibited to us so as to awaken wonder and awe, and to deliver us from the great falsehood and sin of idolatry; but, as we gradually come to learn the actual history of created things, we shall discover that the grandeur of the Divine acts transcended all the resources of human thought and speech in the earlier ages of human history. Even now, although the genius which God has bestowed upon some great men during the last three centuries, and the exhausting labours He has enabled them to prosecute, have resulted in amazing discoveries of the vastness and majesty of the material universe, and of the wisdom and goodness which have determined its laws, we are only beginning to understand the works of God. "He doeth great things and unsearchable; marvellous things without number."

Now, in the inspired narrative of creation it is intimated that, after the Divine power had been put forth in a magnificent series of creative acts, there was a pause; the system of things which God intended to bring into existence was at last complete; all material laws were finally established; every independent form of life had been originated; and God rested from His works. Henceforth, for ages at least, there was nothing for Him to do but to sustain the universe He had made, to watch over the development of all the forces which at His word had begun to act, to uphold the laws which He had instituted. He rested, and He saw that all His works were good. It is true that He fainteth not, neither is weary; but He regarded what He had created, with the satisfaction and peaceful joy with which man pauses when his cherished purposes are perfectly accomplished, and with which man contemplates the translation of his dreams into facts. An architect who has built a majestic cathedral, a painter who has finished a glorious picture, a sculptor who has carved a noble statue, rests,—not because his genius has been exhausted,—it may even have been developed and exalted by his labour,—but because he rejoices when his idea has assumed a permanent form of grandeur or beauty. And so God rested,—found delight in His material and spiritual creation: He crowned it with the highest and most wonderful honour, declaring that even HE thought it good.

Into the depths of that Divine delight who can hope to penetrate? "God is great, and we know Him not." To Him, as to us, the consciousness of perfection must be a source of blessedness. From eternity He had known His power, His wisdom, His justice, and His love. In the solitude in which the Godhead dwelt, before there were any creatures to gaze on the Divine glory or to be governed and sustained by the Divine hand, there was perfect and infinite joy. And yet it is hard for us not to think that there is another element of blessedness in the actual exercise of omnipotence, and in witnessing its effects; in the adjustment by infinite wisdom of the forces of the visible creation, and the comprehension by an unlimited and faultless knowledge of all the activities of created life; in the outflowing of the eternal love upon the innumerable orders of moral creatures, and in the vision of their holiness and joy, God saw that His works were "good." He contemplated them not with the passionless unconcern which we are too disposed to attribute to an infinite being, but with positive delight.

II.

Even in Jewish times there were indications that man might have fellowship with the rest of God.

On the weekly Sabbath, which commemorated the rest of God, man himself was required to rest, and so the thoughts of the devout were naturally led to a calm and happy meditation on the Divine works, and to thanksgivings for all that God had made,—thanksgivings in which man rose into communion with God's own joy over His creation. Those who heartily honour the work of the artist have no remote or imperfect fellowship with the satisfaction which he himself finds in the exercise and achievements of his genius.

In the ninety-fifth Psalm, God speaks of His own "rest" as one which man might share.

III.

In the Christian revelation the possibility of this high communion is far more perfectly revealed.

I repudiate the dreams of Pantheism, even when they are baptised with the Christian name, and when the dreamers speak a language richly coloured with the characteristic terms of the New Testament Scriptures. Though penetrated and transfigured by the light descending from the higher regions of revealed truth, and looking warm and gorgeous as the clouds of sunset, the theory is mere mist and vapour still. But the soberest interpreter of the Gospels and of the apostolic writings, will reverently acknowledge that there are passages of unfathomable depth which foreshadow a blessed union between all holy beings and their Creator. For men there are "exceeding great and precious promises," and though our relationship to God in Christ gives to these promises a peculiar emphasis and richer meaning, we cannot but believe that for other ranks of moral beings there is a corresponding though, perhaps, an inferior bliss. "To him that overcometh will I give to sit with Me on My throne, even as I also overcame and am set down with My Father on His throne." We are "predestinated to be conformed to the image of His Son." We are "joint heirs with Christ." All believers are "living stones," in the temple of which, "Jesus Christ Himself" is "the chief corner stone." In Christ "dwelleth all the fulness of the Godhead bodily," and "ye are complete in Him." "The glory which Thou gavest me I have given them." "Our fellowship is with the Father and with the Son Jesus Christ."

The preparations for our final communion with the Divine joy are already around us. We shall share God's rest, for we share His work. He inspires us with love for the souls of men and with keen solicitude for their everlasting salvation. "The glorious gospel of the blessed God" is "committed" to "our trust." In preaching it, multitudes of saints have undertaken and sustained heavy labours, and endured severe persecutions. All who preach it earnestly, learn something of the yearning compassion for men which prompted Christ Himself to take the form of a servant, and to "become obedient unto death, even the death of the cross." They have "great heaviness and continual sorrow of heart," because of the ungodly. Christ left heaven to save mankind; and they, though "having a desire to depart," are content that their entrance into glory should be delayed in order that they may continue to persuade and entreat men to be reconciled to God. An apostle could even speak of "filling up that which is left behind of the afflictions of Christ for His body's sake, the Church."

Our earthly work is the prophecy of our heavenly reward. Called to take a part in effecting the salvation of men, we shall share the bliss with which their salvation will fill for ever the heart of God. The "cross" is ours as well as Christ's; and "the joy which was set before Him" is ours too.

The "new heavens and the new earth" are emerging from the darkness and chaos of the world's moral condition to a grandeur and splendour infinitely transcending the glories of the material universe; but in this new creation God is not acting alone. Not by His word merely, but also by human toil and suffering, is the mighty and everlasting structure rising to its ultimate perfection. And when the brighter heavens and the fairer earth are "finished, and all the host of them," and shall lie under the eye of God in their consummate and incorruptible beauty, and He shall declare that they are "good,' the humblest and obscurest of those who have contributed to the great result, shall share the Divine satisfaction, and rest with God from their work.

It is terrible to think that with such an inheritance within our reach, any should "fall" after the "example of" those who lost Canaan and perished in the wilderness. But, to escape a doom of which theirs is but the shadow, it is necessary to "labour." For the "*Word of God*," which we have to receive and obey, is a *living and powerful thing; it is sharper than any two-edged sword;* it *pierces* into the very depths of man's nature; it *discerns*, distinguishes, *the thoughts and intents of the heart.*" What we are, is manifested in the way in which we receive it. We are returning our final answer to the question whether we will serve God or not. His Word has such attributes that the secret of our heart is told by our acceptance or rejection of it. "*Neither is there any creature that is not manifest in His sight*, by whom the Word is spoken; *but all things are naked and open unto the eye of Him with whom we have to do.*" Whether we listen to Him or not, He knows perfectly; and by that knowledge He will determine our eternal destiny. No revision of His sentence will be needed; no reversal can be hoped for. Now is the crisis of our immortal history.

THE SYMPATHY OF CHRIST.

"Seeing, then, that we have a great High Priest, that is passed into the heavens, Jesus, the Son of God, let us hold fast our profession," &c.—HEBREWS iv, 14-16.

THESE verses form, at once, the close of that solemn argument for steadfastness in the profession of faith in the Lord Jesus which occupies the greater part of the third and fourth chapters of this epistle, and the transition to the illustration of the priesthood of Christ, which commences in the fifth chapter, and, after being interrupted by a passage filled with most startling and awful warnings, extends through the seventh, eighth, and ninth chapters, and the first half of the tenth.

I.

"*Let us hold fast our profession.*" This is the brief summary of the duty which is enforced by the whole epistle. To give to this exhortation an irresistible force, the writer has just recalled the disastrous history of the generation which escaped from Egypt. They did not hold fast their profession of confidence in God, but lost their faith and their courage, were guilty of great sin, and perished in the wilderness.

It must be acknowledged that the circumstances of their flight and of their life in the desert, were a severe test of their religious trust and fidelity. When the fugitives saw Pharaoh and his army behind them,—enraged at their escape and resolved to destroy them,—and the sea in front, we can hardly wonder that they were filled with terror and exclaimed that it would have been better for them to have died in Egypt. When, ten months afterwards, the whole nation seemed in danger of perishing through want of bread, I am not disposed to judge them very hardly, or to think they were conspicuous for their distrust above all the rest of mankind, because they cried again, "Would to God we had died in Egypt!" But it seems inexcusable that their unbelief should have continued after repeated interferences of miraculous power. When they wanted water, they lost faith and murmured; when they became weary of the manna, they lost faith and murmured; when the spies returned who had been sent to search out the land of Canaan, and declared how strong the inhabitants were, that they were giants, and that the people of Israel would never be able to overcome them, they lost faith again, and murmured again, and cried again, "Would to God we had died in the land of Egypt!" and they appointed a new chief in the place of Moses to lead them back to slavery. When they saw the Egyptians dead upon the sea shore, they could sing with Moses and with Miriam loud songs of triumph, and when they were assembled at the foot of Sinai they could utter solemn vows, saying, "All that the Lord hath spoken we will do;" but they did not "hold fast" their confidence, and so they were destroyed.

The faith of the Hebrew Christians to whom this epistle was addressed was also exposed to severe trials. They had a whole nation against them. The glorious traditions of their race seemed against them. Their education, all the habits and modes of thought of their early religious life, were against them too. They were in danger of being driven from the temple in which they and their fathers had worshipped, from the altars at which they and their fathers had sacrificed. Reputation, property, life itself, were imperilled by their Christian profession. It was hard for them to hold it fast. They were tempted to conceal their faith in the Lord Jesus, and the writer attaches great importance to the external act as well as to the internal principle. Profession was indispensable if the Christian church was to win new adherents, if the Christian faith was to be upheld against Jewish hatred, if the truth which had been revealed to those who believed in Christ, was to be made known to all mankind and transmitted to future generations. Persecution was no reason for concealing the convictions of the heart. Even to escape loss and injury, they must not "forsake the assembling of themselves together," after the manner of some less courageous and less earnest brethren. Profession of faith was a duty they owed to Christ and a duty they owed to man. It is the same now.

I know that some men plead that they can honour Christ by a quiet, upright, generous life, without any unequivocal declaration of their loyalty to him; but surely, if they stand apart from the church, they must see that their endeavours to do well are not certain to be ascribed to the influence of their Christian faith. Their very excellence may be perverted by others to Christ's dishonour; for they may be pointed to as proofs that there are some who have not faith enough to enter the church, who are as truthful, as honest, as kindly, and as regular too at public worship, as those who have; and that, therefore, a firm and decided devotion to Christ can be of no great importance.

But although there may be some of you whom it may be necessary to remind of the duty of making a profession, and of holding fast to it, there are many more who are in danger, while holding fast your profession, of permitting your inner life to decay. Are any of you already conscious of this?—conscious that you think of the sins you have renounced with less hatred than formerly; confess the sins you commit with less sorrow; strive to live a holy life with less eagerness; read the holy Scriptures with less thoughtfulness and solicitude; engage in Christian work less zealously; give your money for the relief of the poor and the maintenance and diffusion of the Gospel with less cheerfulness; pray to God less fervently; find less joy in contemplating the perfections of His character, and in meditating on the words and the deeds by which He has revealed Himself to man? Are you getting impatient under the pressure of Christian duty, weary of dull and apparently unprofitable endeavours to subdue ill temper, to check hasty speech, to root up some evil passion, to live in unbroken communion with God? If so, take heed! If it was a crime to abandon the profession of faith in Christ because of loss and suffering, what must it be, when fidelity to Him is threatened by no perils, by no penalties, to let the faith itself decay and perish?

II.

Steadfastness in the profession of Christ, steadfastness in the practical obedience which that profession implies, is not impossible,—"*seeing that we have a great High Priest that is passed through the heavens, Jesus the Son of God, who can sympathize with our infirmities, being in all points tempted like as we are, though without sin.*" What a tranquillizing, soothing transition this is from the dark and terrible thoughts of the earlier parts of this chapter. It is like a bright, pure, sparkling stream, singing pleasant music and making the green grass and beautiful wild flowers grow on its banks, in a rugged and desolate country. We come upon it with the same sense of security and joy that a solitary and weary traveller feels who has lost his way among huge mountains and has become alarmed as the darkness is gathering around him, when he strikes upon the path which he knows will bring him safely through the pass and into the valley where he means to rest for the night. It is like the shining rainbow on the retreating storm.

Our "infirmities" may sometimes force us to exclaim that continuance in well-doing is beyond our strength. We are sure to fail. But we have a High Priest who has passed, not through the veil of an earthly temple to stand before a mere symbol of the Divine presence, but has passed through the heavens to stand before the very throne of God. And while pleading there for us, He will remember how He, too, was sorely tried; how His human weakness quailed in the presence of suffering; and how He was tempted to turn aside from the work to which He had put His hand, so fruitless and powerless seemed all His endeavours to instruct, to warn, to bless mankind. There was a time when He was exceeding sorrowful even unto death, and when all the forces of His human nature, though rooted immoveably in a Divine stedfastness, were straining and bending like the trees of the forest under the stress of a vehement storm; there was a mysterious agony and an earnest prayer, thrice repeated, that if it were possible the bitter cup might pass from Him. He who has passed through the heavens—our great High Priest—is the man, Christ Jesus, as well as the Son of God. He can be touched with the feeling of our infirmities though without sin,—He was in all points tempted like as we are; tempted by human weariness, by human weakness, by want of success, by the failure of His friends, by the power of His enemies; tempted to abandon His work and leave the world unsaved. Remembering all this, He will not be hard on us, if our infirmities make us shrink from the prolonged and exhausting toil in which serving Him and working out our salvation are certain to involve us.

III.

His sympathy, and His presence in heaven, will render us no service unless we "*come boldly to the throne of grace to obtain His mercy*—or *pity*—*and His grace for timely help.*"

(1) We should notice, in the first place, that it is especially about our *infirmities* that we are told to speak to God. It is with these Christ can sympathize. In the next chapter we shall see that since He Himself was compassed with weakness He "can have compassion" on those in whom weakness has led to sin; but it is not said that He "sympathizes" with sin. He is not "touched with a feeling" of *that*. He pities them that fall. He freely forgives the penitent; in a moment, He receives back into the joy of His love all that yearn for His pardon; but with the sins of human nature He can have no sympathy; with its weakness He can.

It is a very significant fact that we have come to use the word "infirmities" to describe habits and tendencies to which the Scriptures always give a harder name. We use it to denote a fretful, irritable temper, certain forms of selfishness, carelessness of speech, and many other sins besides. It is right enough to speak to God about these, and God will pardon them; but let us take care to call them by their right name; and, meanwhile, let us remember that if we spoke to God oftener about our weaknesses we should have fewer sins needing forgiveness and fewer sorrows needing consolation.

What then are the "*infirmities*" of which the writer speaks? They are those forms of human weakness which make us shrink from painful duty, or make it difficult for us to persevere month after month in well-doing.

There are certain physical conditions in which it is hard to trust quietly in God's love, and to keep the image of Christ in our own character and conduct unclouded. The physical exhaustion which follows severe pain or excessive anxiety and labour, seems sometimes to drain away all our moral strength. The weakness of the flesh makes the spirit weak too. Utter lassitude comes upon us, and strenuous exertion seems impossible. He to whom the angels ministered after His forty days' fast in the wilderness, knows what this infirmity is, and from Him we shall have timely help.

Or the conflict between plain duty and the common instincts and affections of our nature may assume a severe form. We may be required by conscience to abandon prospects of ease and comfort and honour; we may have to incur the distrust and opposition of friends; to inflict pain on those we most dearly love; to imperil or sacrifice the chief joy of our earthly life; to provoke the hostility of powerful enemies,—slander we cannot repel, calumny we cannot silence, reproach which seems just, and which we must be content to bear: it is hard to master and quiet the agitation of our heart, to triumph over natural passions in the strength of a Divine affection; but He who was "tempted like as we are" will give us timely help.

Above all, when we are disheartened by disappointment in our Christian work, when friends melt away from our side like deserters from an army which has been broken in spirit by long marches, or by repeated defeats; when our labours are spoiled by the negligence or mistakes or inconsistencies of those in whom we have confided; when we are thwarted in our best endeavours by secret jealousy, by muttered suspicion, by open hatred; when prayer seems to have no power; when toil seems wasted; when the understandings of men remain unconvinced by the most conclusive arguments, their hearts untouched by the most affecting motives, their consciences hardened against the most startling appeals; when those who had begun to do well turn back into sin, and those who had long been faithful are gradually drifting away from what they once supremely cared for; when no plan of well-doing can command sympathy or aid, no right principle manly support; when the good cause seems baffled on every side, and yet we are called to struggle on, heart and flesh failing;—then, above all, we may turn to Him who seemed to labour in vain and spend His strength for nought, and He will sympathize with our weakness, remembering His own. He will rekindle the sinking flame of courage and hopefulness, by telling us that He Himself had to be bruised and put to grief, to be despised and rejected of men, before He could see of the travail of His soul and be satisfied; it was for the suffering of death that He was crowned with glory and honour. He will not upbraid us in our utmost prostration, but will listen graciously, for He knoweth our frame and remembereth that we are dust.

He will give us "*timely help;*" help, prompt and according to the urgency and greatness of our necessity; for He knows that we shall utterly faint but for His merciful support. If He seems to wait long, let us believe that He answers us sometimes by His very waiting; that He is working for us silently and surely though as yet we see not the effects of His love; and that He is giving us help if our trust in Him has not utterly failed.

When we speak to Him of our infirmities we may speak "*boldly.*" There are many prayers we can offer only with shame and sorrow, whatever may be the strength of our conviction that Christ will answer them. When we confess our *sins;* tell Him that we have left the work undone we longed to have the joy and honour of doing, or have done it badly; that we have violated our vows, broken our resolutions, listened to the lies of the devil, yielded to the passions of the flesh, dishonourably bowed the knee to the usurped authority of the world;—we must hide our face and sink before Him into the dust. But of our "*infirmities*" we may speak "*boldly.*" They awaken His sympathy, not His indignation; they recall to His remembrance those days and nights of His own earthly history, by which the mighty and glorious company of kings and priests that stand before His throne were exalted to immortal blessedness.

As a child goes to its mother and tells her, not of the faults which need her pardon, but of weariness when the evening comes, and asks to be laid peacefully to rest—or of the heated brain, and parched lips, and languid limbs which are the signs of sickness, perhaps of danger, and asks to be lovingly watched and tenderly comforted and cared for,—so may we go to the throne of grace to obtain pity and timely help, whenever we are conscious that through our infirmities we are in danger of ceasing to hold fast to our profession and to all that profession implies.

I cannot close without asking you to consider the wonderful and perfect harmony in the revelation of God through Christ Jesus, of the most awful and alarming motives to holy living and the loving recognition of all the weakness and sorrow of humanity. While listening to the terrible warnings of the earlier part of this chapter, we might well tremble and be filled not merely with dismay, but with despair. *Now*, the faintest heart may be at peace, and the weakest may look up with hope.

It is by the action of these diverse but not antagonistic spiritual forces that the highest forms of Christian character are built up. If I am affected only by the tremendous energy of the truths which affirm my guilt and my danger, I shall become, at the best, hard and stern in my religious life, and shall serve God with the spirit of a slave; if I am affected only by those which affirm the gentleness of Christ's compassion, the throne of conscience will be built on the drifting sand, I shall be destitute of the resoluteness and constancy of a will which recognises the majesty of the Divine law, and my religion will become a thing of sentimental emotion and intermittent excitement. The true Christian life is at once vigorous and lovely, strong and tender, uniting reverential awe and childlike trust, great fear and great joy; a noble tree, with roots which have penetrated far into dark and hidden depths, a trunk of colossal strength, mighty branches which have wrestled with many a winter's storm; and yet the roots are covered with velvet moss, and the green ivy and the graceful woodbine cling to the trunk and festoon the branches; and over all there is a boundless exuberance of foliage, in which sunlight and shadow make each other more beautiful; and the sweet songs of birds fill it with music by day and the pleasant murmur of summer winds by night.

THE PRIESTHOOD OF CHRIST.

"For every high priest taken from among men is ordained for men in things pertaining to God, that he may offer both gifts and sacrifices for sins," &c.
HEBREWS v, 1-10.

SOME of you may be ready to ask what moral and religious good we may hope to derive from the study of the old Jewish ritual. What have we to do with temples, and priests, and altars, and sacrifices? All these things belong to a remote age; to us they have no significance; let us rather enquire what the New Testament has to say about ourselves, our own duties, and our own destiny.

Let me acknowledge that I am not among the number of those who seem to believe that there is more religious truth in the writings of Moses than in the four Gospels, and that the theory of Christian doctrine is more fully developed in the book of Leviticus than in the epistles of St. Paul and St. John. The habit of turning incessantly to the minute regulations of the old ceremonial, to discover the profoundest disclosures of the mind and will of God, rests on a complete misunderstanding of the ancient system, and it is well if it does not issue in a serious misapprehension of some parts of the more perfect revelation. The directions given to the Jewish priests for the offering of sacrifices are not, I think, to be treated like a set of religious riddles, the answers to which include the deepest truths of the New Testament; nor were the Levitical institutions spiritual hieroglyphics intended to teach Christian people a mysterious, esoteric wisdom which the apostles failed to impart.

And yet I am not disposed to regard the ancient faith and rites of Judaism as worthless to ourselves. When I remember that for more than sixteen centuries the religious life of a nation was sustained and expressed by those singular ceremonies, they at once become an object of practical interest to me—I want to know what there was in them which accounts for their permanence and their power. The interest becomes still deeper when I remember that whatever measure of responsibility the Christian apostles may have assumed in relation to the minute and infallible accuracy of the old Jewish books, it is implied throughout the New Testament that the Jewish system itself was founded by the command of God, and defended through successive generations by His wisdom and power. And I soon discover that, although it is absurd to look into the more elementary revelation for what Christ Himself has not revealed, there is very much in the old Testament system which assists me in understanding New Testament teaching.

The writers of the Christian Scriptures were all Jews: every one of them had lived till manhood in fellowship with his Jewish countrymen,—praying in the temple, offering sacrifices, attending the feasts; and some of their writings were written for readers who had received Jewish culture. Hence the language employed can only be rightly understood by knowing what it meant when used by Jews and addressed to Jews. Words are not arbitrary creations of the human intellect—they grow out of the life and thought of a people; and you cannot know their meaning without knowing something of the people who employ them. If I want to know for instance, what St. Paul meant when he talked about *sacrifice*, I must ask, not what is the meaning of that term among ourselves, but what it meant when Jews used it eighteen hundred years ago—for words change their meaning with the changing creeds and life of men. Hence the institutions of the Old Testament are, to a large extent, a dictionary in which I learn the true sense of the language of the New; but, to use it rightly, it is clearly necessary that we should be very careful not to take our technical theology with us when we turn to the dictionary, but should let it speak for itself.

Again, it is the custom of anatomists to illustrate the structure of the human body—the highest and most perfect form of physical life—by comparing it part by part with the structure of inferior animals; and they tell us that they can detect many instructive analogies of formation and function between certain parts of the human body and certain parts of the body of many creatures whose physical organisation seems at first sight to be altogether unlike our own. The simpler structure of the animal enables them sometimes to solve questions which had quite baffled them in investigating the more complex structure of man. And so the more elementary form of religious life among the Jews will sometimes assist us in comprehending some of the more mysterious and difficult parts of the Christian faith. Only, again, it is clearly necessary that we should not imagine that the Old Testament is the same as the New,—as rich, as complicated, as profound in its revelation of God and of our relations to Him,—but should take it just as it stands, and try to learn what the temple, and the priesthood, and the sacrifices were, in the old times, to the people among whom they were instituted.

And now, let us see how the writer of this Epistle illustrates one aspect of the work of the Lord Jesus Christ from the functions of the Jewish High Priest, and let us remember that in his teaching as well as in his direct exhortation he has before him one great end, of which he never for a moment loses sight,—preventing these Jewish Christians from drifting back to their old faith.

"*Every High Priest being taken from among men is ordained*—or appointed—*for men in things pertaining to God, that he may offer both gifts and sacrifices for sin.*" In other words, his primary function is, not to teach, but to present to God the expressions of human homage, and to offer sacrifice for human sins: and he belongs to the race which he has to represent in the Divine presence. He must be a man himself, that he may "*have compassion on the ignorant and on them that are out of the way—being himself also compassed with infirmity*" which sometimes betrays him, too, into sin—and so he has to "*offer sacrifices for his own sins as well as for the sins of the people.*"

The Jewish Christians only needed these brief hints to recall to their minds the central figure of their ancient worship. At once, the High Priest stood before them with his unique sanctity, his high prerogative of entering once a year into the hidden sanctuary where for ages there was a visible symbol of the Divine presence, and where he, the representative of the whole nation, of the meanest and most guilty, as well as of the greatest and holiest among them, stood in an awful sense face to face with God. They saw in him, in the office he held, in the duties he discharged, this great fact visibly set forth—that man was not denied access to God: even when they had grievously sinned, when they were suffering dreadful chastisements for their offences—their country desolate, their cities burned with fire,—still the High Priest went into the Holy of Holies, and God permitted him to approach the mercy-seat. And the priest who was thus suffered, as the representative of the whole people, to stand in the presence of Jehovah, was not an angel, but a man; not a sinless man either, but compassed about with infirmity like the weakest of his race. He had to commence the solemnities of the great Day of Atonement by divesting himself of his gorgeous robes, and offering a sacrifice for the sins of himself and his family, acknowledging that he was a sinner, and so telling the nation that a sinful man might draw near to God.

I do not think that in ancient times good men saw much more than this in the office and duties of the High Priest, though in later ages there were unmistakeable indications that the office was to culminate in a higher and more permanent appointment. What they saw in the sacrifices I must reserve for another time; but even this was a great thing. The institution of the Priesthood, maintained by visible rites and ceremonies the conviction, that access to God was granted to every man, no matter how guilty; for the representative of the religious life of the people, himself exposed to temptation, could enter into the court of the temple where the presence of the Holy God was peculiarly manifested.

The whole significance and worth of the High Priesthood depended upon the fact that it was of Divine appointment. The High Priest was set apart, "*called*" by God Himself to discharge the functions of his office. He was not appointed by man, for then his appointment would only have indicated man's yearning after God; he was appointed by God, and therefore his appointment indicated that it was God's own will that man should have access to the Divine presence. "*No man taketh this office to himself, but he that is called of God, as was Aaron.*"

These, then, are the two principal ideas of the first four verses: first, that the Jewish High Priest, appointed to offer gifts and sacrifices for sin, was a sinful man himself, and able therefore to think compassionately of sinners,—and, secondly, that he was appointed by God, and therefore his functions were not a mere expression of human want and solicitude, but a proof that God Himself wished men to draw near to Him.

And now see in what manner the writer shows these faltering and hesitating Jewish Christians how unnecessary it was for them to turn back to the ancient faith, and that they had in their new faith all, and more than all, they had in the old.

I.

First, Were those ancient priests appointed by God Himself to their priestly office? Christ, too, is Priest by the same authority. He "*did not glorify* Himself *to be made a High Priest*"—did not assume the office or the name unbidden. According to their own interpretation of their own Scriptures, the Messiah—and they acknowleged that Jesus was the Messiah, though they were hankering after the comfort and strength of Jewish ceremonialism,—the Messiah was the Son of God; and God had said to Him, "Thou art a Priest for ever, after the order of Melchisedek;" a greater thing *that*, than to be in the line of the Aaronic priests.

I cannot believe that in thus asserting on Christ's behalf a Divine appointment to the Priesthood, the writer was merely making use of absurd Jewish prejudices to confirm his readers in the Christian faith. The passion for a Priest—a Divinely appointed Priest—seems to be an instinct of the human soul. I think most men will say:—There are times when I am so disheartened by the consciousness of my moral weakness, when the contrast between the Divine purity and my own sinfulness seems to me so appalling, that I have no courage to speak to God myself; times when I can perfectly understand how it is that my Roman Catholic brother clings to his saints to intercede for him, and to his priests to pronounce the absolution of his sins; times when I am unutterably thankful—having a better and purer faith—that Jesus Christ is the representative of the whole human race, specially of all that obey Him. Yes, what the High Priest was to the Jew, Jesus Christ is to me. The conscience-stricken Israelite who was tormented by the remembrance of his wrong-doing and was passionately crying out to God, "Cast me not away from Thy presence," saw the Priest cleanse himself, offer sacrifices for himself and the people, and then enter into the place set apart as the very presence-chamber of the Most High. What did that mean? What *can* it mean, might the sinful Jew exclaim, except this, that I, poor, guilty, miserable man that I am, have not lost all hope of the Divine help and pity? the priest yonder goes into the Holy of Holies, by God's own appointment, for *me*, for I too am a child of Abraham, and have my share in all that the High Priesthood represents.

If, at this moment, the brave though unhappy race which is struggling to throw off the crushing despotism of Russia, were invited to send a representative to the English court, to the French court—what would it mean? Why, as soon as the heroic people, who seem to have found inspiration and hope in their very misery, immoveable resolution in the very desperateness of their cause, discovered that one of their leaders was received in Paris and another in London, they would see in these facts the clear proof that it was the determination of two great empires to redress their wrongs and to assist them in the fight for freedom. What would it matter to them that in one wild skirmish after another, they were miserably defeated, and driven for their very lives into the dark forests of the land they have resolved to save?—the presence of their acknowledged and invited representatives in the capitals of England and France, would be a firm rock on which to rest their confidence that their miseries and wrongs had touched the heart of two nations which could give them efficient support, and that therefore the emancipation of their country was certain.

When I see Christ at the right hand of God I reason in the same way. What does His presence yonder in heaven mean? "*He glorified not Himself in being made a High Priest.*" He was appointed to it by God. He is the great Representative of our religious life; of *mine*,—for I, too, am a man; of mine, for I am a sinful man, and He came to save sinners. Why is He in heaven at all, except that God is on my side, not against me,—on my side when I am beaten, as well as when I am victorious; wants to help me; is resolved to do it, if I will only let Him? And when the darkest and stormiest hours come, I may forget all my danger and trouble, and master all my dread lest God Himself should forsake me, by looking unto Jesus—the Divinely-appointed Head of the human race, through whom we may all, even the worst and the weakest of us, return to God.

II.

But, secondly, the Jewish High Priests were not only appointed by God, they were men themselves; and their humanity, with all its moral weakness, gave great additional significance to their approach to God in behalf of their brethren. We can conceive of an angel being constituted the religious representative of mankind, and even his appointment to that office would be a proof of God's mercy; but the heart has greater peace now that a man, sharing our own infirmities, stands before God for us. We feel that God is not keeping our race at a distance, as being too far gone in sin to possess, as yet, free access to Him: and if our own nature thus approaches God in the person of our Representative, we feel more confident that all our difficulties and perils will be sure to awaken the Divine compassion. To recur to the illustration I used just now,—it would be something if the English government appointed an Englishman, and the French government a Frenchman, to be the representative at their respective courts of the Polish people,—but it would be far more, if two patriotic leaders of the struggling nation, of Polish blood themselves, were invited to represent their countrymen. The *humanity* of the Jewish priesthood was an essential element of the spell which their office possessed for the hearts of the Jewish race.

And, by the way, I am inclined to think that the doctrine recently promulgated with authority by the Romish Church concerning the sinless conception of the Virgin Mary, will, by removing her further from the sympathies of men, ultimately issue in weakening the attraction of her intercession. Part of the charm of the intercession of the Virgin and of the saints has been derived from this, that their imperfections when on earth seemed likely to make them more compassionate now to sinful men than Christ could be, who knew no sin; and this semi-deification of the Virgin, if practically accepted by the members of the Romish Church, will, to a great extent, destroy the more confiding trustfulness with which their prayers have hitherto been offered to her. If their present creed be true, she was as pure from all evil as Christ Himself, pure not in life merely, but by the very mystery of her birth.

But to return: the true ground of sympathy lies, not in common sin, but in common struggles and common weakness. The man who has been exposed to trials like my own, if his nature was as sensitive to their influence as mine, will feel for me, whether he was more or less successful than I have been in resisting temptation to wrong-doing. It is not sin that makes a man compassionate, but the consciousness of weakness, teaching him how hard it is not to sin. It is not by distrusting God in times of suffering that our pity for other men in their sorrows is made more tender, but by passing through and feeling the terrible power of the sufferings by which their faith is tried.

Already, in two remarkable and touching passages, the writer of this Epistle has told his readers that Christ can sympathize with their weakness on account of His personal sufferings and temptations: He was made in all points like unto his brethren; He can be touched with a feeling of our infirmities: but now he returns to this most important truth, and recalls to their remembrance that scene of agony in which the sorrows of the

Lord Jesus appear to have reached an almost intolerable intensity, and His strength seems to have been almost overborne and exhausted. "*In the days of His flesh when He had offered up strong cryings and tears unto Him that was able to save Him from death*"—from death into which He was fast sinking through the greatness of His mental suffering,—"*He was heard*," and His fear was calmed and subdued. There are no details given here of the sufferings in Gethsemane; they were too well known to all Christian people for it to be necessary to narrate them; but the reference is clearly to the agony of that dreadful night.

Perhaps we are hardly able to speak at all about the source and nature of these sufferings. No human eye rested on Him through the struggles of that terrible hour: even the disciples who were elected to watch with Him slumbered; and too little is told us to afford any sure ground even for speculation on the elements of His mysterious sorrow. I think, however, that this passage affords a hint that it was the prospect of all that was to come upon Him on the following day—the anticipation of the depths of anguish into which he would be plunged when He realised on the cross His brotherhood with a world of sinners, His union with a race which had grievously dishonoured God, His intimate relationship with creatures whose crimes had aroused the divine anger though their miseries had touched the divine pity;—the vivid anticipation of the hitherto unknown horror of losing for a little time the vision of God's face through His profound realisation of the wickedness and wretchedness of mankind; I think it was this which filled Him with a dismay which made Him shrink,—not in the constancy of His resolved will,—but in the infirmity of His sensitive affections, from the completion of His work. Do you not think that when the Son of God hung on the cross, having been betrayed by one of His own disciples for thirty pieces of silver, denied with curses by another, rejected and mocked at by the people He had loved so well, given up to popular fury by the guilty weakness of the Roman governor, hunted to death by the malignity of the Jewish priests, He must have had a most awful vision of the terrible evil of sin—must have *entered into it*, as His holy soul had never entered before. As He hung there, with the darkness of death deepening around Him, must not His compassionate heart have realised with a fearful and horrible intensity what death had been already to millions of the human race—what it would be to millions more—until, just as we ourselves, when deeply meditating on the miseries of others, sometimes sink into a wretchedness like theirs and seem to share their woe, so He, pure as He was and beloved of God, felt for a time as though He were descending into the dreadful gloom, in company with all who had died with the crimes of a wicked life haunting them, and the terrors of God's judgment seat and a dreary eternity confronting them? All the anguish and horror of the whole race was upon Him; and as though He too were among the guilty and condemned, He cried, "My God, my God, why hast Thou forsaken me!"

I suppose He saw all this before Him in that lonely hour in Gethsemane, and He was filled with a sorrow which threatened to end in death: and with strong cryings and tears He appealed to God—"O my Father, if it be possible, let this cup pass from me, nevertheless not as I will, but as Thou wilt."

And then an angel came and strengthened Him, not at the end of the conflict as in the wilderness, but in the very middle of it; and being in an agony, He prayed more earnestly, and though using substantially the same words, yet there is a change, now it is—"O my Father, if this cup may *not* pass from me, except I drink it, 'Thy will be done.'" And a third time He offered the same prayer.

"*He was heard:*" not that the object of His fear was removed; but the fear itself was calmed and subdued; He was able to look forward without dismay to all that the morrow would bring. "*Though He was a Son, He learned obedience by the things He suffered.*"

And now, will any one venture to say that the argument about Priesthood, which culminates in a truth like this, might have been well enough for Jews, but has no practical interest for us? For the Jews it must have had a force of which we can hardly conceive; for it lays hold of precisely those circumstances of humiliation in the life of Christ which, when contrasted with the visible splendour and grandeur of their own early faith, made them ashamed of their Christian profession, and transforms these circumstances into an argument of infinite pathos for trusting in Christ still. They too had their "*fear*"— a fear of isolation from the religious and political life of their countrymen,—of personal suffering and danger; but this fear, according to the inspired writer, had been anticipated and provided for in Christ's own history, and they might go to Him and tell Him of it all.

And for us Gentiles, living in an atmosphere of doubt and of controversy, it seems to me a fact worthy of very serious thought, and suggestive of many reflections of great value in relation to the intellectual troubles of our time, that in an Epistle evidently intended to assert and vindicate the preeminent dignity of the Lord Jesus Christ, the writer does not shrink from those parts of Christ's earthly history which might seem at first sight most unfriendly to his purpose. Beginning with the proof that the Messiah of Jewish hope was the object of angelic worship, was the Creator of all material things, and upheld them all by the word of His power, he insists here with an impassioned earnestness on the very conflicts and sufferings which most clearly prove Him to be bone of our bone and flesh of our flesh. This writer was no fanatic, bending or concealing, in his eagerness to glorify the object of his adoration, all adverse circumstances so as to establish his own theory.

No, this old argument has not become obsolete: its form may have been determined by the intellectual and moral peculiarities of an age which has passed away, but its substance must be of infinite value to the human heart so long as the world in which man lives is darkened with suffering, and man himself is conscious that the vision of this suffering is an agony and a terror. Would to God that I knew how to tell you all that these words seem to mean!—but you will never find it out till the time comes when your soul is so lacerated by your own griefs, or by the physical tortures, and the moral anguish, and the comfortless desolation of myriads of mankind, that you are ready to think that God, in the height of His perfect and eternal blessedness, must be incapable of sympathizing with the misery of the human race, or He would never have permitted such sorrows to come upon it; and then, when heart and flesh are failing,—then, in the breaking up of all faith in the Divine goodness, you will discover that there is here an immoveable rock on which you may stand firm when floods of great waters are heaving darkly and tumultuously around you. It is not merely the calm pity of the ever-blessed God, who has been surrounded through bright millenniums with the songs of angels crowned with everlasting light and making sweetest music with their harps of gold, that watches over the destinies of men; there is One at His side in yonder palace of eternal joy,—the brightness of His glory, the express image of His person,—who Himself once sank into a deeper darkness than ever made you tremble, and realized the awful weight and burden of human wretchedness as you have never realized it; One who, in a world of misery, stood alone in an awful supremacy of woe, as now in a world of glory He stands alone in a splendid supremacy of bliss, whose title was, "The man of sorrows, and acquainted with grief," whose symbol of dignity, the crown of thorns, marked Him out as the very chief and king of a suffering race; One who being Himself Divine, and having left heaven to accomplish a work which had been present to the Divine mind from eternity, and in which all the previous movements of the Divine government closed and culminated, shrank and shuddered in His weakness when the crisis drew near, and offered up prayers and supplications with strong cryings and tears unto Him that was able to deliver Him from death. In Him,—in the pitifulness of His heart,—in the fervour of His sympathy,—who will not rest with unshaken and victorious confidence? Having passed through such a history, and risen at last to the perfection of power, of authority, and glory, He must be touched with a feeling of our infirmities, and will confer eternal salvation on all them that obey Him.

IGNORANCE AND APOSTASY.

"Of whom we have many things to say, and hard to be uttered * * * Leaving the principles of the Gospel of Christ let us go on unto perfection * * * It is impossible—if they shall fall away to renew them again unto repentance." HEBREWS v, 11—vi, 8.

It appears from the first verse of this passage that the analogy between the priesthood of Melchizedek and the priesthood of Christ presented difficulties to the minds of Jewish Christians more formidable than were involved in any of the discussions in the earlier part of the Epistle. Those difficulties were occasioned principally, perhaps, by the habits of thought which had been formed and strengthened by the religious discipline and inspired books of Judaism.

Melchizedek occupies no great space in the Old Testament Scriptures. His name occurs only twice—in the narrative of his meeting with Abraham after the recovery of the prisoners and spoils which had been carried off from Sodom and Gomorrah by the marauding chiefs of certain Eastern tribes, and in the 110th Psalm, in which it is declared that the Messiah was to be a Priest "after the order of Melchizedek." To claim for him any kind of superiority over Aaron, over Moses, over Abraham himself, would be likely to startle an ordinary Jew. Aaron was the head of a line of priests which for sixteen centuries had worn the sacred vestments, and stood before the mercy-seat on behalf of the Jewish people. Moses was the patriot and lawgiver by whom their fathers had been emancipated from Egyptian bondage and organised into a nation. From the fidelity of Abraham to Jehovah, had flowed all the distinctions which constituted the heritage of the Jewish race—their temple, their sacrifices, their priests, their prophets, the miracles which had been wrought to defend them from their enemies, all the wonderful interferences of Divine power and wisdom by which the nation had been raised to secular greatness and delivered from shameful captivity, all their hopes of a future glory, which should surpass even the splendour of Solomon's reign and exalt a Jewish prince to the empire of the world. The writer hesitates, therefore, at the very threshold of what he has to say. It will be hard for him so to present the truth as to make it clearly understood; and, what makes the case worse, those whom he is addressing have become "*dull of hearing.*" Time was, when they had greater quickness and readiness of perception—their minds were open once, to receive whatever new teaching might come from authorized instructors; they had been candid, eager to know the truth, disposed to make any effort to deal with it fairly and to grasp it firmly. But their intellectual clearness had been injured by the decline of their moral and spiritual character. What they knew already about Christ had involved them in troubles, conflicts, and losses; and there was no anxiety to know more. Their minds had gradually been closing up. Jewish prejudice, spiritual declension, had made them not only indifferent to any new revelations of Christian doctrine, but positively indisposed and almost incompetent to learn any more. "*Considering the time*" that they had believed in Christ, they ought to have so mastered the characteristic truths of the Christian faith as to have become able to teach others; but, instead of this, they themselves still needed to be taught some of its elementary principles. They were like little children still, needing "*milk*," incapable of living on "*strong meat.*" It would not do for anyone who taught them to speak as though they had made any great progress. Everything must be made very simple. The greatest care must be taken to prevent misunderstanding. What ought to have been obvious must receive abundant illustration. What ought to have been long familiar must be frequently reiterated.

Their ignorance was the result of sin. They had become weary of the troubles into which their new faith had brought them; and they did not care to learn more about it. They had also permitted their old faith to regain much of its power over them, and so not only had their love for Christ, and their devotion to Him, become less fervent, but the clearer religious light which had once shone in their intellect, had been darkened.

I.

I wish you to consider whether the very inadequate knowledge of Christian truth existing among ourselves is not traceable to similar causes. "*Ye ought to be teachers;*" and yet is it not the common confession of many Christian people that they need to be taught again "*the first principles*" of the gospel? They make the confession without shame; they seem almost to think that there is some kind of virtue in it. I believe that if they had lived eighteen hundred years ago, and an apostle had told them that he wanted to speak to them about Melchizedek, but found it hard to present the truth in a form sufficiently clear to be quite intelligible, they would have said that they would greatly prefer that he should leave the whole subject untouched; that they liked the simple gospel,—the simpler the better; that what they wanted was "milk;" that they had no taste for difficult questions; that they liked to have their hearts moved; that this doctrinal teaching of which, unfortunately, he and some of his brethren seemed so fond, was quite above them, and did them no good; that there were many things in his sermons "hard to be understood;"—that they wished he would be more "obvious;" and that a Christian teacher was bound to be constantly repeating the elementary facts and truths of the Christian faith.

Now this inspired writer refuses to listen to any thing of the kind. He does not for a moment admit that it was any fault in him to be reaching constantly after those Divine treasures which lay beyond the comprehension of some of his readers "*Ye ought to be teachers.*" The cause of all the difficulty is that you have become dull of hearing. You are babes—when you ought to be strong men.

There is something positively ludicrous, were it not very sad, in so many Christian people—good sort of people too—clinging to the idea that it is quite the right thing for them to continue to the end of their days " babes in Christ :" they seem to think that there is something very touching, very beautiful, and very humble in all this. But, "for everything there is a season and a time for every purpose under heaven :" "a time," no doubt, "to be born;" a time for the sweet beauty and pathetic helplessness of infancy—a time to be fed on milk, to be folded in warmth day and night, to be defended from the cold wind, the rain, and the snow, to be touched softly and tenderly, and to lie passive in the arms of love; and, perhaps, some of you mothers have been sorry when your feeble, delicate darlings began to show that this pleasant time was passing by, and that the restlessness, and the movement, and the self-assertion, of a riper age had come;—but still, none of you are anxious that your sons and daughters of twenty years' growth, should affect in their speech the lispings of infancy, and in their countenance its innocent simplicity,—should still need the same harmless food and the same gentle care. Depend upon it God is no more anxious that your spiritual infancy, with all its peculiar charms, should be perpetuated : you may perpetuate its weakness, but its beauty soon passes away and returns no more.

Is not our inadequate knowledge of Christian doctrine, like that of these Jewish Christians, a sin rather than a necessity? Let me put it to some of you—directly and most seriously— whether you have ever given a tithe of the labour to mastering those truths which lie beyond the elementary principles of our faith which you gave to mastering those elementary principles themselves. What a sinner needs to know in order to obtain the Divine pardon and the baptism of the Holy Ghost, is simple enough;—some things which the believer needs to know, if he is to become a perfect man in Christ Jesus, are "hard to be understood:" and yet some of you remember the intense anxiety and the serious toil with which you endeavoured to learn the first, but are perfectly aware that there has been no corresponding effort to learn the second. You not only read, but studied, and prayed over "The Rise and Progress," "The Anxious Inquirer," and "Come to Jesus,"—but I should like to know what other books—books written to develope the deeper contents of the Christian revelation to those who are already in Christ—have ever had anything approaching the same thought and care. And is not one of the reasons this—that you have been conscious of no such desire to attain holiness as you once had to obtain safety? You were passionately eager to become one of the servants of Christ, because to be in His service was essential to your deliverance from danger; but you have felt very little concern to learn how you may serve Him well, or to know those truths by which your strength for serving Him would be augmented. The little you have discovered of what a Christian ought to be, has occasioned you sorrow enough, and you find it trouble enough to maintain your religious life at its present level; you have no heart either to study or to strive after any higher ideal of Christian character. You are content to remain in your present state—and when, "*considering the time*" you have been believers, "*you ought to be teachers, you have need that one teach you the first principles of the oracles of God.*" Let it be understood that, as a rule, inadequate Christian knowledge is the result of a defect of Christian earnestness; that the incessant craving for mere "milk" is a proof that there has been no spiritual growth; that the incapacity of getting beyond "first principles" is a sin, not a misfortune, much less a Christian grace,—and we may hope that there will be some increase in the Christian intelligence of our churches, and in the vigour and depth of popular religious books, and popular preaching.

The second cause of the absence of progress in the knowledge of these Jewish Christians may also be paralleled among ourselves. They had been drifting back in heart and in practice to the old Jewish religion, and so their intellect had become less able to comprehend Christian truth. I cannot stay to explain the philosophy of this—the explanation is easy enough to all who are accustomed to observe the history of their own minds; and, without any philosophizing, everyone may see that the understanding must gradually become incapable of thinking aright on a spiritual faith, if passions and prejudices are gradually strengthening in favour of a ceremonial and external religion. The minds of these Christian Jews had been silently more and more possessed with the pomp and show of their temple service and with dreams of national glory, and their capacity for apprehending the deeper truths of the Christian revelation was rapidly diminishing. And so some of us, I fear, have been drifting back into mere worldliness, and are less familiar with the disclosures of the unseen world which are the objects of faith, than when we began to believe. Our intellectual activity is almost confined to the sphere of things "seen and temporal" because our chief care and efforts have ceased to be directed to things "unseen and eternal." We do not live in the region of spiritual realities, and, therefore, our habits of thought unfit us for acquiring spiritual knowledge. The man that lives among his books finds it hard to understand things which are perfectly simple to men of affairs; the student of the exact sciences finds it hard to appreciate the force of moral evidence; the subject of a despotic government finds it hard to comprehend the excitement and the apparent lawlessness of a free commonwealth; and so, if you are altogether devoted to secular business all the week through,—if, practically, your highest aim in life is to get rich or to live in luxury,—if you are engaged in no Christian work,—if your time for meditation and prayer is very brief, and if you hurry over all the observances which are intended to deepen and ennoble your religious affections,— instead of being teachers, you will "*have need that some one teach you the first principles of the oracles of God.*"

There is a delicate touch of sarcasm in the writer's words; you who ought to be teachers require "*some one*"—*anybody will do*, you have no need of an apostle or an inspired teacher —you require some one or other to teach you the first principles. You have grown unfamiliar with the objects of spiritual contemplation:—anyone who lives a higher and more godly life,— any Christian who is moderately faithful to the responsibilities and honours of his high vocation may teach you the simple truths which you need to learn again.

Unless the traditions which have come down to us concerning the habits of our Nonconformist fathers are altogether inaccurate, there was far more of serious thoughtfulness among them than there is among ourselves. They really cared to learn all that God had taught mankind by the discourses and acts of the Lord Jesus and the writings of the apostles. They held grave discussions on Christian doctrine. They thought in solitude on those high questions which many of us shrink from altogether, or are content to have decided for us by the mere authority of great names or by what is understood to be the common belief of the religious party to which we belong. That this was the temper and habit of their mind does not rest on mere partial testimony: it is proved by the sermons they listened to, which would scatter a modern congregation in six weeks; and by the books they studied, which many of us are accustomed to praise, but which very few of us, I imagine, have read. We often express an earnest longing for Puritan times to come again, and Puritan preachers, and Puritan literature; but if any attempt were made to restore—not the mere form of Puritanism—but even its substantial excellence and power, some who are loudest in expressing these longings would be most indignant and most weary. Our fathers listened for hours, not merely to men of genius like Howe and Baxter and Owen, but to multitudes of "painful preachers," (they were called so in honour, not in scorn), whose only attractiveness lay in this, that with laborious fidelity, though with no brilliance or beauty, they endeavoured, in their protracted sermons, with their clumsy sentences, and innumerable divisions, to establish and to teach the whole system of Christian truth. *We* find it hard to listen for forty minutes to any man who does not amuse us with his humour, or excite us with his eloquence. We have not the hunger which makes us desire truth, no matter how roughly dressed; it must be served daintily and made piquant by fancy or wit. Even some of the best of us ask for "milk," not for "meat." We have yet to learn that we ought to "serve God with the spirit and with the understanding also."

II.

And now how does the writer of this epistle determine to deal with these sluggish Christians. Will he omit all he has to say about Melchizedec? By no means. Does he begin to teach them first principles? No, any one may do that. It is indispensable they should advance; and "*Therefore,*" he says, "*leaving the principles of the doctrine of Christ—let us go on unto perfection,*" or maturity. To the Christian Jew the elementary truths were those which the sacred writer proceeds to mention and on which he does not intend to say any thing.

"*Not laying again the foundation of repentance from dead works;*" their old religious activity with all its observances and ceremonies, as well as their sins, are perhaps, included under this last phrase; before they believed in Christ there was no life in their religious duties. Some of them, indeed, might have been devout Jews, and a certain degree of earnestness and reality might have been present in their prayers and sacrifices; but, speaking broadly and generally, their religious activity was a dead, unspiritual thing.*

The necessity of "*faith in God*" was also one of the first principles; it was this which constituted the very beginning of a truly devout life; they had had faith once in circumcision, in sacrifices, in many sacred rites; but Christ had taught them, as Luther taught the Church of the sixteenth century, to look direct to heaven and to repose all their confidence in God Himself.

And their Christian instructors had had to teach them what "*baptisms*" meant; for Christian baptism was a very great event in the life of an adult Jew, and he had to be made to see clearly that it was an acknowledgement of what his nation had blasphemously denied—the kingship of Christ over earth and heaven; that it was the visible sign to be affixed to all for whom Christ died,—to all who ought to obey Christ's authority: and the Jew would ask for an account of the relation between this

---

* "Yield yourselves unto God as those that are alive from the dead," (Romans, vi, 13), and other similar passages, favour the opinion that by "dead works" the writer means the sins of which the spiritually dead are guilty, the acts proper to and characteristic of their condition. The phrase "dead works" in cap. ix, 14, so evidently involves a metaphor in which the moral defilement of sin is compared to the ceremonial impurity produced by contact with a dead body, that it affords no aid in the interpretation of the phrase in the present passage.

baptism and the baptism of John, to which many had submitted who never came to believe in Christ, and to the cleansings by water common in the ancient system; and so, "*teaching about baptisms*" stood on the very threshold of his acquaintance with Christian truth, though with us, perhaps it lies somewhat farther on.

The Jew had been accustomed to the "*laying on of hands*" in the old system, and he would want that explained when he saw it practised in the appointment of Christian ministers to their office and, probably, in the admission of believers to the Church.

Since Christ had brought life and immortality to light through the Gospel, the new revelation of the future world was one of the first objects of the Jewish convert's lawful curiosity, and he was told what the new faith taught concerning "*the resurrection of the dead and eternal judgment*,"—that judgment which takes place, not in time, else its decisions might be reversed, but in the eternity by which time is encompassed, and is therefore a judgment by which the condition of the soul is irrevocably determined.

The writer says, "*Let us go on unto perfection;*" these are truths which you learnt at the very beginning of your Christian profession: it is not my intention again "*to lay the foundation*" on which all your knowledge and life till now have rested; if there is to be growth of character, there must be growth of knowledge too. We must press on to other truths. And "*this will we do if God permit.*"

III.

And why is he resolved to do all he can to transform their infantine feebleness into mature strength? Why does he insist so earnestly on the necessity of their advancing both in the mastery of truth, and in the development of the religious life to the fulness and perfection for which a richer knowledge of truth is indispensable? Why? Because if they do not go forward their feebleness will become feebler, and what little knowledge they have will dwindle away and disappear. The infant that ceases to grow will soon cease to live. Stagnation of religious life and thought was likely to end in death. There must be a change for the better, or all will be lost. Unless there is progress towards a higher condition, there will soon be apostasy from Christ altogether. If they continue to drift and to drift towards their former state, they will sink into irretrievable ruin and hopeless destruction. "*For it is impossible for those who were once enlightened, and have tasted of the heavenly gift, and were made partakers of the Holy Ghost, and have tasted the good word of God, and the powers of the world to come, if they shall fall away, to renew them again unto repentance; seeing they crucify to themselves the Son of God afresh, and put Him to an open shame.*"

I know how this passage has made the heart of many a good man tremble: but I dare not pass it over for all that. It rises up in the New Testament with a gloomy grandeur,—stern, portentous, awful, sublime, as Mount Sinai when the Lord descended upon it in fire, and threatening storm-clouds were around Him, and thunderings and lightnings and unearthly voices told that He was there. We too, like the ancient people, may well be filled with dread and "stand afar off," thankful that for us, not Moses, but Christ, draws near to the thick darkness where God is; but the vision comes to us as it came to them, "that the fear of God may be upon us, and that we sin not."

Concerning whom is it that the writer affirms that "*it is impossible to renew them again unto repentance?*" I know not how he could have chosen expressions which more forcibly describe the possession of a real and genuine Christian life. Phrase is heaped upon phrase that there may be no misapprehension.

"*Those who were once enlightened.*" "the god of this world hath blinded the minds of those that believe not;" "God who commanded the light to shine out of darkness hath shined in our hearts to give the light of the knowledge of the glory of God in the face of Jesus Christ."*

"*And have tasted the heavenly gift.*" Christ spoke to the woman of Samaria of the "gift of God," which, if she had known, she would have asked of Him, and He would have

---

* 2 Corinthians iv, 4—6.

given her "living water." Paul speaks in the Epistle to the Romans of God's salvation, especially perhaps of justification, as "the free gift." "The gift of righteousness." Peter, in his first Epistle, uses the word "gift" in connection with the manifold grace of God: and in the second Epistle to the Corinthians, Paul speaks, I think, of Christ Himself, in whom is included all that the bounty and mercy of God can confer upon mankind, as God's "unspeakable gift."*

These persons had "*tasted* the heavenly gift," had not merely been offered it, had not merely looked at it, but had had personal experience of it, as the Christians to whom Peter wrote had "*tasted* that the Lord is gracious."† There had been a real interior knowledge of what it is to receive the gift of mercy, the gift of life through the Lord Jesus Christ.

"*And were made partakers of the Holy Ghost;*" of whom it is said elsewhere that He is the "earnest of our inheritance until the redemption of the purchased possession."‡ There is no hint that I see in the passage itself to justify for a moment the hypothesis that the reference is to mere miraculous gifts rather than to the indwelling of the Spirit in the heart.

"*And have tasted the good word of God,*"—had personal experience of how His promises can console the troubled heart, how the assurances of His mercy can loosen the burden of the guilty conscience, how the expressions of His love, the declaration of His will, can quicken and strengthen and exalt the spiritual life of man.

"*And the powers of the world to come,*"—foretastes of future glory, as some suppose; but I think that this phrase, "the world to come," is used here in another meaning. The new religious dispensation which was to follow the advent of the Messiah had received this name among the Jews, and it is often employed in the New Testament as equivalent to the "kingdom of Christ,"—the new state of things which resulted from His death for the sins of mankind, and His enthronement at the right hand of God. The revelation of God in Christ, His consummated atonement for sin, His sovereignty over heaven

---

* John iv, 10; Romans v, 15—17; 1 Peter iv, 10; 2 Cor, ix, 15.
† 1 Peter ii, 3. ‡ Ephesians i, 14.

and earth, the mission of the Holy Ghost, were the shrines of mightier spiritual forces for the regenerating and perfecting of man's nature than had ever been known to the saints of the earlier faith. These "powers of the world to come" had been, not objects of belief, but of consciousness, to the persons here described.

Not only do the expressions themselves compel me to believe that the writer is thinking of those whose Christian life had been a reality—not a delusion—*the place of this passage in his appeal* confirms me in this persuasion. He is exhorting the people who are thus described, to make progress in Christian knowledge and Christian character. Had they been self-deceived,—had they been hypocrites,—he would have charged them, not to "go on unto perfection," but, now at last, to begin a real and honest Christian life. He declares that he shall not "lay again the foundation of repentance from dead works and faith towards God." Had they never been true Christians at all, that was precisely what he ought to have done. He is warning them against "falling away." If their whole religious life had been a deception, it would have been impossible for them to fall away from Christ's service, for they would never have been truly in it. It is by appealing to the dreadful results of the apostasy into which they are drifting that he endeavours to raise them to intensest earnestness. Had he supposed they were hypocrites or self-deceived, he would have had no need to tell them of the ruin which threatened them if they grew worse; he would have startled and terrified them by awful disclosures of their present guilt, their present dangers, and told them that they were condemned already.

No, this evasion will not bear looking into. The writer had present to his mind those who once gave earnest heed to the great salvation, but were now neglecting it, and for whom, if they neglected it altogether, there could be no escape; those who, like their fathers in the old time, had been delivered by the mighty hand of God from a life of miserable bondage, but who, through an evil heart of unbelief, were in danger of perishing in the midst of the hardships of the wilderness, before they reached the promised land. He had before him men who, in former days and in the energy of their earlier devotion, had endured a great fight of afflictions for Christ's sake, but who had need of patience, who must still live by faith, who were half inclined to draw back, and if they did, would draw back unto perdition. He had before him men who were in danger of sinning wilfully after receiving the knowledge of the truth, in danger of treading under foot the Son of God, in danger of counting the blood of the covenant, wherewith they were sanctified, an unholy thing, and doing despite unto the Spirit of Grace,—not by rejecting His outward appeals through Christian teachers and divine providences, but by expelling Him from the heart which had been His temple; men for whom there was the "sorer punishment," the "certain looking for of judgment," the "vengeance" which "belongeth to the Lord," the "fearful thing" of falling "into the hands of the living God."

They had begun to forsake the assemblies of the church; some of them were secretly thinking, perhaps, of the possibility of that silent secession from the church altogether to which all whose religious earnestness was sinking were likely at last to come. They were becoming weary of being Christians at so great a cost, and were fast drifting towards apostasy. Some of their old companions, perhaps, had already renounced their faith in Christ, and their troubles were over. Might it not be desirable to imitate their example? The writer meets them just in that condition, and he warns them that their feet are on the crumbling edge of an awful gulf, whose dark and horrible depths no human line can fathom, and that if they sink they sink beyond the reach of hope. Once in that gulf no merciful hand can touch them, seeing that apostates are guilty of "*crucifying to themselves the Son of God afresh and putting Him to an open shame.*"

But perhaps he means to say that if they apostatize it will be impossible for *man* to renew them to repentance, although all things are possible to God. If he had meant *that* he would have said it. But what need could there be to say that, at all? It is impossible for *man* to renew the soul that is freest from evil passions and from confirmed habits of sin; it is impossible for *man* to renew those who hear the gospel for the first time and have never hardened their hearts by rejecting it. The regeneration of the soul in every case is beyond human power: it would have been absurd for the writer to attempt to add solemnity to his warnings against the darkest crimes by saying that it would be impossible for man to do for those who sinned most daringly what man cannot do for those whose sins are lightest.

"It is impossible" not only with man, but impossible, according to the laws of the human spirit, which God established and which God respects,—impossible with God "to renew unto repentance" those who are in the condition here described. Having known so much of the glory and grace of the Lord Jesus Christ, apostasy with them is a "*crucifying of the Lord afresh, and a putting Him to an open shame.*" The thief that hangs on the neighbouring cross may repent and be forgiven, but if Lazarus whom He has raised from the dead, drives through His hands the cruel nails, and mocks Him in His dying agonies, who will not say that while committing such a crime his heart must be beyond the reach of the mightiest truths in the compass of Divine revelation, and that even the Spirit of all grace must retreat,—grieved, amazed, confounded, —by the unparalleled transgression?

And, I repeat, that according to the thought of the writer of this Epistle, if those who have been once enlightened, and have tasted of the heavenly gift and were made partakers of the Holy Ghost, fall away, they "crucify the Lord afresh;" and while the apostasy lasts the crime is prolonged. They are committing it still. They are in the very act, driving the nails, uttering words of scorn; and, while this continues, they are beyond the reach of human teaching and of Divine grace.

Do you ask me whether it is possible for a Christian man to commit a crime and to sink into a doom like this? I dare not obliterate the tremendous force of this passage by denying the possibility. Far better leave it as it is—an awful hypothesis— to warn us against the danger and the guilt, than venture by fine-drawn speculations, to diminish its practical power. If you ask me how I can reconcile the possibility which seems implied in the passage as it stands, with the merciful promises which assure us of God's keeping if we trust in Him, I answer that these promises are to those who trust, and continue to trust, in God,—not to those who trusted once, but whose trust has now perished: and I answer farther, that I would rather be charged by a whole council of theologians with introducing scientific inconsistency into a theological system, than dare to lessen the terror of a divinely-inspired warning, the undiminished awfulness of which may be needed to save some soul from death.

This, however, I will say—for this is in the passage itself—that the impossibility of renewing unto repentance is confined to those who *are* crucifying—not to those who have done it—but to those who *are* crucifying the Son of God afresh and putting Him to an open shame. If any who have reason to fear that once they did it, now abhor the crime, long to obtain pardon, and to be renewed unto repentance, let them come unto Him who prayed for forgiveness for His murderers, who "ever liveth to make intercession for us," and in you, as the chief of sinners, He will show for an example, and make known to the ages to come the "exceeding riches of his grace."

HOPEFULNESS.

"But, beloved, we are persuaded better things of you, and things that accompany salvation, though we thus speak.

"For God is not unrighteous to forget your work and labour of love, which ye have shewed to His name, in that ye have ministered to the saints, and do minister."—HEBREWS vi, 9-20.

IT is quite after the manner of the writer of this Epistle to introduce the most pathetic encouragements to courageous fidelity immediately after the most awful warnings against the guilt and danger of apostasy. The solemn appeal in the third and fourth chapters to the history of those who escaped from bondage in Egypt but perished in the wilderness through their unbelief, and the exhortation founded on their miserable end, "Let us therefore fear lest a promise being left us of entering into His rest any of you should appear to have fallen short of it," are followed by the declaration that "we have not a High Priest who cannot be touched with the feeling of our infirmities, but one who was in all points tried like as we are," and that when our strength is failing we may therefore "come boldly to the throne of grace," sure of His sympathy, "to obtain mercy and find grace for timely help." And in this passage, though he has severely condemned the Jewish Christians for their want of progress in knowledge and manly vigour, and has told them of the appalling condition into which they will sink, if they continue to drift away from Christ, He speaks to them affectionately of his confident persuasion that, after all, they will continue faithful to their profession : "*beloved, we are persuaded better things of you, and things which accompany salvation, though we thus speak.*"

It is, I think, well worthy of consideration on the part of all who are entrusted with the moral and religious care of others, that throughout Holy Scripture there is the union of kindly, loving hopefulness with strong and even stern rebuke. If we despair of men who have gone grievously wrong, they will soon despair of themselves. Those who have been most successful, in prevailing on others to trust in Christ, have commonly had an ardent and unconquerable persuasion that they should succeed; the eager faith of their own hearts has passed into the hearts of those with whom they pleaded.

I.

And on what does this hopefulness rest in the present case? Plainly there is nothing said to diminish the force of the warnings in the previous verses. The writer does not fall back on an eternal purpose of God which will infallibly secure the salvation of all who have truly believed in Christ. There is nothing to encourage these faltering, hesitating Christians, to hope that since they were once renewed by the Holy Ghost, they may now conceal their faith in Christ, let that faith perish altogether, consult their own safety and peace, by visibly renouncing all association with the church, and yet be sure of being rescued at last from the "cursing" and "burning." He meant what he said when he told them what would be the result of apostasy; and he does not unsay it now. His persuasion that instead of destruction lying before them there was salvation, does not rest on any doctrine which would cancel the threatenings which darken the pages of this Epistle, like the portentous omens of a coming storm. His hope rests on this, that "God is *not unrighteous to forget*" their work and their love which they had showed to His name, in that they had ministered to the saints, and still continued to minister.

By their "*work*," I think the writer meant their Christian life in general. They had been energetic and courageous servants of Christ, and had been zealous in maintaining His honour. There had been not merely faith, but works in harmony with faith. There had been not merely inward emotion of the right kind, but outward and visible acts of the right kind. They had lived a good life; they had done God's will; their "work" had been even in God's judgment an excellent and honourable thing.

And they had been especially remarkable for *ministering to the saints;* that is, by relieving their necessities, standing by them in danger, and showing them sympathy in suffering. Great distress had come upon the churches in Judea—distress so great, that even Macedonia and Corinth had been invited to send them aid; but among the Jewish Christians themselves there had been an openhanded generosity. Those who had little themselves had given to those who had less; those who had nothing to give had yet ministered to their brethren by personal kindnesses and loving attentions. And all this they were doing still. Not perhaps so heartily as in former times, but they were still doing it.

Now, says the writer, God is not unrighteous to forget all this: He remembers and He desires to reward your past fidelity and generosity; this is a reason for being hopeful about you.

This argument may assume two forms:

(*a*) Unless you continue faithful to the end, all your former Christian life and liberality must remain without the eternal recompense God longs to bestow. Your former struggles against many difficulties, your self-sacrifice, your Christian uprightness, your liberality to the saints, will all be unrewarded. The apostasy of the closing days of your life would render worthless the fidelity of all your previous years. You have done so well that if now your energy and usefulness do not fail, you will not merely be saved so as by fire, but will have "an abundant entrance" into everlasting glory. You have already laid up treasure in heaven. Crowns and thrones are there to reward your past toil, to compensate your past shame, and to signalise your past victories. It is not God's will that any who have suffered with Christ should miss the honour and blessedness of reigning with Him. And hence He will do His utmost to keep you from destruction. He has an eternal reward for you, and He will do His best to put you in possession of it.

(b) Or else, perhaps, the argument may be stated thus. Your past fidelity to Christ, and your ministrations to the saints, recorded in God's memory, and certain to receive His righteous recompense, will lead Him to do for you in this life what, but for your former goodness, it would be unreasonable to expect. He will reward your Christian work, and your love shown to His name, by alleviating the severity of your trial, by affording special supernatural aids to your faith and constancy. If, the writer might have said, if I were addressing men who had only recently believed, or who, since they believed, had always been cowards in the time of persecution, had always been inconsistent in moral conduct, had never been kindly and generous towards their brethren, I could have no hope of you; your present weakness would in my judgment be almost sure to issue in spiritual death; but you did so well once, and in some respects are doing so well still, that to you God will manifest unusual forbearance; for you there will be unusual and miraculous assistance; "He is not unrighteous to forget your work and the love ye have shewed to his name."

What a motive there is here for endeavouring to live a life of the highest and noblest kind, for energetic Christian work, for unsparing self-sacrifice, for the freest liberality! By courage, by labour, by generosity, by holiness, we not only augment and exalt our everlasting bliss, secure in the world to come a richer inheritance, a loftier throne, a brighter crown, a diviner joy,— we increase our safety from falling away altogether. We should live up to our most perfect conceptions of what the servants of Christ ought to be, not only that we may have the heartier welcome and the higher approbation when we enter heaven, but that we may be more certain of overcoming the outward dangers and the inward weakness which in future years may imperil the very existence of our religious life.

By the necessary operation of the laws of our spiritual nature, those who have been most faithful to Christ are most likely to come out victorious from the most terrible trials to which they may be subjected; but this is not all. If through many years, you serve God with conspicuous fidelity, He will be so solicitous to confer on you the everlasting reward of your "work" that He will protect you from temptations that would be likely to destroy you altogether; or He will communicate to you more richly the aid of His Holy Spirit to enable you successfully to confront them. Since for you, in consequence of your well-doing, there is reserved in heaven a special inheritance, incorruptible, undefiled, and that fadeth not away, all His power will be exerted that you may be kept through faith unto the salvation ready to be revealed in the last time.

If sometimes you fear that evil days are before you, when you will lose the human supports by which your faith is now sustained—days when strong temptations by which others have been plunged into shame and ruin will assault your fidelity, see in the text one way of making ready for the hour and power of darkness. Abound *now* in the work of the Lord. Minister *now* to the saints; and when the trouble and danger come, God will not forget. He will remember your present love, your present zeal, your present devotedness, and will reward you then by being your strength and shield.

I cannot stop to remove difficulties which some persons may feel about the use of the word "*righteous*" in this place; but can only say, that there is no need for any of us to be more anxious about maintaining the freedom of God's grace than the writers of the Holy Scriptures are themselves. Our sins are forgiven freely by the Divine mercy through Christ; our hearts are renewed freely by the power of the Holy Ghost; all the spiritual energies by which our Christian life is sustained are freely imparted to us by the Divine goodness; when we have done all we are unprofitable servants. And yet, if you have any doubt about the certainty of God's *rewarding* those who serve him well,—if you do not feel that, according to the constitution under which we live, it is a just and not merely a gracious thing for God to recompense a man like Paul for all his labours and sufferings, you have very much to learn about the true teaching of the New Testament. You must find room in your belief for everything for which inspired men found room in their writings; and if you cannot get this sentence into your theology, "God is not unrighteous to forget your work, and the love which ye have showed to His name," your theology needs alteration and readjustment. "Of the Lord shall ye receive the reward of the inheritance, for ye serve the Lord Christ;" "it is a righteous thing with God to recompense tribulation to them that trouble you, and to you who are troubled rest, with us, when the Lord Jesus shall be revealed from heaven with His mighty angels."

II.

Having expressed his confidence that his readers will not drift into apostasy, and assigned the reasons for his hope, the inspired writer exhorts them to renewed energy, and gives a reason for strong and persevering faith in God. "*We desire that every one of you do show the same* diligence" that was manifested in your former Christian life and in your ministrations to the saints which still continue; we desire that every one of you do show the same diligence in relation to the establishment, the strengthening, the perfecting of your hope unto the end. You are becoming discouraged and depressed. Let it be your object now to give to the hope which is beginning to decay the fulness of assurance, and a fulness of assurance which shall last until the object of hope shall be fully attained, "*that ye may not become* sluggish or slothful, *but followers of them who, through faith and endurance inherit the promises.*" This is the exhortation. When their Christian life began, they trusted in the Divine word, they looked for the salvation and eternal glory which Christ had promised them; and if they were to recover from their present declension, there must be the rekindling of the almost extinguished fires of hope. The sufferings and difficulties of the present must be overcome in the strength of a clear and distinct view of the eternal future.

Hope ranks with Faith and Charity as one of the royal elements of Christian perfection. We are saved by hope. Every man that hath hope in Christ purifieth himself even as He is pure. The temptations, and sorrows, and weariness which endanger our fidelity, are to be vanquished, not merely by faith in the consolations which God will now afford, or by the love which rejoices to be found worthy to suffer for Christ's sake, but also by a confident hope resting on the promise of Christ that if we are faithful unto death, He will give us a crown of life; that, if we overcome, we shall be pillars in the temple of God, and go no more out,—shall be clothed in white raiment,—shall eat of the hidden manna,—shall receive the white stone,—shall never have our name blotted from the Book of Life,—shall sit with Christ in His throne, even as He overcame and is seated with the Father in His throne. The heaviest of earthly calamities, the bitterest of earthly sorrows, the sharpest of earthly temptations, will appear to us light afflictions, and but for a moment; we shall perceive that they are all working for us a far more exceeding and eternal weight of glory; if we look not at the things which are seen and temporal, but at the things which are unseen and eternal.

But such a hope, strong enough to exert a permanent influence over the whole character and life, will not rise up in the soul by accident or without great diligence and care. Dazzling but transient visions of everlasting blessedness may sometimes come to men in whom the religious affections are almost powerless. The city of God, with its walls of massive splendour and the brightness and blessedness which they enclose, may be seen for a moment by the imagination even of ungodly men; but the radiant pageant will be as unsubstantial the purple and golden magnificence of sunset, and, fading away, will leave the soul in dim twilight, which will soon darken into perfect night. The hope of which the writer of this Epistle is speaking is not the dream of fancy, but one of the noblest intuitions of the soul. It is permanent in its presence and power,—as different from the momentary excitements of the imagination, as a calm Christian faith from the irrational convictions of the ignorant and the superstitious, or as a deep and genuine Christian charity from the impulses of mere kindly emotion and good-nature.

The diligence which augments and strengthens this hope will carefully avoid all that would stain and corrupt the soul, for it is only the pure in heart who see God in the home in which

God and His angels dwell; it will encourage habits of devotion and of communion with heaven, for it is only those whose affections are firmly set on things above, who can see Christ sitting on the right hand of God and the saints enthroned with Him in bliss; it will subdue the force of those inferior passions which seek their satisfaction in the riches which perish and the honour which decays, for it is only those whose treasures are in the skies,—whose hearts will long and yearn for the glory hereafter to be revealed. The diligence here required will loosen the soul from the interests of this mortal life,—will enlarge those capacities which can not be filled except with the perfect satisfactions which are the immortal inheritance of the saints,—will intensify all those affections which thirst for the vision of God, transformation into His likeness, and communion with His infinite and eternal blessedness.

But the question may arise, Is it not possible for our hope, when thus carefully and diligently perfected, to be ultimately disappointed?—is it not, after all, a wild and presumptuous thing to desire and expect so transcendent a bliss? Is there anything for so great a hope to rest upon,—anything solid and firm enough to sustain all its weight? Yes, is the reply; "*when God made promise unto Abraham,*"—a promise the final developement and fulness of which we are still waiting for,— "*because He could swear by no greater, He sware by Himself, saying, Surely*"—and the word thus translated is the common formula of Jewish oaths—"*Surely, blessing, I will bless thee, and multiplying, I will multiply thee;*" and Abraham believed God's word, and after his faith had stood the test of long delay,— "*after he had patiently endured,—he obtained the promise.*" It began to be fulfilled when Isaac was born.

"*For men verily swear by the greater,*" invoking on themselves, if they swear falsely, the vengeance of some superior power; "*and an oath is an end of all strife*" or gainsaying,—it is the firmest and surest establishment of the truth and certainty of what is promised or affirmed. "*Wherefore God, willing to show more abundantly to the heirs of promise*"—to Isaac and to Jacob that is—and to all who afterwards came to have an interest in what the Divine word had been pledged to bestow, "*the im-*

mutability of His counsel, condescended to mediate"—to become, as it were, a third person between Himself and Abraham, using the form of asseveration by which creatures call down on themselves the Divine curse, "*by*" adding "*an oath*" to His promise —"*that by two immutable things,*"—His own word and the oath which strengthened it,—"*in which it was impossible for God to lie, we may have strong encouragement who have fled for refuge to the hope set before us in the Gospel, which hope we have as an anchor of the soul, both sure and steadfast, and entering into that within the veil—the Holy of Holies—whither a forerunner on our behalf has entered, even Jesus, He having become a High Priest for ever after the order of Melchizedek.*"

The kernel of this argument for sustained confidence in God may, I think, be stated thus:—Long ago, when God called Abraham from his father's house, God promised him many and glorious blessings; the whole history of his descendants—the birth of Isaac, the muliplication of the Jewish race, their miraculous history, the coming of the Messiah—is the fulfilment of the promise; but much yet remains to be fulfilled. The depth and wealth of it have only been partially revealed. In the writings of the prophets, in the songs of the Psalmists, there are indications that the earthly kingdom was to rise into a nobler and grander form : instead of a secular prince, there was to be a Divine ruler—instead of the land which God had given to their fathers, an everlasting and heavenly inheritance. We are the heirs of the promise; the very crisis of its perfect accomplishment has now arrived; we are bound to rest upon it with the same confidence with which Abraham rested, and all the saintly men of the older faith. It is more than a promise. Anticipating the severe and protracted strain to which faith would be subjected, God added to His promise an oath. "By myself have I sworn," saith the Lord, "that in blessing I will bless thee, and in thy seed shall all the nations of the earth be blessed." This rock, the Divine promise, the Divine oath, is the ultimate foundation of all Jewish hope : on this foundation our hope is built. God's purpose is immutable, though as yet we may not be able to see that it is being fulfilled; but as Abraham waited for a long time before he saw even the beginning of the accomplishment of the Divine word, we too must wait. And meanwhile, in the midst of all the tumult and storm by which we are now surrounded, our hope is like a strong anchor, which must hold us firmly till the brighter, calmer future comes; it is an anchor fixed in the very nature, and truth, and glory of God—immoveable as the foundations of His eternal throne; for in His earnest desire to command our trust, He has condescended to strengthen the force of His promise by adding to it that solemn confirmation by which men are accustomed to invoke on themselves the direst calamities if they prove false to their word.

God knew all our infirmity. It ought to have been enough if, once for all, He had told us of the unsearchable riches of His grace. One gracious promise shining out from the darkness should have been enough to attract the vision and to command the confidence of all nations and of all ages. One golden sentence assuring us of His infinite and everlasting mercy ought to have been enough for the faith of all the millions of the human race to rest upon. When burdened with the guilt of sin,—when struggling with temptation,—when exhausted by sorrow,—it ought to have been enough for us if we knew that once heaven had spoken to earth, and invited our perfect and happy trust. Among ourselves, how often has a heart sorely tried, clung for years to a few broken words, hurriedly spoken by human lips, and found in them a spell and a charm which filled the air with music, made a desert a paradise, and enabled hope to defy repeated disappointments, and to rest exultingly in the certainty of a happy future. And a solitary promise should have been enough from the lips of Him who cannot lie. But it was not His will to subject us to the severity of such a test. Like the stars of heaven for multitude are the declarations of His willingness to pardon the sins of the most guilty, and to receive back the wicked into the joy of His love. For those who have known Him, but who have gone astray, there are promises encouraging them to return, and assuring them that God is faithful and just to forgive their sins, and to cleanse them from all unrighteousness; there are loving words for the weak and the weary, for the sorrowful, for the tempted, for the persecuted, and for the dying —words so special and direct in their application to all the vicissitudes of human life, that sometimes we must have felt as though they had been written in the ages long gone by only for *our* use ; that, like some secret treasure which had been hidden for centuries and found by us at last, they had never been intended for the saints who have gone before us, but had been reserved for our own consolation and support; in such wonderful ways has God made provision for our need !

There is another aspect under which we may regard these innumerable expressions of the Divine gentleness and love. They look like the irrepressible yearnings of the Divine nature for our confidence. It is not enough for God that the faith of angels and archangels reposes through age after age on His justice and goodness. He seems as if He could not be content without our faith too. He seems more eager to be trusted than even to be obeyed. The laws of nature shall be disturbed if miracles will only awaken our trust. Angels shall reveal their glory to mortal eyes, if angelic visions will only awaken our trust. His own Son shall leave the throne of His glory and die an accursed death, if the transcendent gift will only awaken our trust. Promise shall be accumulated on promise, revelation added to revelation, if multiplied expressions of His love will only awaken our trust. He who cannot lie, whose truth endureth to all generations, will humble Himself to the level of men whose word may fail unless it is confirmed by an oath ;—and since in that awful height in which He is enthroned He can see above Him none greater than Himself, to whose piercing scrutiny He can appeal for His sincerity, whose vengeance He can invoke if He should ever prove unfaithful,—He will swear by Himself, that His purpose may be manifestly immutable, if the oath which often enables us to rely on the word of a false and treacherous man, will only awaken our trust. Oh, wonder not, that from end to end of Holy Scripture, Faith is invested with an importance which has provoked the hostile criticism of those who understand neither the weakness of man nor the infinite cravings of the heart of God. And let the poorest and feeblest and obscurest of mankind rejoice in this—that if they could consecrate to God's service the wealth of an empire, erect to His honour the costliest temples, offer Him the homage of the noblest genius—all these would give Him less perfect delight than He derives from a faith which vanquishes doubt and stands firm in conflict, and which in death itself fears no evil, exclaiming, "Thou art with me, Thou art my strength and my song, my sun and my shield—none that trust in Thee shall ever be confounded."

MELCHIZEDEK.

"For this Melchizedek, King of Salem, priest of the Most High God, who met Abraham returning from the slaughter of the kings, and blessed him," &c.
—HEBREWS vii, 1-28.

THE inspired writer of this Epistle has already prepared us for the difficulties which occur in this chapter on the priesthood of Melchizedek. He has "many things to say and things difficult to explain," since his readers had become "dull of hearing." To make the subject perfectly intelligible to those who had ceased to give earnest heed to the elementary facts and doctrines of the Christian faith, and who needed to be taught again the first principles of the oracles of God, was no easy task. Of course, this implies that the discussion in itself was somewhat remote from the line of ordinary Christian teaching, else it would not have required thoughtful and disciplined and thoroughly spiritual men to understand it. The special difficulties which were likely to prevent these Judaizing Christians from appreciating and accepting this part of the Epistle were stated in a former sermon; but for ourselves, it is not altogether free from obscurity,—obscurity arising mainly from want of careful thought on the true relations of the Old Testament to the New.

There is hardly anything more curious in the history of Scripture interpretation than the variety of theories on the person and dignity of Melchizedek,—theories chiefly built upon the expressions employed in this chapter. In the early ages of the Church some heretical sects and some orthodox theologians indulged in strange speculations on this subject. By some it was believed that Melchizedek was a manifestation of the Holy Spirit; by others, that he was an early incarnation of Christ

Himself; by others, that he was one of the powers or emanations of God, superior to our Lord, but after the model of whom Christ was afterwards formed. Origen of Alexandria believed that he was an angel; others thought that he was a man, formed before the creation of the world out of spiritual not earthly matter; others, that he was Enoch sent to live on the earth again after the flood. Some conjectured that he was Shem, the son of Noah, following an ancient Jewish tradition, preserved in one of the Targums; others, that he was Ham; while others, again, have thought that he was the patriarch Job.

You will not expect me to discuss these various hypotheses. Though some of the expressions, especially those in the third and eighth verses, are seriously perplexing, I venture to think that, without any attempt to explain away or diminish the force of the writer's language, only interpreting every phrase in the light of the two passages concerning Melchizedek in the Old Testament, and in the light of the writer's own purpose, we may be able to see that he does not wish us to suppose that Melchizedek was anything more than a good man, King of Salem, and the recognized representative and priest, in his own country and times, of the Most High God.

To correct the errors, confirm the faith, and animate the courage of those Jewish Christians who were disheartened and depressed by the absence of visible glory in the history of Christ and in the constitution and position of the Christian Church, it has been shown already that, personally and by His works, Christ is greater than the angels whose ministry had thrown a supernatural splendour around the ancient institutions of Judaism; that by His relationship to God and His rank in God's spiritual "house," Christ, the Son of God, is greater than Moses, who was only God's servant, though the founder and lawgiver of the Jewish commonwealth, and the great patriot and hero of Jewish story; and that from Christ we are to receive a nobler "rest" than that into which Joshua led the tribes of Israel after their long wanderings in the wilderness. And now the writer begins the contrast between the priesthood—not the person, but the priesthood—of Christ, and the priesthood of Aaron and his successors, and is about to show that the priesthood of Christ is far loftier and more glorious.

He commences his argument by an appeal to a remarkable event in Abraham's history. Many years before this event occurred, Abraham, in obedience to a Divine call, had left the land of his birth and his father's house; he had received those promises which were the foundation of all the privileges and distinctions of the Jewish race; already a special Divine providence watched over him; quite recently, after his separation from Lot, God had told him that the land of Canaan—northward, southward, eastward, and westward—was to belong to him and his children, and that his seed were to be as the dust of the earth.

The story about Melchizedek may be told in a few sentences. Abraham's nephew, Lot, had gone to feed his flocks in the rich and fruitful plains of Jordan, and was living in Sodom. The cities in that neighbourhood had been subdued by the chiefs of certain Eastern tribes, and for twelve years had served Chedorlaomer, King of Elam. In the thirteenth year, there was a revolt against the power of the stranger. But Chedorlaomer, with the chiefs that were in alliance with him, came and utterly overthrew the chiefs of Sodom, Gomorrah, and the neighbouring cities, and carried away many prisoners and considerable booty. Lot was among the captives; and his wealth, which he had loved so well and was so selfishly eager to increase, was in the hands of the invaders. Abraham heard of the calamity, followed the victorious army, overtook it in the north-western borders of Palestine, fell upon it by night, and completely routed it. Lot and the other prisoners and all the spoil were recovered. As Abraham was returning to the south, Melchizedek met him and brought forth bread and wine for the refreshment of the patriarch and his followers—in which hospitable act, by the way, some expositors have ingeniously or absurdly found a prophetic anticipation of the Lord's Supper. In the narrative in Genesis, Melchizedek is described as "King of Salem,"—which was probably the country around the hills on which Jerusalem was afterwards built—and "priest of the Most High God;" and he blessed Abraham, and received a tithe of the recaptured spoils.

There is no hint in the narrative that any superhuman dignity belonged to this Canaanitish king; and yet the story is very remarkable, especially to those whose habits of thought on all religious subjects have been formed by Jewish institutions. Here is a Canaanitish king, about whose reign and subsequent history not a solitary fact is known, recognised by Abraham himself as God's priest,—receiving tithes from the illustrious head of the Jewish nation,—assuming the right to bless him. It is also rather significant that some years afterwards, when Abraham was commanded to sacrifice Isaac, he was directed to go into the land of Moriah and offer his son for a burnt-offering on one of the mountains there; and this was in the very district over which I have said that Melchizedek probably reigned. The name he bore was eminently suggestive: he was "Melchizedek"—"king of righteousness:" his title was suggestive too: he was "King of Salem"—"king of peace." Who is this mysterious stranger? Whence did he receive his sanctity? From what priestly ancestors did he spring? When did he assume his priestly functions?—when did he lay them down?— to whom were they transmitted? As a priest, he stands before us "*without a genealogy;*"* he belongs to no consecrated line; the commencement of his priestly functions is not connected with the death of any predecessor, the close of them is not marked by the appearance of another who succeeded him. A priest, "*without*" a priestly "*father,*" "*without*" a "*mother*" belonging to the sacerdotal line; without a definite consecration signalizing his entrance into his office, without successors indicating that his functions had ceased,—held a position altogether unlike that of the priesthood that ministered in the Jewish temple,—belonged to altogether a different "order." He was a king as well as a priest.

It was these circumstances that made the priesthood of

---

* "Without descent," *i.e.*, without a pedigree on which to rest his right to the priestly office.

Melchizedek unique. And they had attracted notice long before this Epistle was written.

In the Psalms, an inspired writer fixes on the underived and untransmitted and royal priesthood of the King of Salem as the highest representation of the priesthood of the Messiah; and just as the kingship of a Jewish monarch is sometimes described, in the same book, in language which passes, by imperceptible gradations, into a vision of royal grandeur and authority which no earthly prince could ever possess, so the priesthood of Melchizedek is idealized and exalted until it transcends in dignity and permanence the measures of a merely human ministry. "Thou art a priest *for ever* after the order of Melchizedek."

In the 72nd Psalm the inspired poet presents the true idea of a king anointed by God to reign over His people; and the magnificent representation of a sovereign, who should "judge the people with righteousness and the poor with judgment,"—who should "save the children of the needy and break in pieces the oppressor,"—"in whose days the righteous" were to "flourish,"—who was to "have dominion from sea to sea, and from the river to the end of the earth,"—whose "name" was to "endure for ever," and to "continue as long as the sun,"—in whom men were to be "blessed," and whose glory was to "fill the whole earth;"—this magnificent representation of the ideal king of the chosen race could not possibly become an actual fact in the history of any mortal prince; but in it all the kings of the Jewish nation were to recognise the grandeur properly belonging to the crown and throne of the king of God's people—the sublime and perfect conception to which their government was to be conformed.

And the priesthood of Melchizedek is similarly treated in the 110th Psalm. Because of its peculiar characteristics it is employed to denominate the everlasting priesthood of the Messiah. As Priest of the Most High God, the Canaanitish king stood apart from all the consecrated descendants of Aaron, deriving his dignity from none, transmitting it to none; his royal priesthood was the noblest visible approach to the everlasting priesthood of the Son of God; and the Psalmist therefore speaks of Christ as belonging to the same priestly order, and as fulfilling the idea which in the priesthood of Melchizedek was represented in an inferior form.

It is with these two passages before him that the author of this Epistle proceeds to contrast the order of priesthood which derives its name from Melchizedek with that which derives its name from Aaron; and the facts contained in Genesis are blended with the idea of Melchizedek's priesthood which in the Psalm is developed from those facts. This is not an unnatural process. If, for instance, it had been the business of any inspired writer to contrast the kingship of Christ with the kingship of heathen monarchs, he might have said that Christ was a king after the order of Solomon, and proceeded to refer to certain facts in Solomon's history, and to quote those passages from the 72nd Psalm which I quoted just now, to show that the kingship with which Solomon was invested was, according to the *idea* of it, a universal and everlasting sovereignty; the monarchs that rule over the nations of the world rule over a limited territory, but it is testified concerning this King that He has dominion from sea to sea: *they* die and pass away, but *He* shall live, and His name shall endure for ever; Solomon "*is made like unto the Son of God, and abideth*" a King "*continually.*" In such a discussion there would have been a blending of what was true only of Solomon with what was true only of that loftier Prince whose royal greatness Solomon imperfectly and temporarily sustained. There is, I repeat, a similar blending here: in some parts of the chapter the writer speaks of what was actually true of the priesthood of Melchizedek, as borne by the human king of Salem; in other parts he loses sight of the man and sees only the Divine conception of an everlasting priesthood, which Melchizedek personally could not possess: in other words, following the example of the 110th Psalm, Melchizedek "*is* made *like unto the Son of God, and abideth a priest continually.*"

And "*now consider how great this man was, unto whom even*

the patriarch Abraham gave the tenth of the spoils." "*The sons of Levi who receive the office of the priesthood have a commandment to take tithes of the people according to the law;*" the priests have this acknowledged symbol of supremacy over their brethren, who come, like themselves, from the loins of Abraham; but here is one who does not belong to the Jewish priesthood, nor stand in the line of their descent, who "*received tithes from Abraham*" himself, and whose dignity is therefore higher than their own. Not only did he receive tithes from Abraham, but he "*blessed him that had received the promises: now without contradiction, the less is blessed by the greater,*"—the son by the father, the people by the priest; and, therefore, in this memorable meeting Abraham himself assumes a position inferior to that of the King of Salem.

Nor is this all. By Jewish law "*men that die receive tithes, but there,*"—and now the Canaanitish king of Genesis becomes the Melchizedek of the Psalms—"*there he receiveth them of whom it is witnessed that he liveth;*" eternity being essential to the true idea of the priesthood of Melchizedek. Just as a writer asserting the dignity of the kingship of Solomon, though that dignity could not be attained by Solomon himself, might say, on the ground of the 72nd Psalm, when referring to the gifts that were brought to him, here a king received tribute concerning whom it is said that "they shall fear Thee as long as the sun and moon endureth, throughout all generations." This everlasting dominion, though impossible to Solomon, was according to the Psalm, an essential element of the divinely-appointed sovereignty of which Solomon's was a transient and imperfect anticipation.

Nor is this all, "*as I may so say, Levi also, who receiveth tithes, payed tithes in Abraham, for he was yet in the loins of his father when Melchizedek met him.*" Honour among the Jewish people, being strictly hereditary, all the privileges of the race being regarded as simply the inheritance of the descendants of Abraham, the throne being limited to the descendants of David, and the priestly office to the descendants of Aaron, this argument would have a greater force for Jews than it may have for some of us. What promises Abraham received, his descendants were taught to regard as given to them; what homage he paid might also be fairly regarded as paid by them. The idea of the strict unity of a family in the person of its head was more familiar to their minds than it is to ours. Levi, therefore, paid tithes in Abraham; and the Jewish priesthood itself acknowledged in that act the superior priesthood of Melchizedek.

The remaining part of the chapter, the substance of which I shall presently proceed to give, is much simpler. The things "hard to be uttered," are contained in the first ten verses; and I repeat that the difficulty in those verses arises from a want of thoughtful and deep reflection on the ancient revelations of God to man. But let me say that there is the greatest possible difference between the apostolic method of developing the profound spiritual meaning of certain Jewish institutions and the practice of many modern and ancient interpreters. Nothing can be more childish or irrational than the ingenuity of some learned men in discovering the whole substance of Christian doctrine in some of the circumstances of Jewish ceremonies, and in some of the incidental phrases of Old Testament history. Their whole scheme of interpretation is purely arbitrary. On the other hand, I am prepared to say that I have never yet found in the New Testament any allusions to the ancient Jewish Scriptures, any illustrations derived from the ancient Jewish ritual, which, when seriously and patiently studied, have not proved to be logically and philosophically just. The books of Moses and the prophets are never treated by the inspired writers as affording materials out of which an ingenious fancy has license to construct unsubstantial demonstrations of truths which the authority of Christ and of His apostles sufficiently authenticate; but as containing imperfect and elementary revelations—hints and foreshadowings—in which a mind that has comprehended the general structure and purpose of the ancient system may recognize the outlines and anticipations of the fully-developed Christian faith.

But to return to the eleventh verse of the chapter—the

prophecy, in the 110th Psalm, of the coming of a priest after the order of Melchizedek, is still present to the mind of the writer; and he asks—"*If, then, the Levitical priesthood—for upon* the basis of *it the people received the law*"—it was the very foundation and centre of the whole Jewish constitution—"*if, then, the Levitical priesthood*" perfectly answered the ends for which the priestly office was instituted, "*if perfection were by it, what further need was there that a different priest should arise after the order of Melchizedek, and that he is said to be not after the order of Aaron?*"

If the Aaronic priesthood had been perfectly effective, there would have been no such indication in the ancient books as that contained in the 110th Psalm, that a priest was to arise after the order of Melchizedek. And then, referring back to the parenthesis in the 11th verse, in which it is said that the whole Jewish constitution was based on the Jewish priesthood, he adds—"*if the priesthood is changed, there comes of necessity a change of the whole law,*" under which the Jewish people lived. And that such a change *has* come about is certain, for "*He of whom these things are spoken*—that is, in the 110th Psalm—*belongs to a different tribe, of which no man has ever devoted himself to the altar. For it is plain that our Lord,*" whom these Jewish Christians acknowledged to be the Messiah, though they did not perceive all His glory, or understand that by His coming the old system was abolished, "*it is plain that our Lord has sprung out of Judah, of which tribe Moses said nothing concerning priesthood. And it is yet far more evident that the law has been changed*—*if,* according to the prophetic Psalm, *after the similitude of Melchizedek, there ariseth a different Priest, who is appointed, not according to the law of a carnal commandment*"—that is, whose functions, authority, and power are regulated by a system which necessarily recognized the frailty and imperfections of the persons by whom it was to be administered—"*but after the power of an endless life,*"—having prerogatives and conferring blessings to which the everlasting existence of the priest himself is indispensable, for he testifieth, "*Thou art a priest* for ever, *after the order of Melchizedek.*

For in this change of the law "*there is a disannulling of the commandment going before*,"—an abrogation of the preceding system,—"*on account of its weakness and unprofitableness,—for the law perfected nothing*,"—its precepts could not sanctify the life,—its sacrifices pointed to an end they could not attain,—its priests could effect no real reconciliation to God,—its kings could not establish on earth the true kingdom of heaven; and with the abolition of the old system there is "*the bringing in of a better hope, by means of which we draw nigh to God.*"

The contrast is not yet closed. "*Those priests were made without an oath, but this*" priest of prophecy who is now come, even the Lord Jesus Christ, "*with an oath, by Him who saith to Him, The Lord sware and will not repent, ' Thou art a Priest for ever after the order of Melchizedek;' and inasmuch as not without an oath He was made priest, of so much better a covenant hath Jesus become surety.*" Nor is this all. "*They truly are many priests because they are not suffered to continue,*" that is in their priesthood, "*by reason of death; but He, on account of His continuing for ever, hath an unchangeable priesthood. Wherefore also He is able to save to the uttermost them that come to God by Him, seeing He ever liveth to make intercession for us. For*" it was also in harmony with all our great necessities, in harmony with all our hopes of present communion with God, and everlasting blessedness in His presence, "*that we should have such a High Priest, holy, harmless, undefiled, separated,*" by His personal purity, "*from our sinful race, and made higher than the heavens, who hath no need day by day, as the high priests, to offer sacrifices, first for his own sins, and then for the people's; for this*"—that is, as the context plainly indicates, offer sacrifice for the sins of the people—"*this He did once for all, when He offered up Himself. For the law maketh men high priests who have infirmity, but the word of the oath, which was after the law, maketh the Son High Priest, who is perfect for evermore.*"

And now, perhaps, some may be ready to ask, Of what service can it be to us to give time and strength to this elaborate contrast between the priesthood of the descendants of Aaron, and the priesthood of the Lord Jesus Christ? What need is there to remind us that Jewish priests were compassed with infirmity, while He having passed through the sufferings and conflicts of His earthly life is perfected for evermore,—that they had to offer sacrifices day by day for their own sins as well as for the sins of the people, while He needeth to offer no sacrifices for Himself, and by a solitary sacrifice atoned for the sins of all mankind,—that they died and passed away, transmitting their priesthood to others, while His priesthood permanently remains with Himself,—that they were appointed without an oath, while He is appointed with an oath, and is therefore the surety of a better covenant? What need is there to prove to us from the ideal priesthood of Melchizedek that He to whom that priesthood in its perfect form belongs, must be greater than Abraham, upon whom Melchizedek conferred a blessing,—greater, therefore, than all Abraham's descendants, whose honours were derived from their ancestor, and could not rise higher than the fountain whence they sprang? What need is there to show to us that, according to Jewish modes of thought, Levi himself, the father of the priestly race that ministered in the Jewish temple, virtually paid tithes to Melchizedek, and so acknowledged the superiority of Melchizedek's priesthood? What need is there to satisfy us that the ancient law has passed away by appealing to a prophecy which indicated that the Aaronic priesthood, the centre of the Jewish constitution, was to give place to a priesthood of a different order; and to the fact that the Messiah, in whom the functions of both king and priest were united, belonged to a tribe whose members had no right to minister at the altar? Why could we not have the positive truth concerning the glory and the permanence of Christ's priestly office placed before us apart from the obsolete errors and superstitions of these Judaizing Christians?

(1) I answer, that the laborious carefulness of this inspired writer in discussing and removing the errors which prevented these persons from acknowledging that their old law had passed away, and that all the blessings it conferred were now to be found in a nobler and more lasting form in the Lord Jesus, is an instructive and affecting example of how we are to

endeavour to bring men to a true religious belief, and a right state of heart in relation to Christ. Stern rebuke for sin, awful warnings for those who are drifting into apostasy, but calm, patient reasoning, for the removal of rooted prejudice and error,—this is what the contents of this Epistle recommend. The Christian teacher must never be satisfied with general statements of positive truth, but must endeavour to displace whatever erroneous opinions prevent the reception of the truth.

He must not denounce mere intellectual misapprehensions, except so far as they are the obvious result of wilfulness, cowardice, or irreligion. He must be patient with the most irrational follies of the human mind, though he must be resolute in condemning all the sins of the human heart.

(2) There is a warning in these arguments against a very common danger. The religious life of the Jewish race had been associated through many centuries with a particular system of religious observances, and it needed, not merely the authority of inspiration, but elaborate instruction, nay, it needed the destruction of Jerusalem itself by the armies of Titus, to prevent the Jewish members of the Christian church endeavouring to perpetuate a ritualism, the use and power of which had now departed. They still clung to their temple, their sacrifices, and their priesthood. They could not relinquish observances which were sanctified and made venerable by the glorious memories and by the sacred traditions of sixteen hundred years. Had not the ceremonial law ministered to the holiness of prophets and psalmists and pious kings and thousands of forgotten saints? Why then should it be abandoned? That the changing times required changing forms of religious service, that the new thoughts which had come from Christ required new expression, that the new life required new forms for its free growth and visible manifestation, this was what they could not understand; this is what vast numbers of Christian people in every succeeding age have been unable to understand. Institutions which for centuries rendered service to God, customs which through many generations were the fitting vestments of spiritual thought and feeling, may become obstacles to the free progress of God's truth, and

solemn mockeries of the interior religious life. And yet their antiquity, and the sacred associations which cluster round them, make it hard to remove them out of the way, except by angry and violent revolt, by bitter and exasperating controversy. It may be proved that at one time the Romish Church, spite of its corruptions, rendered noble service to Christendom; and when Luther and his friends were in rebellion against the Romish see, I can perfectly understand how it was that numbers of good men listened with horror to his denunciations, and recoiled from all fellowship with his enterprise. Illustrious saints had worshipped at the altars of the church, famous theologians, who had confuted dangerous heresies, had been among her faithful sons, heathen nations had been Christianized by her missionaries, millions of humble and uncultivated souls were receiving some sort of spiritual guidance from her services and her priests;—it was perilous, it was rash, it was irreverent, to assault so august, so venerable an institution.

And yet it was necessary. And Luther, by presuming to dispute the supremacy of the Bishop of Rome, which in its beginnings might have been harmless and even beneficial to the church, but which now had become a fearful calamity and curse, prevented foul stagnation and mortal disease corrupting and destroying the religious life of Christendom.

I can quite understand how it was that even good and great men like the English Reformers failed to purify their Service Book from all Romish errors, and yielded ecclesiastical supremacy to the crown. I might admit that greater security and greater immediate visible progress may have been secured to the Reformation movement by its alliance with kings, and that the Prayer Book was admirably adapted to the religious life of a people who were being led out of Romanism into a clearer, truer faith. But see how hard it is now to effect any further progress! To touch the baptismal service seems an insult to the long procession of devout and godly men who have stood at the English font and given thanks for the spiritual renewal of successive generations of English children; and the salvation of the living is imperilled that the memory of the dead may not be dishonoured

If we impeach the alliance of Church and State, we are surrounded at once by a great cloud of witnesses—dignified bishops, learned theologians, lofty saints. These illustrious men worshipped and died in a church, organized and governed by acts of Parliament and deriving its revenues largely from public law; why should not we? And there are majestic cathedrals, whose vast and solemn spaces have been filled through century after century with measured chant and lofty song: there are village churches before whose altars our fathers have bowed through many generations, and in the shadow of whose towers their dust awaits the morning of the resurrection. Admirable materials these for poetry, and precious, too, for enriching the common thoughts and lives of men, but utterly useless in relation to this controversy.

That subjection of the church of Christ to secular authority— I want to know, not whether good men have tacitly or expressly sanctioned it, but whether Christ approves it. These magnificent cathedrals, these ancient churches,—I want to know, not whether they afford beautiful imagery to the poet, or even whether our ancestors found religious culture within their walls, but whether it be true or no, in our own times, that through the law of patronage, through the necessities of a national church, through the structure and contents of the Book of Common Prayer, sermons are preached in multitudes of these sacred buildings, week after week, by men whose teaching points towards Rome, by men who have lost or are losing faith in the supernatural elements of the Christian revelation, by men who are destitute of religious life altogether.

And yet, though this be proved, there are tens of thousands of good men, over whose nature long custom and reverent antiquity have cast such a spell that they find it as difficult to venture upon the freedom of a church untrammelled by State control, as these Jewish Christians found it to escape from the obsolete institutions of their old religious faith.

I wish that we ourselves knew nothing of this injurious bondage to the past; but I believe that if our fathers had not had the courage and wisdom to found our free churches for us, few of us would have the vigour and boldness to do it for ourselves. Among ourselves, custom asserts too frequently an illegitimate authority, and tradition takes the place of common sense and an intelligent study of the true necessities of our times. We, too, have sacred phrases which derive all their consecration from lips that we know could sometimes err; and old observances which we shrink from violating, though their wisdom and authority cannot be demonstrated. We, too, have to learn that the language and the customs which may have been the best possible to former generations, may now obscure our religious thought and impede our religious action: we may be assisted in learning this by the Epistle to the Hebrews and a thoughtful study of the errors against which its argument is directed.

(3) It is of some importance to us, I think, to be reminded that the Christian faith did not come into the world abruptly and without due preparation; but that, through all the ages of human history, Divine providence and Divine revelations had been educating the intellect and heart of mankind for the reception of Christ. The great thoughts of the New Testament have their roots at the very gate of the garden of Eden. The glory which shines from the face of Christ had shed a dim twilight on the darkness of previous centuries. A whole nation had been consecrated to the developement of imperfect anticipations of the final manifestation of God. This ennobles the teaching of Jesus and His apostles; this supplies a separate and independent evidence of their Divine commission. How was it that for sixteen hundred years one religious faith continued to exist among the Jewish people, spite of their restlessness and vacillation, spite of their impatience under its yoke, spite of their inability to appreciate its moral and spiritual dignity,—how was it that this faith survived the invasion of foreign armies, subjugation to foreign kings, captivity in foreign lands? How was it that from Moses down to John the Baptist the same religious principles were steadily proclaimed, the same mysterious hopes clung to, through all the vicissitudes of their national history and by all their authoritative religious teachers—by kings, warriors, shepherds, priests; by men of lofty genius, by men whose only power was

derived from their commission as the prophets of God? How was it that, at last, when the spirit and aims of this protracted system of discipline were unintelligible to all the nation besides, a few peasants and fishermen rose up, and, in spite of the fierce hostility of all the authorities in Church and State, founded new religious institutions, in which all that had been believed and hoped for in previous ages, suddenly assumed a transcendently glorious form, received its obvious interpretation and perfect fulfilment?

The Old Testament, with its ceremonial and predictions, was hardly less essential to the mission of the apostles than the history of Christ. If you tell me that the imagination of the early Church created the four Gospels, I ask whether the Church also invented Moses and the prophets? Of the apostolic band, it was essential that all should tell the same story: if this was the result of close conspiracy, I ask whether Abraham, Moses, and David were also in the plot? If you tell me that the raising of Lazarus was a fiction, though the priests that crucified the Lord believed it, and Judas, who betrayed Him, had no secrets to tell to expose the knavery of his former Master and brethren, I will show you another miracle: here in the epistle to the Hebrews, I see an ancient Faith out of which the life has gone, being carried to its sepulchre, and a Christian writer stops the funeral procession, touches the bier, and the lips of the dead religion open and bear testimony to the greatness and glory of the Lord Jesus Christ.

(4) Finally, This story of Melchizedek has another use: It reminds us that even in ancient times the knowledge and service of the true God were not limited to the chosen race. It was a Canaanitish king who was priest of the Most High, and to whom Abraham religiously devoted a tenth of his spoils. In after times the light that shone with the brightest lustre in Jerusalem sometimes penetrated far beyond the limits of the Jewish people. It shone in the streets of Nineveh when Jonah preached there; and the Ninevites repented of their sins. It shone in Belshazzar's court when Daniel prophesied there; and Babylon was compelled to acknowledge the only true God.

And we may cherish the hope that fragments of early revelation floated down all the divided streams of national history, and reached multitudes of souls of whose humble reverence for an almost unknown God nothing is recorded in history sacred or profane, but who, loving the light that reached them, faint as the light was, shall not enter into condemnation; and that so, from the east, and the west, and the north, and the south, out of nominally heathen lands, many shall come and sit down with Abraham, Isaac, and Jacob in the kingdom of heaven.

This story of Melchizedek, with all the truths that underlie it, is another proof, standing on the very title page of Jewish history, that "God is no respecter of persons," and never has been; but that "in every nation he that feareth Him and worketh righteousness is accepted with Him."

WHAT IS A TYPE?

"Now, of the things which we have spoken this is the sum: We have such an High Priest, who is set on the right hand of the throne of the Majesty in the heavens," &c.—HEBREWS viii, 1-5.

THE discussion concerning Melchizedek has now closed. The writer has shown that the Jewish Scriptures themselves indicated that the priesthood of the descendants of Aaron was not to be perpetual, but was to give place to a priesthood of a higher order,—a priesthood underived, untransmitted, and having a dignity and authority with which mortal men could not be invested. And now he tells his readers that "*the principal thing*" of which he is speaking is, that "*we have a High Priest who sat down on the right hand of the throne of the Majesty in the heavens;*" who is "*a minister*" not of an earthly temple, "*but of the true tabernacle which the Lord pitched, and not man.*" That He cannot be a mere earthly priest, nor present mere earthly sacrifices, is shown in the next two verses. "*Every High Priest is ordained to offer gifts and sacrifices; and so Christ,*" if His priestly name and office are not an idle form, "*must also have somewhat to offer: but if He were on earth He would not be a priest*" at all, for a tribe, a family to which He did not belong, had been appointed and consecrated "*to offer gifts according to the law.*" He is, therefore priest in another sanctuary, and offers other gifts: and what these are the next verse informs us; the service of the Jewish priests is devoted to the "*example,*" or visible illustration and shadow of "*heavenly things,*" as may be suggested indeed by what God said to Moses when "*he was about to complete the tabernacle, 'for see,' said He, 'that thou make all things according to the pattern showed to thee in the mount.'*"

These words appear to me a general introduction to the contrast which the writer now proceeds to draw between the old covenant and the new,—the access to God granted in the Jewish temple, and the access to God granted to Christian believers through Christ,—the numerous Levitical sacrifices, and the great sacrifice once offered for the sins of mankind. Already he has vindicated and illustrated the glory of the Lord Jesus Himself, as being greater than angels, greater than Moses. He has also shown that, according to Jewish prophecy, Christ is not only a priest, but a priest belonging to a loftier rank than that of Aaron and his sons; and now the first part of the Epistle is about to close by a profoundly interesting illustration of the superiority of the Christian dispensation itself to that religious constitution which these Jewish believers were longing to perpetuate. The personal supremacy of Christ above all who had to do with founding or maintaining the ancient system has been made clear; the superiority of His priesthood to that of the sons of Aaron in permanence and in the solemnity of the consecration by which He was appointed to it, has also been shown; and the whole argument of the Epistle for steadfast loyalty to Christ, and against apostasy to Judaism, is about to be crowned and completed by the contrast, which extends to the middle of the tenth chapter, between the inferior promises and the merely symbolic institutions of the old covenant, and the nobler and eternal blessings which belong to the new.

There is one expression in these introductory verses to which I wish to call your most thoughtful attention. The writer does not dwell upon it; but it is developed and illustrated in the next two chapters. The institutions of Judaism are represented as visible illustrations, "*shadows of heavenly things;*" the very forms of the sacred vessels of the tabernacle were made after a pattern which was shown to Moses in the mount, and the whole ritual was a revelation and a prophecy of spiritual and eternal realities.

This sentence is plainly of the very gravest importance in reference to the relation between the institutions of the ancient worship and the great truths and facts of the Christian system; and, as that relation has been greatly misunderstood, and is still perhaps most imperfectly and even incorrectly conceived, by many Christian people, I wish to explain it as clearly and as briefly as I can. All that follows in the argumentative part of this Epistle will be a mere riddle and perplexity to thoughtful persons, if the general principle which this expression affirms is not grasped with firmness and accuracy.

I.

To understand it aright there are, I think, three very simple facts which need to be carefully considered and constantly remembered.

(1) The first is, that the Jewish system was intended for the culture of the religious life of the Jews themselves.

I find, on reading the Old Testament Scriptures, that for about sixteen hundred years before Christ came, the descendants of Abraham, Isaac, and Jacob, were living under a civil polity and maintaining ritualistic observances instituted by God Himself. No matter whether the idea of offering sacrifice originated with man, or was given at first by Divine revelation; no matter whether the resemblances between the Levitical ceremonies and the rites of certain pagan systems were numerous or few; the declarations of holy Scripture are perfectly unambiguous that the whole of the Jewish system had God's sanction. It is equally certain that while many parts of the Levitical law may have rested on social or sanitary grounds exclusively, there were other parts which were religious in their principle and purpose. There was a temple for worship; there were sacrifices for sin; there were consecrated priests. Through generation after generation the appointed victims were consumed on the altar; festival after festival the outer courts of the sanctuary were crowded with worshippers; year after year the High Priest entered with reverence and fear and awe into the Holy of Holies.

Now, it seems to me incredible that all this should have been a mystery without meaning to Moses, to Aaron, to Samuel, to David, to Isaiah, and to all the prophets; incredible. that the tens of thousands of holy men who took part in these solemn rites, should have connected them with no moral or spiritual truths. If it be alleged that this cumbrous and stately system was altogether unintelligible till Christ came,—a riddle, without a solution till then,—I can only ask, For what purpose did it exist at all? Perhaps it may be said that it is an additional aid to our faith to discover in these Jewish rites, curious and even profound anticipations of the fully-developed Christian faith; but, if that had been the solitary object of these institutions, it would surely have been enough if the ceremonies had been performed, once for all, when the people were at Sinai, or when Solomon came to the throne, or if they had been solemnly enacted once every hundred years. If they were simply unintelligible prophecies of Christ,—prophecies which could not be understood until Christ came,—what need was there that, day after day, year after year, century after century, they should be still repeated? Moreover, it is singularly unfortunate, if the ceremonial system had no meaning for the Jews themselves, and reserved all its wealth of instruction for Christian times, that this very system proved a very perilous hindrance to the Christian faith in the first age, and that ever since, it has been to so large an extent a difficulty requiring to be explained, instead of an independent source of instruction on Christian doctrine or practice. *We* understand it imperfectly; if the Jews before Christ did not understand it at all, it has certainly proved a very remarkable and uncompensated failure. It is surely far more reasonable to suppose that the Levitical institutions had a religious meaning for the Jews themselves, and exerted a real and powerful influence on their religious life.

(2) The principles of true religion have always been the same as they are now, ever since man sinned and God determined to effect his redemption through the incarnation, death, resurrection, and glory of the Lord Jesus Christ.

I do not say that those principles were revealed at first as clearly as they are revealed now; but that, although our knowledge of God and of His salvation is much fuller than Adam, or Abraham, or Moses possessed, what was true in their times is true still; that, if God taught them anything, He must have taught them substantially the same things He has taught us, although the teaching was clear only when it dealt with the most elementary truths, and became obscure when it passed beyond them. As far as it went, the revelation of God to the Jewish race must have been substantially identical with His revelation to ourselves. For instance, it was as true then as it is now, that there is but one God,—that His character is holy, and that His law requires man to be holy too :—that man has sinned, needs God's forgiveness, and that whenever God forgives, it is because man's relation to Himself is derived from the suffering of another on man's behalf. These things have been always true, and although they have not always been revealed as fully and clearly as they are now, yet if man received in ancient times any knowledge of God—of God's moral attributes, of God's will; and of his own moral condition and the means of escaping from his guilt and ruin; these truths, whether they were more dimly or more distinctly communicated, must have had a place in Divine revelation. The forms in which truth of this order is clothed may vary,—the measure of man's knowledge of it may vary: but the truth itself is invariable.

And that, as a matter of fact, the same truths substantially that we believe now—not all of them, perhaps, but, so far as they went, the same—were believed by God's saints in the old times, is sufficiently plain from this, that their actual spiritual life was so like our own, that many Christian people—erroneously, as I am compelled to think—suppose that the book of Psalms, in which the devotion of the Jewish saints is uttered, contains a full and adequate expression for the religious life of the Church in all ages.

If, from some remote world, an angelic visitor were to bring fruits and flowers precisely like those with which we ourselves are already familiar, it would be a fair inference that the elements of the soil in that unknown orb were the same as they are here,—that there was heat there like that in which our own flowers blossom and our own fruits ripen,—that there was an atmosphere there like our own, and rain. And so, if we knew nothing of the revelation which God had made to the Jewish people, there would be enough in the Book of Psalms alone, to convince us that it was substantially the same as the revelation He has made to us; for in that book the moral and spiritual results of the ancient revelation are preserved to us, and they are of the same kind as the results of the revelation made to ourselves. David knew as well as we know that the gods of the nations are idols, and that Jehovah is the sole Creator of the heavens which declare His glory, and of the earth which is full of His goodness. He knew that sin was intolerable to God, and, under the consciousness of his guilt, cried passionately, "Cast me not away from Thy presence." He knew that though "God is angry with the wicked every day," "there is forgiveness with Him that He may be feared," and could sing with tranquil joy of the blessedness of the man "whose transgression is forgiven, whose sin is covered."

If, then, the Jewish system was intended for the religious instruction of the Jews themselves,—and if religious truth remains the same through all ages—it follows necessarily that we may expect to find in the institutions of Judaism the same truths which are more fully and gloriously revealed by Christ Himself and the inspired writers of the New Testament.

(3) This conclusion is confirmed, and the necessary limits of it suggested, by the fact that Judaism is always represented in the New Testament as a system intended to discipline and educate men for the coming of Christ.

If the Jewish institutions were introductory to the Christian revelation, they must surely have been in essential harmony with it, and have taught substantially the same truths. If they were intended to discipline the Jewish people for Christ's coming, their spiritual influence must have been in harmony with that of the faith of Christ, and must have formed the spiritual life after the same model.

And yet, since they were only introductory, and formed only a preparatory discipline, we cannot suppose that the Jewish saints—even the wisest and holiest—found in them all that we find in the four Gospels, and the writings of the apostles. The Jewish institutions, according to the language of this Epistle, were not full disclosures of Divine truth; they were pictures or delineations—"*shadows of heavenly things*"—but still heavenly things were actually revealed through them.

II

And now, keeping these three principles in mind, it will not be difficult to perceive what we ought to understand by the typical character of Old Testament ritualism, and of Old Testament history.

According to the use of the writers of the Christian Scriptures, if an ancient ceremony was obviously intended by God to reveal to the Jew a certain religious principle or truth, that ceremony is treated as a type of the Christian *fact* in which the same principle or truth is now revealed.

For instance, take those words of our Lord's in which He says, "Destroy this temple, and in three days I will raise it again," words which according to the evangelist, referred to the temple of His body. Are we to suppose that the connection between the body of Christ and the Jewish temple was purely arbitrary? Or was there any outward resemblance between them which justified the Lord Jesus in speaking of the one as a type of the other? By no means.

Try to imagine yourself a Jew—a devout Jew—who had come out from among the idolatries and superstitions of Egypt, into the wilderness. He knew that the gods which were worshipped by the Egyptians were mere creations of the human imagination, that their visible forms were the work of human hands. He knew too, that the Jehovah he worshipped had created all things; the thunder was the symbol of His voice, and the lightning of His vengeance. He reigned in the highest heavens, was infinite in power, and in wisdom, and perfect in holiness. Occasionally He had appeared to the saintly men of his race; to Abraham in the old time; to Moses more recently; but was not God too great and awful to be accessible to common men? Could even the holiest expect that He would be always near to them?

The tabernacle, constructed by God's own appointment, was the answer to all his apprehensions. In the centre of the camp, surrounded by common dwellings, though composed of more costly materials as became the Divine glory, there was a tent which was to be regarded as God's dwelling-place. It was divided into separate courts, and the innermost sanctuary was to be entered only by the high priest, and by him only once a year; but still, there was the Divine home standing among the common homes of the nation: into the outer court all the people might at any time have access, and into the inner court of all—the very presence-chamber of Jehovah—the high priest entered as the representative of all the people. The tabernacle first, the temple afterwards, was a visible sign of how near God was to man, that no immeasurable interval separated the Highest of all from our sinful race, that in no unexpected vicissitudes of human history was He far away; He had made a home among the children of men. This was the obvious truth which the tabernacle and temple taught the Jewish people; and the very same truth, in a far more wonderful, impressive, and glorious form, was taught by the presence of Christ in the world in a human body. That body, the vesture of a Divine person, taught all that the temple taught concerning God's nearness to man, and taught it far more fully. And for this reason, Christ could fitly appropriate to the one the very term which denominated the other.

I do not wish to anticipate the discussion of the Jewish sacrifices which occupies the next chapter, but perhaps these afford a still simpler illustration of the principles I am anxious to establish. For instance, when a devout Jew looked upon the sacrifices which were slain for the sins of the whole nation on the great day of atonement, what impression would they produce on his mind? Are we to suppose that he foresaw that the time would come when God Himself, in the person of Jesus Christ, would stoop to shame and death that human transgression might be forgiven? I think not; whatever intimations of this kind may be found in the Psalms and the Prophets, came long after the sacrificial system was first instituted, and must have been, till the coming of Christ, very mysterious and dim. But he saw in the sacrifices a visible declaration, made by the Divine authority, of the ill desert of

What is a Type?

sin: he saw also that it was God's will that sin should be forgiven, and forgiven, not on account of any great and noble works wrought by the repentant sinner himself; for to offer the animal sacrifices for the sin of the whole people, required no self-denial worth considering on the part of any individual, and the forgiveness which might be obtained when they were offered, was plainly the free, undeserved act of the Divine mercy. Conviction of the evil of sin, trust for pardon in the grace of God, and not in any atonement to be effected by their own right doing, were naturally encouraged by these annual offerings. Nor was this all: the whole Jewish nation was gradually familiarized with the idea that by God's appointment forgiveness of sin was connected with the sufferings of a victim guilty of no offence against the Divine law.

But these same truths lie at the very basis of the atonement made by Christ for human sin; and these same spiritual results, conviction of the evil of sin, simple trust in the Divine mercy for pardon, are encouraged by His death. And hence Jewish sacrifices are typical of Christ's atonement.

The same principle which determines the typical character of religious institutions and ceremonies determines also the typical character of historical narratives. The fancy of theologians has run wild in attaching spiritual meanings to Old Testament stories, and, by a natural reaction, many thoughtful men have come to think with unmitigated contempt of all typical interpretations of historical facts, whether in the lives of individual saints or the vicissitudes of the Jewish nation. The innumerable wives of Solomon have been spiritualized into a typical representation of the innumerable virtues of his character; Samson's meeting a young lion has been made typical of Christ's meeting Saul on his way to Damascus; Jacob's purchasing of the birthright by red pottage, of Christ's purchasing heaven for us by His own red blood, and Jacob's being clothed in Esau's garment when the blessing was obtained, of Christ's being clothed in our nature when the purchase was effected. All these fanciful analogies are unworthy of the dignity of holy Scripture; a system of interpretation dealing in such puerilities and arbitrary conceits as these, must manifestly be utterly vague and uncertain. On such principles anything may be brought out of anything.

But if, in God's government of the Jewish people or His providential ordering of an individual life, any principle is obviously revealed, which is exemplified in a higher form in the present spiritual relations of mankind, a typical element may be fairly recognised.

An Old Testament type is the exhibition, in an inferior form, of a truth, a principle, a law, which is revealed in a higher form in the Christian dispensation.

THE NEW COVENANT.

" But now hath He obtained a more excellent ministry, by how much also He is the mediator of a better covenant, which was established upon better promises," &c.—HEBREWS viii, 6-13,

THE sermon last Sunday morning was intended to establish and illustrate the great principle which should govern all our inquiries into the relations between the Jewish temple and the Christian church. The institutions of Judaism were the "shadows of heavenly things." To us, the heavenly things themselves have been revealed. In the verses which we have to consider now, the contrast in detail, between the old covenant and the new, which forms the close of the argumentative part of this Epistle, commences, and this contrast involves some of the most interesting and important questions of Christian theology.

The word "*covenant*" has a very technical sound, and seems to belong rather to scholastic theologians than to ordinary Christian people; but I do not think we can do without it. The idea it represents is simple enough. The Jewish people held a certain relationship to God; and the word "*covenant*" is used to denote the basis and terms of that relationship. God conferred on them very wonderful privileges, and to retain these privileges they were required to obey His laws; Moses was the "*mediator*" of the covenant; he told the people, in God's name, the blessings which it was in God's heart to bestow upon them, and he told them also what conditions they had to fulfil in order that God's intention might be accomplished. These conditions were deliberately accepted; so the covenant was established.

But Christ, it is affirmed, has obtained a "*ministry*" as much "*more excellent*" than that of Moses as the new covenant is better than the old; and that the relations between man and God, established by Christ, are better than the relations established by Moses, is the subject of the remaining part of this chapter, and extends to the middle of the tenth.

I.

It may assist us to understand this discussion if we consider what the Mosaic covenant was, in its essence and purpose.

(1) The law given to Moses was not the original foundation of the high distinctions which belonged to the Jewish race. The history of the chosen people did not begin when they stood at the foot of Mount Sinai and listened with terror to the voice of God. Several hundred years before, Abraham had obeyed the Divine call, had manifested an immoveable faith in the Divine word, and had been told that his descendants were to be numerous as the stars of heaven and the sands of the sea shore, were to become a great nation, and were to be the source of blessings to all mankind. God did not wait until the Jewish nation had shown their fidelity to His law, before He promised to give them the land of Canaan, and to raise up among them the Messiah. These promises were theirs before the law was promulgated. Already they had been delivered from bondage in Egypt; already they had been separated from the rest of mankind; already the greatest of the prophets had been sent to them; and all the religious privileges which were inseparable from the fulfilment of the Divine promises to Abraham, privileges which were the pride and glory of the Jewish race, rested, not on the Mosaic law, but on the Abrahamic promises, which the law did not and could not annul.

(2) Although what is elsewhere called the "inheritance" of the Jewish people was not a reward for their obedience to the Divine law, that inheritance would prove a curse instead of a blessing to them if they were disobedient.

It was not because of their own goodness that they were called out from among the other nations of the earth, to stand nearer to God and to prepare for the coming of Christ; but, having been called, it was necessary that they should be loyal to the Divine authority. It was not because of their own obedience that they received the promise of the land of Canaan as a Divine gift; but having received that promise, it was necessary, if God's name was not to be dishonoured, that they should renounce the worship of idols, and present to the world the noble spectacle of a devout and upright people. From the nature of the inheritance which belonged to them as the descendants of Abraham, it could not be theirs in all its wealth and glory unless they were faithful to God.

An earthly king does not receive his crown and throne as the reward of his excellence; he derives it from his ancestors; but, being a king, he is bound to govern justly and righteously.

Paul was not called to the apostleship because of his personal merit; but, being called to the apostleship, he was bound to be zealous, courageous, and laborious in discharging its duties; and the blessedness and honour conferred upon him by his appointment would not only have been lost, they would have given place to the most appalling misery and shame, if the responsibilities of his vocation had not been faithfully discharged.

And so, the high distinctions of the Jewish people were originally derived from God's promises to Abraham; but, if these distinctions were not to be their ruin and disgrace, it was necessary that they should bear themselves worthily of their noble and yet perilous position.

(3) Hence it was that, when the race was about to be organized into a nation, God gave them a law—a law which presupposed the promises they had long possessed, and was intended to make them worthy of the position which belonged to them already, and to enable them to attain all the honour which that position placed within their reach.

There was serious cause to fear that the descendants of Abraham, if left to the simple institutions which had been sufficient to sustain the religious faith and holiness of their fathers, would be guilty of sins so enormous, that God would be constrained to punish instead of blessing them. Their moral sense had been corrupted by their protracted slavery and by their long familiarity with the vices which always flourish in the shadow of idolatry. Their faith in the God of their fathers had been enfeebled, and the effect of the tremendous manifestations of His power in connection with their deliverance from Egypt, was not likely to be lasting. And so the law was added "because of transgressions." It was necessary, since their whole moral and religious nature had been so injured, that clear and definite precepts should be given to them from heaven, and should be accompanied by such external signs of the awful greatness of Jehovah as should make them fear to disobey. It was also necessary that the principles of the true religion should be visibly embodied in sacred buildings, sacred persons, sacred rites, sacred days; and as they now required a national constitution, it was an additional advantage that they should receive that, too, from heaven, and that the principles of the true faith should be interwoven with all the customs and appointments of their secular and political life.

Therefore, God gave them the ten commandments, forbidding idolatry, blasphemy and irreverence; asserting His supremacy as the sole Creator of the world, and instituting a sacred day to commemorate the completion of creation; forbidding disobedience and irreverence to parents, murder, adultery, theft, false witness, and surrounding with the Divine protection the rights of property and the sanctities of the family. In addition to these great precepts there were laws punishing specific crimes against God and against men; there were regulations, some of which are almost unintelligible to us, which were intended, by the sheer force of the Divine authority, to expel from the Jewish nation the vices, the superstitions, and even the follies of surrounding races. Nor was this all. Knowing that even if they were faithful at heart, there would be transgressions, not only of significant ceremonial requirements, but of the moral law itself,—recognizing the necessity of developing and confirming the sense of guilt and encouraging a trust in the Divine mercy, God instituted priesthood and developed the system of sacrifice. There was provision, therefore, not only for the right ordering of the life of the people, but, both in the law itself and in the ritual, there was provision for arousing the sense of sin, and leading the penitent to confess his wrong-doing and to hope for God's forgiveness.

Had the people been faithful to this law, I do not mean by obeying perfectly all its moral precepts, but by honestly and earnestly endeavouring to obey them, and by a devout and trustful use of all its provision for human imperfection, the whole history of the Jewish nation would have been different. There would have been no division into two hostile kingdoms, no tyranny of wicked princes, no chastisement inflicted by heathen nations, no captivity in Babylon. The Jews would have been in fact what they were meant to be, a "peculiar treasure" unto God, though all the earth is His; "a kingdom of priests, a holy nation:" "but they continued not in my covenant, and I disregarded them, saith the Lord."

II.

What security is there that any better fate will attend God's last and great endeavour to confer blessings on our race? The present relations between man and God rest ultimately upon the promises made to us through Christ, just as the relations of the Jews to God rested on the promises made to them through Abraham. The Jews were born members of a nation inheriting glorious distinctions, and yet could not derive any advantage or joy from their position, unless they were faithful to the Divine law; we too are born into a Divine kingdom, but without faith and holiness we must lose all the honour and blessedness which are thus put within our reach. For the Jews there was an earthly Canaan,—promised to them not on the ground of their obedience, but on the ground of their descent from Abraham; and yet, through their sin, the land flowing with milk and honey became a desert, it was cursed with barrenness, it was destroyed by invading armies, and at last it was lost altogether; for us there is a Divine and immortal rest, a home in heaven, an inheritance incorruptible, undefiled, and that fadeth not away; it is promised to us, not because of our personal excellence, but because of the atonement of the Lord Jesus Christ, and yet unless we are pure in heart we cannot see God either here or hereafter; into the city of God nothing can enter that defileth.

So far then there is an analogy between our position and the position of the Jewish race; but here the analogy ceases, and a contrast begins. To us, as to them, promises have been given which do not rest on our personal holiness, but which cannot be fulfilled unless we are holy. To us, as to them, an honourable position has been given, not on the ground of our obedience, but which cannot be retained unless we obey. Where then is the contrast between their case and ours? The writer states it with transparent clearness, in words quoted from Old Testament prophecy.

To the Jews God gave promises, and then an outward law requiring obedience; to us God has given promises, and an inward disposition inclining us to obedience. The privileges which belonged to the descendants of Abraham became their curse, because they did not keep the law which was proclaimed at Sinai; but the privileges which belong to us, who are one with Christ, become our everlasting joy and glory, because God has given us the Holy Ghost to make us meet for the inheritance of the saints in light.

That the Jewish race might not lose, through their sins, the inheritance bestowed on them in Abraham, God gave them the law: that we may not lose, through our sins, the inheritance bestowed on us in Christ, God has given us the Spirit. They were not to obtain the right to their peculiar distinctions by obeying the law; the law was intended to prevent them losing what was theirs without their obedience: we are not to obtain the right to the blessings of the Christian dispensation by the work of the Spirit; the Spirit has been given that the redemption, which is God's free gift to us through Christ, may not be lost.

The promises to Abraham were the foundation of all the privileges of the Jewish people, and the law was given that they might not be the worse instead of the better for God's goodness: the work of Christ is the foundation of all the merciful economy under which we live, with its promises of present pardon and everlasting glory, and the Spirit has been given that we may not be the worse instead of the better for the death of Christ and the revelation of God's mercy. It is not without significance that the coming of the Holy Ghost was delayed till the day of Pentecost, which, according to the belief of the Jews, commemorated the giving of the Mosaic law.

It is not difficult for us to imagine the dark and gloomy fears which would trouble the hearts of thoughtful and devout Jews in ancient times, when they considered all the crimes of which the Jewish nation had been guilty, and all the miseries with which those crimes were punished. Spite of the goodness of God to Abraham, spite of the promises which were the basis of their national life, generation after generation had turned aside to the worship of false gods, and the whole people, instead of being conspicuous for fidelity to Jehovah, and conspicuous for the peace, happiness, and prosperity which that fidelity would have secured, had been conspicuous for their sins, and conspicuous for their national troubles. And might it not be the same in that future age to which the hope of the nation was continually directed?

When the Christ came for whom they were hoping, might He not come in vain? Might He not fail, through human perverseness, to establish the kingdom of heaven, as Moses had failed by his institutions to constrain the people to obey the voice of God? And so, as the promise of the land of Canaan, though fulfilled, had brought the nation no joy, might not the promise of the Messiah, though fulfilled, fail utterly to secure the higher blessings which were hoped for from His coming?

The fullest answer to these apprehensions is given in the passage from Jeremiah, quoted in the verses we are now considering. The old institutions, received through Moses, had not been successful in making the people fit for their exalted vocation; but a new system is to be established. Had the first "*been faultless*" no place would have been sought for the second: the announcement of a new covenant is the condemnation of the old: in "*finding fault*" with the nation, in rebuking them for their grievous sins, and declaring His intention to resort to new means for securing their obedience, God virtually pronounces the system under which they had already lived to be a failure. "*Behold the days come, saith the Lord, when I will make a new covenant with the house of Israel, and with the house of Judah; not according to the covenant that I made with their fathers in the day when I took them by the hand to lead them out of the land of Egypt; because they continued not in my covenant, and I regarded them not, saith the Lord. For this is the covenant that I will make with the house of Israel after those days, saith the Lord; I will put my laws into their mind, and write them in their hearts: and I will be to them a God, and they shall be to me a people; and they shall not teach every man his neighbour, and every man his brother, saying, Know the Lord: for all shall know me from the least to the greatest. For I will be merciful to their unrighteousness, and their sins and their iniquities will I remember no more.*" And since God had spoken of a "*new covenant,*" He had "*made the first old; and that which is being made old, and is getting into old age, is nigh unto vanishing away.*" In the ancient Scriptures themselves, there were intimations that the Mosaic institutions were not to last for ever.

In these verses the contrast between the Jewish and the Christian dispensations is drawn in strong, bold lines. It is necessary, perhaps, to remember that even under the Mosaic covenant the power of God purified the souls of men, and the "true light" enlightened them; but external law was the great characteristic of the system. It is necessary to remember, too, that even under the Christian system there are precepts to be obeyed as well as mysterious spiritual forces to be yielded to; but it is the presence of the Spirit of God in the soul of man that constitutes its supreme distinction and glory.

"We believe in the Holy Ghost,"—believe, not merely that in remote centuries and remote lands He revealed to prophets and apostles the glorious perfections and holy will of God, but that He abides with the church and with every member of it, always and everywhere. But for His permanent presence in all who believe in Christ, the splendid titles bestowed on all

Christians would be cruel irony, and the precepts requiring perfect conformity to the image of Christ, a mockery of our weakness. To illustrate in our own lives "the mind that was in Christ Jesus," the Spirit that God gave to Him "without measure," must rest upon us also. To be His brethren, we must be "born of the Holy Ghost." No Divine sonship, in the highest sense of the term, is possible to us unless by the Spirit we are made "partakers of the Divine nature;" no priestly sanctity unless our souls are made pure and white by His grace; no regal dignity unless we are ennobled and made strong by "the exceeding greatness of His power." By special acts of illumination the Spirit established the church, even as God founded the material universe by special acts of creative power; and the church is sustained in the freshness of life, and beauty, and glory, by the permanent and ordinary operations of the Spirit, just as the planets are kept in their orbits and the stream of created existence kept from stagnation by the constant and ordinary exertion of God's omnipotence. The church, without the presence of the Holy Ghost, would sink back into spiritual death and ruin—as the universe, without the presence of God, would return to its original darkness and chaos.

THE OLD SANCTUARY.

"Then verily the first covenant had also ordinances of Divine service, and a worldly sanctuary. For there was a tabernacle made; the first wherein was," &c.—HEBREWS ix, 1-5.

ALTHOUGH in the course of this Epistle the inspired author illustrates and explains the meaning and purpose of some of the most important of the institutions of Judaism, it was not his intention to write a dissertation on the ancient ritual. He wrote to prevent apostasy, not to interpret the Mosaic system. The Epistle is an argument, an appeal, addressed to Jewish believers, who were in danger of falling away from Christ. The writer speaks of the angels, whose ministry had glorified the ancient faith, and of Moses, and of Melchizedek, and of the Jewish priesthood and the Jewish sacrifices, only to exalt the honour of the Lord Jesus and the superiority of the Christian church to the Jewish temple.

It was not necessary, therefore, that he should write a commentary on the book of Leviticus; it was sufficient for his purpose that he should select those institutions and ceremonies which had the strongest hold on the heart and the imagination of the Jew, and prove that nothing would be lost by surrendering them all for Christ; that, whatever may have been their value in former ages, they had now become obsolete; that Christ had actually conferred the blessings which they imperfectly symbolised.

Hence it is that many of the most singular institutions of the Mosaic law are not mentioned at all in this Epistle, or if mentioned, mentioned without any explanation. Concerning the golden candlestick, and the table of shewbread, and the altar of incense, and the ark of the covenant, and the cherubim of glory, the writer says it is not necessary or important that he should "*speak one by one.*" His reference to them is merely an introduction to what he has to say about the ritual of the great day of atonement. To explain what he has left unexplained, and to speak "one by one" of those things which he passed over, will be an interruption, therefore, of the current of his argument; but I do not know that I can have a better opportunity than that which is afforded by the exposition of these verses, for offering some observations on a very curious and interesting subject; and I shall, therefore, ask you this morning to try and understand the use and meaning of those parts of the tabernacle furniture which are mentioned in this passage.

I shall not occupy your time with any description of the form of the sanctuary—you can understand that far better from the engravings of it in books which are in almost everybody's hands;—nor shall I detain you with any account of the various materials which entered into its structure. I wish to speak of the religious significance of the sacred things which are spoken of in these verses.

The tabernacle was regarded by the Jewish people as the dwelling-place of Jehovah. Not that they believed that the Divine presence was limited to this material structure; they knew that if they ascended into heaven He was there, and that if they descended into the dark regions of the dead He was there. But, in His great and wonderful condescension, He had commanded them to construct for Him a tent, which was to be pitched among their own tents in the wilderness; and afterwards they built Him a temple conspicuous among all the buildings of Jerusalem for its majesty and splendour. The Sanctuary was to be honoured as God's palace and home. There His priests were to minister. There the sacrifices He had commanded were to be offered. It was a visible and Divinely-appointed testimony that He who inhabited eternity, and whose throne is in the heavens, was very near to the Jewish people—accessible in all times of trouble and fear, and willing to receive the adoration and thanksgivings of sinful men. Lofty and majestic are the words in which Solomon, on the day that the temple was consecrated, acknowledges at once the glory and the condescension of God. "The Lord said that He would dwell in the thick darkness. I have surely built Thee a house to dwell in, a settled place for Thee to abide in for ever. . . . Will God indeed dwell on the earth? Behold, the heaven and heaven of heavens cannot contain Thee; how much less this house that I have built? Yet have Thou respect unto the prayer of Thy servant, and to his supplications, O Lord my God; to hearken to the cry and to the prayer which Thy servant prayeth before Thee to-day: that Thine eyes may be open toward this house night and day, even toward the place of which Thou hast said, My name shall be there: that Thou mayest hearken unto the prayer which Thy servant shall make toward this place. And hearken Thou to the supplication of Thy servant, and of Thy people Israel, when they shall pray towards this place; and hear Thou in heaven, Thy dwelling-place; and when hearest, forgive." The theory of the thoughtful Jew was no doubt this—that as the Omnipresent God revealed Himself more fully to His angels in heaven than to all His creatures besides, so he revealed Himself more fully to those who worshipped Him in the tabernacle or temple, than to all mankind besides.

And now let us examine the innermost chamber of the sanctuary; that into which only the High Priest was ever permitted to enter, and he only once a year; the chamber which is called the "Holy of Holies," or the "Holiest of all." This was regarded as the very home of God on earth. The central object in this chamber was the "*ark*"—a chest of acacia wood, rather more than two feet broad and high, and about three feet long, covered on all sides with plates of the purest gold. This chest was made to be the depository of the two tables of stone, on which the fundamental laws of the Jewish commonwealth were written. For a thousand years the ark was preserved; but when Jerusalem was overthrown by the Chaldeans, it perished. There is a singular legend contained in the second book of Maccabees, to the effect that the prophet Jeremiah commanded the tabernacle, and the altar of incense, and the ark, to follow him to the sacred mount whence Moses beheld the heritage of God, and, finding a cave there, he hid them, and closed up its mouth; and those that went after him could not discover the cave; and Jeremiah declared that they should not be found till God gathered His people again and received them into His mercy. There was no ark in the second temple.

What thoughts would the ark be likely to convey to the Jewish people? It was the "*Ark of the Covenant;*" it contained those laws which came from the lips of Jehovah Himself, and were afterwards written by His finger, when the peculiar relationship was established between Him and the Jewish nation. It reminded them that they were His people, and that He was their God. When false prophets rose up, perverting and corrupting the simplicity and purity of the institutions which God had given to their fathers, they would be warned by the awful sanctity with which the tables of the law were invested, against all departures from their early faith. Whatever mystery might surround the nature and attributes of Jehovah, this they knew, that He had once spoken to the chosen nation, requiring their love and service, forbidding idolatry and crimes of violence and lust; and these same commandments were laid up still in the most holy place.

The law of God was the revelation of His own character as well as the guide of human conduct. When they worshipped, they worshipped him from whom the holy commandments came. And they were reminded, too, that by the voluntary act of their fathers, the Divine law had been solemnly accepted, and that all the successive generations of the Jewish race were under its authority.

The laying up of the tables in the ark, and the placing of the ark in the Holy of Holies, were a most significant declaration (1) of the holiness of God's character, and (2) of the covenant into which the Jewish nation had entered, to be holy too.

According to the original institution, nothing was placed in the ark, excepting these two tables of stone, and there was nothing else in it when Solomon placed the ark in the temple. But in the 16th of Exodus, Moses directs Aaron to take a "*pot*" of "*manna,*" and to lay it up before the Lord for after generations; and, apart from this passage in the Epistle to the Hebrews, it seems probable that this command was interpreted as requiring that the pot of manna should be placed *in* the ark. And so, the "*rod*" of Aaron, which miraculously budded, blossomed, and brought forth fruit, in vindication of the priesthood of his house, was ordered to be laid up before the testimony (Numb. xvii., 10), to be kept for a token against those who had resisted his appointment; and this too was afterwards understood as requiring that the rod should be placed in the ark itself. You remember the story of this rod. Korah, Dathan, and Abiram had dared to contest the authority of Moses and Aaron, and their sin had been punished by earthquake and fire. The people, who seem to have shared the discontent, and to have encouraged the presumption of the men who had ventured to impugn the Divinely-appointed priesthood, murmured at their punishment, and more than fourteen thousand perished by the plague. To set the question for ever at rest, the princes of the several tribes of Israel were required to bring their rods—the symbols of their authority—and to lay them before the ark of God: he whose rod blossomed was to be the object of God's choice for priestly service; and in the morning, the rod of Levi on which Aaron's name was written, was found to have become miraculously fruitful.*

As the tables of the law were a perpetual testimony to the holiness of Jehovah, and a perpetual memorial of the obligations assumed by the Jewish race at Sinai, the rod of Aaron, whether

---

* "The section of the Levites, whose position brought them into contact with the tribe of Reuben, conspired with it to re-assert the old patriarchal system of a household priesthood. The leader of that revolt may have been impelled by a desire to gain the same height as that which Aaron had attained; but the ostensible pretext, that the 'whole congregation were holy' (Numbers xvi, 3) was one which would have cut away all the distinctive privileges of the tribe of which he was a member." (Plumptre in *Smith's Dictionary of the Bible.*) Korah and his companions of the tribe of Levi, were enraged at the limitation of the higher functions of the priesthood to the family of Aaron, and were ready in their revenge to imperil the sacredness of the whole tribe.

placed before the ark, according to what seems to have been the original intention of the Mosaic precept, or within it, was a most significant declaration of the peril of approaching God wilfully and presumptuously in any other way than that which He had instituted. It was also a declaration of the certainty of God's accepting the ministrations of the priests whom He himself had chosen.

Equally obvious, I think, was the meaning of the pot of manna. It was a perpetual testimony to the people of Israel of the infinite resources and ceaseless vigilance of the Divine Providence. When times of famine came, prayer for food would be offered with stronger confidence, when it was remembered that the manna was in the Most Holy Place, and had been laid up there by God's own command. He was not so great as to be indifferent to the physical wants of His creatures—He was not so powerless as to be unable to help them if the drought or the blight destroyed their harvest. In ancient times He had remembered the hunger of their fathers in the wilderness, and the windows of heaven had been opened to supply them with bread.

Over the ark was a plate of solid gold, called in our English Bible the "*mercy-seat*," and at the two extremities of this golden plate were "*the cherubim*," their faces turned towards each other, but bending downwards as in the act of adoration. This was the most mysterious and awful and glorious part of the Holy of Holies itself. "There I will meet with thee," said God to Moses, "and I will commune with thee from above the mercy-seat, from between the two cherubim which are upon the ark of the testimony." Ex. xxv, 22. And it is said in Numbers vii, 89, "that Moses heard the voice of one speaking to him from off the mercy-seat, that was upon the ark of the testimony, from between the two cherubim." In the 80th Psalm it is written, "Thou that dwellest between the cherubim, shine forth;" and in the 99th, "The Lord reigneth; let the people tremble; He sitteth between the cherubims; let the earth be moved."

It is remarkable that no description is contained in the Books of Moses of these wonderful figures that were bowing before God day and night in a ceaseless act of adoration; and the descriptions of the cherubim in other parts of Holy

Scripture vary considerably. This, however, seems certain, that they were symbolic forms, in which were combined the highest kinds of created life known to us. The ox, which was the symbol of strength and labour,—the eagle, which was the symbol of the loftiest freedom and the utmost rapidity of motion,—the lion, which was the symbol of regal majesty,—were united with the human form, the symbol of the highest and noblest kind of life, of intelligence, and moral freedom. In the reverential homage of the cherubim, the whole creation is represented as bowing before God. "All His works praise Him." He is compassed about with perpetual and everlasting worship. All strength, all majesty, all wisdom, confess that He is God over all, blessed for evermore.

But while the Jew was reminded by the presence of these symbolic figures in the Holy of Holies, of God's everlasting glory, he was reminded by the golden covering of the ark, that even sinful men might venture to adore Him. It is very generally acknowledged that the word "mercy-seat," as applied to this plate of gold, is likely to lead to misconception. It suggests the idea, that it was regarded as the throne of Jehovah. But there is nothing either in the word itself or in any of the allusions to the thing in Holy Scripture, to justify this. There is a sublime and reverential indefiniteness in all that is said concerning the presence of Jehovah in the Holy Place. He dwelt between the cherubim : their visible homage and the cloud of glory testified that He was there: but no material thing is spoken of as the seat of His throne. What we call the "mercy seat" was the golden covering of the ark, on which year by year the blood was sprinkled that the sins of the nation might be atoned for. The name applied to it in the Hebrew Scriptures includes two ideas. The root from which it is derived permits us to regard it as suggesting its twofold purpose—as shutting in the contents of the sacred chest, and as receiving year by year the blood of atonement; and the LXX translators have, I think, most happily represented the Hebrew word by two Greek words, meaning "*a propitiatory covering.*"

And was there not a fitness in the blood of atonement being sprinkled on the covering of the ark? The ark contained the ten commandments, which the penitent Jew felt that he had broken;—those commandments represented all the precepts which God required him to obey, and many of which he knew he had transgressed. Indeed, the whole of the Book of the Law was in later times placed there. When he cried to the God who dwelt between the cherubim, the presence of the law, which was holy, just, and good, in the ark beneath, reminded him of his guilt; it was an awful testimony against him; it might well have driven him to despair; but on the very covering of the ark was sprinkled year by year the atoning blood; and although his conscience forbade him to think that the sufferings and death of a bullock or a goat could really expiate his sin, he knew that God would not have instituted the ritual if he had not intended to forgive.

You will have noticed the peculiarity of the expression at the commencement of the fourth verse; "*which*"—that is, the Holiest of all, "had *the golden censer,*" or rather "*the golden altar of incense.*" Of the Holy Place it is said, in the second verse, "wherein *was the candlestick and the table, &c.*" The change of expression is significant. The writer does not mean to say that the altar of incense was *within* the Holy of Holies, but that the altar of incense *belonged* to it. That altar actually stood in the Holy Place, but more truly belonged to the Holy of Holies itself. It is very wonderful that any man who had read this Epistle intelligently, could imagine for a moment, that it was possible for the writer to have been so ill-informed as to have believed that the altar was actually within the most sacred inclosure. Apart altogether from inspiration, the intimate and profound knowledge of the Jewish system which the whole of the Epistle indicates, renders it absurd to suppose that on such a simple matter as the position of the altar of incense, the writer could have blundered. It would to my mind be just as reasonable to infer from some peculiarity of expression in Lord Macaulay, that the great historian had erroneously imagined that the Spanish Armada came against this country in the reign of Charles I., or to infer on similar grounds that Dr. Livingstone was under the impression that the island of Madagascar formed part of the African continent.

This altar, made of acacia wood and overlaid with gold, was not used for ordinary sacrifices, but was a stand for the vessel in which the sacred frankincense was burnt. Its position which, according to the directions in Exodus, was to be before the ark of the testimony, though not in the Holy of Holies, was an indication of its peculiar sanctity; and on the great day of atonement this was the only thing, not contained in the innermost sanctuary, which was sprinkled with the atoning blood. The offering of incense is a natural symbol of adoration; and it is plain that it was so regarded by the Jewish people. "Let my prayer" said the Psalmist, "be set before Thee as incense;" and in the vision of Isaiah, when the seraphim had cried "Holy, holy, holy, is the Lord God of Hosts, the whole earth is full of his glory," the temple was immediately filled with clouds of incense. Morning and evening the vessel on the golden altar was to be lighted with live coals taken from the altar of burnt offering.

Consider for a moment what these provisions of the Jewish ritual plainly taught. There was not only atonement for sin and the possibility of forgiveness, as exhibited in the great annual sacrifices; but day by day the burnt offering symbolically represented the duty and the possibility of consecrating body, soul, and spirit to God. And even this was not all. The guilty might tremble to approach the holy God with songs of praise and words of adoration; they might fear that this would be presumption, which He would resent and punish. The holy angels behold His face and may worship Him day and night without ceasing, but for sinful men to aspire to this supreme privilege and blessedness might seem an offence against the divine purity. But no; he who has entered into the spirit of the burnt offering may venture without fear to speak to God of His high perfections and to offer adoration. Obedience may be followed by worship. Self-consecration will kindle in the soul reverence, and awe, and wonder, and gratitude, and joy; and God will not refuse the homage.

"*The table and the shewbread*" were also in the Holy Place. This table, like the altar of incense, was made of acacia wood and overlaid with gold. Every Sabbath day twelve unleavened loaves were placed upon it,—one for every tribe,—and the loaves were sprinkled over with frankincense. Although nothing is said about wine, the vessels which had to be made for the table seem to prove that wine was placed with the bread. All the vessels were of gold. The idea symbolised by this singular appointment is indicated, I think, in Leviticus, where it is said that the shewbread, or "the bread of the presence," was an offering from the children of Israel. Wine and bread represent the two principal articles of human food. They stand for all the things which support the life of man. They represent that which all men, rich and poor, must have, if they are to live at all. And the covering of the table, week by week, with bread and wine, seems to me a natural form of acknowledging God as the Author and Giver of all common blessings. As the manna in the ark was a continual testimony in God's name to the power and goodness of the Divine providence, the bread and the wine on the table in the Holy Place was a continual recognition of that providence on the part of man. "All things come of thee." "Thou openest thine hand and satisfiest the wants of every living thing." "Thou givest corn and wine." And in the acknowledgment that God gives the means of life, there is an implied acknowledgment that life itself should be devoted to Him.

Only the "*golden candlestick*" now remains for notice. One or two passages both in the Old and New Testaments are commonly quoted, as illustrating its meaning and purpose; but I confess that these passages do not appear to me very pertinent. We are thrown, I think, on our own conception of what would be the natural impression produced by it on the minds of devout Jews. In later times it was the custom to keep the lights burning all day as well as all night; but the original law required that they should be lit in the evening and *dressed* in the morning. And you will remember that Samuel heard the voice of God before the lamp of God went out in the temple, implying that it was not kept continually burning. I believe that the later custom helped to conceal the natural meaning of the appointment.

If the priests had had any duties to discharge at night in the

Holy Place, I should have felt no necessity to make any inquiry at all about the significance of the seven lights; the impossibility of performing the sacred functions in total darkness would have been an adequate explanation. But there was no midnight ritual: why then, when the curtain, which was thrown aside during the day to admit the light of heaven, was closed for the night, was not the holy place left in darkness? There seems to me to be a perfectly obvious and natural answer. The Holy Place was in the thoughts of every devout Jew when he longed for the mercy of God to forgive his sin, or cried to Him for consolation in time of trouble. It was there that, day by day, the priests offered the incense, which was the visible symbol of all supplication and worship. That was the chamber in which the Lord received the prayers and homage of the nation, as the Most Holy Place was His secret shrine. And would not the lamps that burnt there during the darkness, and filled it with light, seem to say to every troubled soul, that God never slumbered nor slept; that the darkness and the light are both alike to Him, and that at all times He is waiting to listen to the prayers of His people? It is in perfect harmony with this explanation, that the seven lights of the ancient candlestick, no longer united, however, in one stem, are used in the Apocalypse to represent the churches. Christ "*walketh* in the midst of the seven golden candlesticks;" in a world that has forgotten God, and forgotten Him so long that it might well despair of ever being able to conciliate His favour, and believe that He had forsaken for ever the race which had so ungratefully and presumptuously sinned against Him, the Churches of Christ bear a continual testimony to His presence and gracious activity.

It can hardly be expected that we should be able to understand perfectly all the institutions of Judaism. They answered their purpose in sustaining the religious life of a long line of holy men, and introducing into the thought and literature of the chosen race elements of Divine truth, without which the revelation of God in Christ would have been hardly intelligible: but they have passed away; their aspect has become strange and unfamiliar; and it requires a vigorous intellectual effort to place ourselves in the position of the people to whom they were given. But it is of some importance that we should understand them sufficiently, to be able to show that the Jewish ritual was not an unmeaning and superstitious pageant. Contempt for Moses is inconsistent with a true reverence for Christ.

And, however foreign to our own intellectual habits may be the sacrifices, and altars, and incense, and priests of the Jewish faith, a knowledge of the transcendent excellence and power of the religious belief of the Jews, when compared with that of any other ancient people, will suggest caution and hesitation in challenging the religious institutions by which that belief was developed and sustained. Judge the system by its results, and it will demand respect. Even if it were granted that there were dreary times in Jewish history, when the mass of the people were as superstitious and as immoral as the common people of Assyria, or of Persia, or of Greece, or of Rome, it might still be asked, Where, among the greatest nations of antiquity, can there be shown a long line of men like that to which the Jews can point,—maintaining with faultless unanimity and unwavering faith, the unity of God and the perfection of His moral attributes,—investing moral laws with divine authority,—penetrated with a sense of the evil of sin and the exceeding beauty of holiness? Where else can there be shown a succession of men who, through age after age, through sixteen centuries of glory and of suffering, proclaimed a theology so noble, a morality so pure; and endeavoured, by national institutions, religious ceremonies, sublime and pathetic eloquence, and immortal songs, to exalt and purify the moral and religious life of their country? However unintelligible the Mosaic ritual may seem to one who has not entered into the spirit of the people for whom it was constructed and the times to which it belongs—this at least will be confessed, that it was the centre and inspiration of the grandest and purest religious thought of the ancient world.

But again, I say, the institutions of Judaism have passed away. The fulness of time has come. Inarticulate symbols have given place to the Divine Word manifest in the flesh. We need no earthly tabernacle to assure us of the condescending interest of the Most High in the conflicts, and joys, and troubles, which make up the life of man: God himself has become such an one as ourselves; partaker of flesh and blood; tempted in all points as we are, though without sin. We need no golden candlestick to fill with rich and tranquil light the darkness of a Holy place, and to remind us that the Eternal God is ever ready to listen to the sighing of the contrite and the prayer of the needy; for Christ ever liveth to make intercession for us, and we know that He fainteth not, neither is weary. We need no table with its loaves and wine to remind us that all our earthly possessions should be consecrated to God, and that our life itself belongs to Him: we have another table which tells what God has done for us, and looking upon its pathetic symbols we exclaim, "We are not our own, we are bought with a price;" we "know the grace of our Lord Jesus Christ," and "whether we live we must live unto the Lord, or whether we die we must die unto the Lord." No golden altar of incense is needed to assure us that the worship and the petitions of sinful men are acceptable to God: we have heard it from the lips of the Son that "whatsoever we ask in His name" shall be given, and that "the Father himself loveth us;" we have received "power to become the sons of God," and "the spirit of adoption" is ours. We need no cherubim to tell us of God's majesty, and to testify that all created things reveal His wisdom, power, and goodness: we have seen Him ourselves, and the splendour of the heavens has become pale,—sun, moon, and stars have lost their light in the presence of the glory of God as revealed in the face of Jesus Christ. No miraculous manna need be preserved as a memorial for all generations of the bounty of divine Providence: we know that God has given us Christ, and that "with Him He will freely give us all things." No ark of the covenant is necessary to remind us that between us and God lasting relations have been established, of mercy on His part, and duty on ours: in Christ, God and Man are for ever one. Wonderful indeed was the divine compassion which covered the tables of the law requiring a perfection of which man always failed, with the most sacred symbol of mercy,—uniting the precepts which uttered rebuke while they gave guidance, with the atonement which justified the hope of pardon; but for us tables of stone and propitiatory covering are alike unnecessary : Christ in His stainless purity, Christ in His unfaltering obedience to God, Christ in His love for man, Christ is our law ; and when our neart sinks and faints as we contemplate His bright perfections, when we are ready to cry out in despair that the tables of stone and the thunders of Sinai could not so appal the heart of the guilty as the vision of His living holiness, that no human words, though written by the finger of God, could require or describe a devotion or a purity comparable to His,—we discover with amazement and joy, that by the very perfection which dismays us, He is atoning for all our transgressions, and that the sublime culmination of His love and obedience in His agony and death, accomplishes for man a complete and everlasting redemption. In Him the highest revelation of law is associated, not with the symbol, but with the reality of atonement. The shadows of heavenly things have disappeared ; the first covenant, with its ordinances of divine service, and its worldly sanctuary, have become old and vanished away ; " the law came by Moses, but grace and truth came by Jesus Christ."

JEWISH SACRIFICES.

"Now, when these things were thus ordained, the priests went always into the first tabernacle, accomplishing the service of God." &c.—HEBREWS ix, 6-9.

As I said last Sunday morning, the first five verses of this chapter,—in which the writer speaks of the Holy Place, with its golden lamp and table of shewbread, and the Holiest of all, with its altar of incense and its ark, and the tables of the covenant, and Aaron's rod and the adoring cherubim,—are introductory to the exposition, extending through the verses of this chapter to the middle of the tenth, of the contrast between the Jewish sacrifices and the sacrifice of the Lord Jesus Christ. It will assist us in understanding the course of this argument if we are able to place distinctly before us the original character and significance of the expiatory offerings of the ancient law; their character and significance, I mean, as apprehended by religious and thoughtful men before the time of Christ. It is an inversion of the true order of the investigation, to begin by filling the mind with all the truths revealed in the New Testament, and developed by the speculations and controversies of a long succession of uninspired theologians, concerning the atonement of Christ, and then to examine the Jewish ritual to discover symbolic anticipations of the doctrine.

If it be objected that without the clear light of the Christian dispensation, the ancient ceremonial is unmeaning, this is to impeach the wisdom and goodness of God, by whose authority it was sustained for sixteen hundred years; and the objection is based on forgetfulness of the fact, that elementary teaching, though less extensive in its range, ought plainly to be more easily intelligible than subsequent and higher revelations. The

Jewish system was a discipline and preparation for the Christian; exhibiting the same principles by simpler methods; taking less for granted; addressing men who knew little, and needed to be taught as we teach children, by diagrams and models, in which the highest truths and laws are illustrated in their most elementary forms. The natural order of the investigation is to attempt to discover, first, what impressions were produced, what instruction was conveyed, by Jewish institutions in Jewish times; then to consider how the Christian revelation has exalted and perfected the Jewish. The system of Moses did not presuppose the knowledge of the teaching of Christ and of the apostles; *their* teaching presupposed a knowledge of the teaching of Moses.

It is not necessary, nor would it be possible in a single sermon, to give a complete account of the innumerable offerings instituted or regulated by the Levitical law. The writer of this Epistle is thinking principally, if not exclusively, of one class of sacrifices; sacrifices in which the idea of atonement for sin was so conspicuous as to give them their distinguishing name. In the burnt-offering the idea of atonement was subordinate to the idea of the complete surrender and devotion of the soul to God; in the peace-offering, the idea of atonement was subordinate to the idea of joyful thanksgiving and happy fellowship with God: in the sin-offering the idea of atonement was supreme.

I do not propose to illustrate the details of the ritual connected with sacrifices of this class, but to consider the relation, as it would appear to a Jew, between sin-offerings and moral transgression.

It is a common impression that whenever a Jew had committed an ordinary moral offence against the Divine law, he had only to bring the appointed sacrifice and offer it with the appointed ceremonies in order to obtain the Divine forgiveness. The passage in the fifty-first Psalm, in which David exclaims, "Thou desirest not sacrifice, else would I give it," is popularly interpreted as meaning, that for the crimes of which David had been guilty no sin-offerings could be accepted, though for less serious transgressions atonement could easily be made. But since the conscience vehemently protests against the morality of a system which is supposed to provide for the cancelling of sin on the condition of offering an animal sacrifice, many persons believe that in addition to the sin-offering, it was necessary that the guilty man should be truly penitent; some go further still, and believe that forgiveness was not to be obtained unless the faith of the penitent associated his sacrifice with the atonement afterwards to be accomplished by the Lord Jesus Christ. Such persons must be greatly surprised, that although page after page in the books of Exodus, Leviticus, Numbers, and Deuteronomy is filled with ceremonial directions, there is not a word to remind the man who has brought his sin-offering to the priest, that the atoning efficacy of the sacrifice will depend either upon his penitence or his faith: an examination of the law will remove these difficulties and correct the common errors which involve the whole subject in obscurity and confusion.

Sin-offerings formed a part of the appointed ritual on certain great religious days, when they were offered on behalf of the whole nation, and could not possibly be supposed to secure by themselves the actual pardon of sin. They were also offered in certain special and occasional circumstances, on behalf of individuals or on behalf of the whole people, and then it is distinctly declared that on their being offered, the particular offences for which they were to atone should be forgiven. I shall speak of the second class first.

I.

There were, I say, certain transgressions of the Divine law which were not only to be atoned for by the sin-offering, but which were actually to be forgiven when the offering had been presented and slain, and the altar sprinkled with its blood.

(1) If the High Priest or the head of any of the tribes violated, through ignorance, any of the ritualistic or ceremonial precepts, when he discovered his fault, he was to bring a bullock for a sin-offering, and the offence was to be blotted out. If the whole congregation committed a similar offence, the same sacrifice made atonement and secured pardon. If any of the

common people committed a similar offence, a goat or a lamb effected the same results.

There was also the special case of a man having in certain specified circumstances unconsciously or involuntarily incurred ceremonial defilement. This was likely to happen so frequently that a lighter atonement was accepted; a lamb or a kid, or, if the man was poor, two turtle doves or two young pigeons, or even a small quantity of fine flour, effected atonement, and also obtained forgiveness. In all these cases there was no moral element at all, for there was no voluntary transgression. In all these cases, too, it was the ceremonial law that had been violated. No moral gilt had been incurred, and it was reasonable and just that the unintentional ceremonial failure should be cancelled when the ceremonial compensation had been presented.

(2) Again, if a man had knowingly failed to bear testimony in a court of law against men whom he knew to be justly accused of a crime, he was required to confess his sin and to bring a lamb or a kid for a sin-offering, or if he was poor, two turtle doves, or two young pigeons, or a small quantity of fine flour; and then his sin was to be forgiven. The moral element in this case would generally be very slight and insignificant. Desirable as it is that all who know anything that would inculpate a guilty man should bear their testimony at his trial, I suppose that there are many circumstances which most of us would regard as morally releasing us from the obligation to volunteer adverse evidence; and many suppose that it was for the neglect of this, that the offering was to make atonement and obtain pardon. But even if the law refers to the case of one who has actually been a witness in court, but has been silent on what would have demonstrated the guilt of the accused, the silence would commonly be occasioned by natural affection, by friendship, by generous compassion for the guilty; and, though a sin against the State, would, when morally considered, be a very slight offence; the telling half the truth when a man had promised to tell all, equivocation, falsehood, perjury, could not be cancelled by the offering of a lamb, or by any offering at all. The concealment of damaging evidence to which the

provision of the law points, was not an act of falsehood, but a want of adequate zeal for the infliction of just penalties on the guilty. If the man's repentance of his omission was sufficient to lead him to confess and to provide the sacrifice, his failure might well be forgiven. This law is an indication of the firmness and resoluteness with which the whole nation was to unite in the administration of criminal justice, rather than of any tendency in the Jewish law, to relax moral obligations by promising forgiveness, on the bare ground of a ritual sacrifice, to what we call sin.

(3) If a man had sworn an oath to do good or to do evil, the force of which he did not at the time perceive, which he was unable, unwilling, or forbidden by the Divine law to perform, he had to bring the same sin-offering as in the case last mentioned, and was assured of forgiveness. Among ourselves, if a man "pronounce with his lips" words whose meaning and purpose he does not apprehend, utters a vow in a state of intoxication, for instance, utters it under some transitory delusion, utters it under the influence of deception practised upon him by others, it would not be considered binding at all. His soul is under no obligation; his lips, not his will, have offended. But the Jewish Lawgiver, solicitous for the sanctity of holy things, does not permit him to retreat from his oath, without acknowledging his involuntary error, and bringing the appointed sacrifice; then he might retreat and be forgiven. This cannot be regarded as a case of a moral offence actually forgiven because a sacrifice has been offered.

II.

There was another class of sacrifices very similar to the sin-offerings, to which it is necessary I should refer for the sake of completing my argument—I mean the trespass-offerings. There has been great division of opinion among scholars on the exact distinction between the two. Professor Fairbairn has, I think, defined the characteristic of the trespass-offerings very accurately in these words,—they "were offerings for sins in which the offence given, or the debt incurred by the misdeed, admitted of some sort of estimation and recompense; so that in addition to the atonement required for the iniquity, in the one point of view, there might also, in the other, be the exaction and the payment of a restitution."* There were cases in which the trespass-offering was not, and could hardly be, accompanied with any compensation for the offence, but I think that the essential characteristic of this class of sacrifices is exactly described in the extract.

(1) If through ignorance any man kept back from God what ought to have been consecrated to Him, the omission was to be atoned for by bringing a ram of an adequate value (to be determined by the priest) for a trespass-offering, and property equal in worth to a fifth more than he had wrongfully though ignorantly withheld. The sin was committed in ignorance; when discovered, the man was to make ample amends; and when the sacrifice was offered, he was to be assured of pardon.

(2) Again, if a man, unconsciously—not through ignorance infringed any ceremonial law, he was regarded as having incurred a debt to God, and this was forgiven on his offering a ram which the priest should pronounce to be of adequate value.

Ignorance in the one case and unconsciousness in the other removed the moral element altogether from these offences; compensation was offered where compensation was possible; and since the transgression was altogether an external, not a spiritual thing, it was forgiven on the bare condition that the external ceremonial was fulfilled.

(3) For certain offences knowingly committed, trespass offerings, with pecuniary compensation, secured pardon.

If a man who had received property in trust was guilty of fraud, in relation to it; or committed a fraud against his partner in business; or dishonestly kept lost property which he had found; or by an oath unjustly deprived another of property; or, finally, by any deception, or by any high-handed wrong-doing, enriched himself at another's expense,—he was to bring a trespass offering and restore the property, adding to it a fifth of its value, and the sin was to be forgiven. It is rather

---

* Fairbairn's Typology, II. 341.

startling to find that actual pardon was promised for crimes like these upon making compensation and bringing the sacrifice; but a little consideration may perhaps diminish the surprise. It is clear that the law did not apply to those whose crimes had been detected by others, or could be punished by public justice. Severer penalties than these were inflicted by the magistrate. The thief, if brought before the public tribunals, had to restore according to circumstances, twofold, fourfold, or fivefold what he had taken, or was sold into bondage. Breach of trust, or denying the possession of property that had been found, was punished by requiring the restitution of double its value. But if a man guilty of any of these crimes had not been brought before the magistrate, or, through defective testimony, or judicial feebleness or corruption, had escaped the penalty, this law of the trespass offering appealed to his conscience to make public confession of his guilt, to implore God's pardon by sacrifice, and to make adequate compensation to him who had been wronged. If conscience responded to this appeal, if he was able to overcome the natural shame which would prevent him from publicly acknowledging his crime, if he restored the property, augmented by a fifth of its value, his repentance might surely be accepted as genuine. He could give no further proof of the reality of his sorrow, than this voluntary confession and voluntary restoration. He was therefore assured of forgiveness.

But this is not an instance of a crime being pardoned simply on the ground of a sacrifice being offered; the consequences of the crime were voluntarily and completely repaired, a heavy pecuniary penalty was voluntarily borne, and public shame was voluntarily endured, in obedience to the Divine law. Nothing is said in the rubric of the trespass-offering concerning the necessity of repentance to make the sacrifice effectual; the reality of the repentance is naturally and justly taken for granted. The object of the law was to encourage restitution when wrong had been done, to remind the wrong-doer that the Divine displeasure had to be averted, as well as compensation given to the victim of injustice.

(4) A trespass-offering formed part of the ritual at the cleansing of a leper; perhaps to indicate that as his leprosy

had separated him both from the civil and religious life of the nation, he had been obliged to neglect duties which he naturally owed both to God and man; in the trespass-offerings the debt was acknowledged that it might be cancelled.

(5) A similar reason, perhaps, may be alleged for the trespass-offering which the Nazarite had to offer if he accidentally became unclean; he had failed, though not by his own fault, in discharging a debt to God which he had voluntarily undertaken, and as in the last case, the debt was acknowledged in the trespass-offering, that it might be cancelled.

(6) There was one other case in which a trespass-offering was required. If a man committed adultery with his slave, the crime was not to be punished by the death of both, as was the law when both were free; but there was to be a scourging, not of the woman only, as our version has it, but perhaps of both, or still more probably of the man only, and then he was to bring a trespass-offering, and to be forgiven. This assurance of pardon apart from any guarantee of repentance for a real crime, stands alone in the Jewish law; its exceptional position would justify us, I think, in passing it over in a general estimate of the efficacy and results of animal sacrifice. Perhaps we ought to regard the provision as primarily intended not to provide atonement and secure pardon, but as one of the numerous arrangements by which the Mosaic system endeavoured to soften and to elevate the condition of the slave. It is clear that the relation of a master to his slaves involved the same evils in the early ages of the world that it involves now; and the Jewish Lawgiver, unable to break down the atrocious system by the force of mere authority, so regulated it as to diminish its hardships and gradually to develope a recognition of the indestructible right to personal freedom of every man who has not been guilty of a crime. The scourging was the physical penalty of the offence; the trespass-offering reminded the wrong-doer that he had both violated the rights of another and provoked the anger of God. But the difficulty of this case I frankly admit.

Speaking generally, neither sin-offering nor trespass-offering could, when offered by an individual, assure forgiveness to the guilty for any sins committed either against God or man. They removed ceremonial defilement which had been unavoidably, involuntarily, or unconsciously incurred, but provided no atonement and secured no pardon for intentional violation of even ceremonial precepts. They gave rest to the conscience for unconscious trifling with holy things, or neglecting to aid in the administration of justice; but provided no atonement and secured no pardon for breaking solemn vows, or disregarding the sanctity of an oath. They gave assurance of God's forgiveness, when, through ignorance, God's claims on property had not been satisfied, and this only on condition that more was consecrated to Him on the discovery of the offence than the law originally required; but provided no atonement and secured no pardon for intentional sacrilege. In certain special cases of injustice, they obtained God's mercy, when the wrong had been actually undone by voluntary restitution to the injured, and the shame of public confession had been voluntarily endured; but provided no atonement and secured no pardon for the innumerable sins against God, or against man, which cannot actually be undone by subsequent acts of reparation: the only moral offences which God forgave on the mere offering of a sacrifice, were offences freely acknowledged, offences not symbolically, but actually, atoned for and cancelled by voluntary restitution. God forgave, only when by the voluntary act of the guilty, the victim of injustice no longer suffered from the crime.

If when a man had told a lie, or committed a sensual sin, or intentionally neglected any religious duty, he had been directed to procure a sacrifice—no instruction, however clear, however authoritative, however solemn, to the effect, that apart from interior repentance and trust in the Divine mercy the sacrifice would be unavailing, could have prevented men coming to regard the mere ceremonial act as an easy means of blotting out the moral offence. Iniquity would have been established by a law. The moral sense of the nation would have been enfeebled and paralyzed by the natural influence of its religious institutions.

III.

What provision was there, then, in the Levitical system for recognising the idea of atonement in connection with the pardon of moral offences? Men sinned against the moral law in those days; how were they assured of the possibility of obtaining the Divine forgiveness?

The anger of God against moral transgressions was revealed more awfully at Mount Sinai than it had ever been revealed before; was there not also a clearer revelation of the divine mercy? There was.

It is, I think, a very significant fact that no mention is made of sin-offerings before the giving of the Mosaic law. In the previous sacrifices, the idea of expiation, if recognised at all, was vague and indistinct. The slaying of an animal and the burning of it on an altar was a common mode of worship from the very earliest times; but there is not a solitary hint, so far as I know, before the establishment of the Levitical system, that the sacrifice had any atoning power, real or symbolic.

Apart from an express Divine revelation,—and no such revelation is recorded as having been given in patriarchal times,—I do not see how the death of a lamb or a bullock could have been regarded as possessing expiatory significance or value, although it was a very natural form of confessing that the worshipper deserved the death he had inflicted, and of deprecating the Divine displeasure.

That sacrifices were offered as soon as man was driven out of Eden, that they were offered in connection with sin, is no proof that they were regarded as expiatory, but only that the worshipper confessed his own guilt or the guilt of others and implored God's mercy, by a rite which he knew that God approved. When the evil of sin was more emphatically revealed in the Mosaic dispensation,—although the old burnt-offering was still retained, and atoning significance, though subordinate to other purposes, was now, for the first time, distinctly ascribed to it,— a new offering with a new name and a new ritual was instituted specially to represent the idea of expiation. The sin-offering appears for the first time in the Levitical law.

When offered by individuals, it had no power, as I have already proved, to atone for sin; not even a symbolic expiation for moral offences was attributed to it. But there were a few occasions on which it was offered by public law and for the whole people. To these we will now direct our attention.

(1) The daily sacrifices in the temple were not sin-offerings, but burnt-offerings; the morning and evening lamb exhibited the idea of atonement only faintly and in connection with ideas of a different order. It was the same with the double sacrifices offered on ordinary Sabbaths.

But, at the commencement of every month, special rites were celebrated, and in addition to special burnt-offerings, a kid of the goats was to be publicly offered for a sin-offering. A public sin-offering was also part of the appointed ritual at the passover, and at pentecost, and at the feast of trumpets, and every day during the feast of tabernacles; and, on the great day of atonement, the whole ritual centred and culminated in offerings to which an expiatory significance is distinctly ascribed. At specified times, therefore, during the year, and at the commencement of every month, expiatory sacrifices for sin were offered for the whole people. It is, however, the great annual expiation that was specially present to the writer of this Epistle in the passage to which our attention is directed this morning; the idea of the public sin-offering was most clearly exhibited in that remarkable ritual, and in it we shall be most likely to discover what the real effect of the sin-offering was supposed to be.

Most of the religious festivals of the Jewish people were bright and cheerful. Their ordinary Sabbaths were days of rest but not of melancholy; and their feasts were times of great rejoicing. But on one day of the year they were to "afflict" their "souls" by "a statute for ever." In the sacrifices of that day there was "a remembrance again made of sins every year." The rubric for these annual ceremonies is most minute and, on the whole, easily intelligible. Omitting some of the details of the ritual, which were however unusually significant, the ceremonial of the day may be briefly detailed.

The High Priest, who, as the religious representative of the nation, sustained the most prominent part throughout the ceremonies of the day, first laid aside the gorgeous robes in which he ordinarily discharged the functions of his office, and clothed himself in plain, white linen; for it was a time of humiliation, not of pomp and majesty. He then brought the living animals appointed for the sacrifices of the day, and presented them at the door of the tabernacle. The lot was cast to determine which of the two goats, together constituting the sin-offering for the people, was to be slain; and which was to be afterwards sent away into the wilderness. A bullock having been slain as a sin-offering, to make atonement for himself and the priesthood, the High Priest entered the Most Holy Place, closed against even him all the year beside; and with streaming incense ascending from the censer in one hand, he stood before the mercy-seat, and before the adoring cherubim, and before the cloud of glory above the ark: with the other hand he sprinkled the blood of the bullock on the mercy-seat, and then again sprinkled the blood seven times on the floor before the ark.* After this he came out; the special work of expiation for himself and the priesthood had been accomplished. The goat destined to die for the people having been slain, he returned to the innermost sanctuary, and, as before, sprinkled the blood first on the mercy-seat, and then seven times on the floor before the ark. By his first entrance he was said "to make an atonement" for his own sins, and by the second for the sins of the people; and since by their iniquities the very sanctuary of God had been defiled, he was to sprinkle the blood both of the bullock and the goat seven times upon the altar of incense, "to cleanse it and hallow it from the uncleanness of the children of Israel." This having been done, he laid both his hands upon the head of the living goat, and confessed over it "all the iniquities of the children of Israel, and all their transgressions, with all their sins, putting them on the head of the goat," and then sent it, by a man appointed for the purpose, into the wilderness.

The great work of expiation was now consummated. The

* Some suppose that the High Priest entered the Holy Place first with the incense, and then a second time with the blood. The rubric is not quite clear.

High Priest divested himself of his linen garments, purified himself with water, arrayed himself in his splendid robes, put on his ephod of crimson, purple, and gold, and his breastplate flashing with precious stones. He then offered a burnt-offering for himself and a burnt-offering for the people, the atoning element in which was on this day emphatically recognized; and, passing over some significant but less important rites, the solemn ceremonial was over.

There are four or five facts which seem to me very obvious and certain in relation to this annual ceremonial.

(1) The sins confessed on that day by the High Priest were not mere ceremonial offences, nor offences against Jehovah considered as the political head of the Jewish people. When the High Priest was charged to confess with such solemnity the iniquities, transgressions, and sins of the nation over the head of the goat, it is surely inconceivable that the confession referred to mere ceremonial lapses, for every one of which there was, I think, an adequate ceremonial atonement. Nor is there any hint that there was any intention to distinguish between sin as an internal act, a spiritual offence, a crime against God, as the moral governor of mankind, and sin as a mere external and political offence against the laws of the nation of which God was the true King. The language of confession is as full, as comprehensive, as exhaustive, as language could possibly be; and not a single part of the ritual can be pointed to as suggesting an idea of the re-adjustment of the merely political relations between God and the Jewish people. The expiation, if expiation there was, had to do with sin, in the truest and deepest sense the word can bear.

(2) The sin confessed on that day was considered as expiated, really or symbolically, by the appointed sacrifice. Aaron made atonement for himself and his house, and then for the whole nation. They were very familiar with the idea of atonement. When they had unintentionally transgressed a ceremonial law, the private sin-offering atoned for and cancelled the offence. When they had unintentionally become ceremonially unclean, the sin-offering restored to them free

access to the courts of the Lord. They had been forbidden to eat blood, because "the life of the flesh is in the blood, and I have given it you upon the altar, said Jehovah, to make an atonement for your souls; for it is the blood that maketh an atonement for the soul." The life of the animal stood for their life; its death was an expiation for their offences. And although the atoning element was always present in the animal sacrifices, it received peculiar emphasis in the offerings of this particular day. The very name of the principal sacrifices gave prominence to the idea of expiation; they were sin-offerings. The language used in instituting the service gave prominence to it; again and again it is said that the rites of that day were to make "atonement." The peculiar ceremonies gave prominence to it; the sending away of the goat into the wilderness with the sins of the nation on his head—to indicate their complete removal, and suggesting to our minds the idea afterwards expressed by the Psalmist, "as far as the east is from the west, so far hath He removed our transgressions from us," —forced into distinct and unambiguous prominence, the idea that atonement was being effected for the sins of the nation.

(3) No one could suppose that the slaying of the one goat or the sending of the other into the wilderness actually expiated the offence of the whole people. As individuals, they were accustomed to bring costlier sacrifices for single transgressions, for involuntary transgressions, for transgressions against the merely ceremonial law; it was impossible for them to believe that the innumerable sins of all the people of Israel, during a whole year, could be truly atoned for by a comparatively insignificant offering. In this lay the safety of the whole service. Had they been permitted to bring individual sacrifices for individual offences against the moral law,—sacrifices offered at the cost of the individual offender,—there would have been an irresistible tendency to regard the expiation as real and complete. But the two goats of the great day of atonement were provided at the public cost, they did not impose a burden on a solitary individual among all the thousands of Israel; and yet they were to

expiate innumerable offences. The symbolic character of the expiation could not fail to be recognised.

(4) No one could suppose that these annual sin-offerings, by their own intrinsic efficacy, secured actual forgiveness for any, even the least, offence against the Divine law. "Without the shedding of blood there was no remission of sin," but it is an error to suppose that "where blood was duly shed, in the way and manner the law required, remission followed as a matter of course."

There is a very noticeable difference between what is said by Moses about the public sin-offerings and what is said about the private sin-offerings. When an individual brought his sacrifice to expiate an involuntary offence against the ceremonial law, it is said that by offering the sacrifice "the priest shall make atonement for him, as concerning his sin, and *it shall be forgiven him*." When the trespass-offering was brought for any of the specified moral offences I have already noticed, it is said, "The priest shall make atonement for him before the Lord, and *it shall be forgiven him*." The ceremonial offence was blotted out when the ceremonial compensation was offered; the genuine repentance of the man that brought the trespass-offering for an offence in which a moral element was present, was taken for granted because he had voluntarily met the hard conditions associated with the sacrifice, and therefore he was assured of pardon. There is no such assurance of forgiveness for the sins which were expiated by the annual ceremonial. Atonement was made, but remission did not necessarily follow. No man could dream that remission necessarily followed. The two ideas of atonement and pardon, though associated, are distinct. Atonement is the condition of pardon; but whether pardon shall be granted as soon as atonement is made, depends on the existence or absence of moral hindrances to forgiveness in the sinner himself. God is *free to forgive*, because acknowledgment has been made of the evil of sin; but other conditions must be met before forgiveness is actually bestowed.

(5) The necessity of repentance in connection with the great act of expiation was most impressively taught by the law that

on that day, the people were "to afflict their souls." Common work was to be suspended as on the weekly Sabbath; there was to be a holy convocation, and the people were to spend the day in sorrow and humiliation for all their sins. He who thus fulfilled the law, but he alone, would be able to find in the solemn ritual assurance of the Divine mercy; and although his conscience would find no satisfaction in the sacrifices themselves, as though they were an adequate expiation of his offences, he would be able to rest in the conviction that for reasons, too deep and mysterious perhaps for the human intellect to discover, but perfectly satisfactory to the infinitely and only "wise God," forgiveness was certainly assured to all who sorrowed for their sin in connection with the symbolic acts of confession and atonement.

IV.

I find that this sermon has already extended far beyond the limits I anticipated, and must postpone the exposition of the text. In the future discourses on this Epistle I shall not, I think, have any occasion to task your strength as I have tasked it this morning and as I tasked it last Sunday; but I cannot close without calling your attention to the irresistible argument afforded by this discussion for the truly expiatory character of the death of the Lord Jesus Christ. The evangelical doctrine of the atonement does not rest, as some seem to suppose, on the artificial refinements of uninspired theologians, or on weak analogies drawn from the imperfect operations of human governments, or on the etymology of a few Greek nouns and verbs, or on the exact force of one or two Greek prepositions.

At the very gates of the fair garden which man lost by his transgression, sacrifice began to be offered when man appealed to the Divine mercy and gave thanks for the Divine goodness. Whether instituted by a direct Divine command, or, as some suppose, suggested by the instincts of the human heart, this form of worship was manifestly acceptable to the Most High. When the descendants of Abraham were organized into a nation, and the law of God was more fully revealed, and the hope of salvation strengthened by new institutions and promises, the idea of expiation for sin, by means of death, was one of the most prominent characteristics of the religious system which was to develope the thought and life of the chosen race. The idea was so presented that no sanction was given to the fatal delusion that, by the mere blood of the sacrifices, transgression of the moral law could be atoned for, or that, by mere external rites, the impenitent sinner could escape from the just penalties of his crimes. The moral sense of the guilty was strengthened by the very institutions which suggested and justified the hope of God's forgiveness. But the idea of expiation, by the blood of innocent victims,—and of expiation as the necessary condition of the Divine pardon, was wrought into the very structure of the religious faith of the Jew. He might miss the meaning of every other part of the Mosaic system, but not to recognize *this* was impossible. It was forced upon him in a thousand forms; he could not escape it. And, however miserably the Mosaic institutions may have failed in disciplining a truly righteous and godly nation, they did not fail in carrying this idea into the intellect and heart of the Jewish people. It coloured their language,—it gave form even to their superstitions. It was as deeply rooted in their souls as the conviction that they were an elect race, called of God to higher distinctions than the proudest nations of the heathen world possessed.

When Christ came, and when His apostles began to preach the gospel, not to the Jews only but also to the Gentiles, the idea of expiation re-appears in the new and nobler faith. If it had been erroneous, there should have been a resolute and uncompromising controversy with the tremendous falsehood; or at least a careful avoidance of every expression, every allusion, that could even appear to sanction and was likely to perpetuate it. To tell me that the language of the New Testament which teaches me that Christ by His death truly atoned for the sins of mankind, was an accommodation to Jewish prejudices, is not only to impeach the authority of the ancient faith, which reveals the more clearly the signs of its Divine origin the more profoundly it is studied, but to insult the understanding and slander the integrity of Christ Himself and His apostles.

"Accommodation to Jewish prejudices!" The suggestion is, I repeat, an insult to the *understanding* of the founders of the Christian faith. Had Christ been anxious for that, there was no need for Him to transfer into the new faith the false theology of the old. It would have been easy and comparatively harmless, to flatter Jewish patriotism and leave Jewish formalism unrebuked. He would not have healed the sick on the Sabbath, nor justified His disciples for plucking the ears of corn as they passed on the Sabbath through the corn fields. He would never have spoken of the destruction of the temple. He would have commanded His disciples to perpetuate its services. Had He been anxious for "acommodation to Jewish prejudices," He would have been punctilious in observing the external customs which they honoured, while He silently undermined the erroneous elements of their belief. It is not the manner of Jesuitical reformers to preach the false and pernicious principles of the system they wish to overthrow, and to treat lightly or trample under foot its external observances. The popular mind cares far more for the visible ceremony than for the invisible conviction. Christ might have escaped the malice and cruelty of His enemies had He only taught another doctrine, while He carefully honoured the outward form of their superstition. "Accommodation to Jewish prejudices!" Was Paul anxious for that? Did he talk about the atonement in connection with the death of Christ merely to humour the adherents of a theology which he himself disbelieved;—he who made light of circumcision, and asserted that the exclusive privileges of the Jew were over; that nothing was common or unclean; that under the law in which the Jews boasted, they had been in bondage for sixteen hundred years, and that through Christ alone could they become free? The idea, that the apostle who taught these things, and taught them so boldly, not to say harshly, would, in teaching any Christian doctrine, swerve a hair's breadth from his own convictions to curry favour by accommodating his language to Jewish prejudices, is simply absurd. Had he wanted to do that, he must have been destitute of the most ordinary sense not to have seen that there were easier ways of doing it.

And the suggestion is a slander on their *integrity*. If on such a point as this, they hesitate, equivocate, cut and trim their words to sanction a portentous error, my faith in their honesty is gone.

But it was no Jewish prejudice which gave form and colour to their teaching. It was a truth, and one of the deepest truths which the ancient institutions exhibited and the ancient prophets taught. Moses came from God, and he by symbolic rites, revealed that "without the shedding of blood, there is no remission of sins;" and in due time Christ came, and by the Eternal Spirit offered himself without spot to God—died the just for the unjust—was wounded for our transgressions, bruised for our iniquities,—and now we have redemption through His blood, even the forgiveness of sins, according to the riches of His grace.

ACCESS TO GOD.

"Now when these things were thus ordained, the priests went always into the first tabernacle, accomplishing the service of God," &c. —HEBREWS ix, 6-14.

WE have in these verses an authoritative declaration of what God intended to teach the Jewish people, by certain well-known arrangements in their tabernacle. To the Holy Place, the priests had free access at all times. Every week, every day, they were there "*accomplishing the service of God,*" offering the incense, lighting and dressing the golden lamps, changing the shewbread. But a veil separated "*the first tabernacle*" from the second, the Holy Place from the Holiest of all. The sacred ark, with its propitiatory covering, the mysterious cherubim, and the cloud of glory, was concealed, not only from the people, but from the consecrated priesthood. Even the High Priest himself was not suffered to enter the inner sanctuary, except on the great day of atonement.

The nation was not excluded altogether from the immediate presence of God—for the representative of its religious life stood once a year face to face with the visible symbols of the Divine Majesty but, except on that solitary occasion, even the most sacred acts of worship were to be celebrated in the less sacred enclosure.

I.

The exclusion of the very priesthood from the Holy of Holies, the appointment of a chamber of inferior sanctity as the place where the most sacred rites of the ceremonial service, with only one exception, were to be observed, is declared to have signified "*that the way into the Holiest of all* * *had not yet been made manifest.*" That "*first tabernacle*,"—separated from the Most Holy Place by heavy curtains which were never drawn aside except by the High Priest, and by him only once a year, and even then in connection with an unusual ritual of most oppressive solemnity,—would have been altogether unnecessary, if there had been free access to God. While it stood, priests and people were constantly taught that though God was nearer to them than to all mankind besides, they could not yet enter into the closest and most blessed communion with Him.

I think that this inspired and authoritative interpretation of what was meant by the division of the Jewish sanctuary into the first and second tabernacles, the Holy Place, and the Holiest of all, is of the very greatest value in illustrating the principles which should guide us in considering all the parts of the Levitical system.

(1) We learn, beyond all question, that the arrangements and institutions of Jewish worship were intended by the Holy Ghost to have a religious significance. The Spirit revealed Divine truth by inspired prophets. The same Spirit revealed Divine truth in the structure of the material sanctuary. The modes of communication varied; the source and substance of the revelation were the same. It was not mere human fancy, it was not a desire on the part of Moses to assimilate the religious ceremonial of the Jewish people to that of the surrounding nations, which led to the establishment of the Levitical ritual; the arrangements were a vehicle and instrument by which the Holy Ghost made known religious truths.

(2) The simplicity and obviousness of this interpretation of the division of the tabernacle into two chambers, confirms very strongly the principle on which I have so frequently insisted throughout these discourses, that in determining the symbolic meaning of the ancient services we should inquire What was the impression they would naturally produce on the Jews themselves?

---

* Or, rather, "*The way into the Holy Places*," i.e., the *true* Holy Places.

What the Holy Ghost "*signified*" by excluding not only the people but the priests from the inner sanctuary, might have been seen by any Jew of ordinary intelligence. There was nothing recondite in the arrangement. It was intelligible to men wholly ignorant of the truth which was unrevealed before the coming of Christ. It must have produced, even upon those who never asked themselves its meaning, the designed impression. Every Jew knew that even the High Priest was permitted to enter the Holy of Holies only once a year, and that the other priests were never permitted to enter it at all; every Jew, therefore, would feel that free and habitual access to the immediate presence of God was checked by Divinely-appointed institutions. This impression he would have, spite of any arbitrary and fanciful meanings which his religious teachers might suppose they discovered in the structure of the Holy Place and its relations to the Holiest of all; and this impression would have been naturally produced on our own minds had no inspired writer told us what the Holy Ghost signified.

We have here an authoritative illustration of the manner in which we should interpret the symbolic institutions of Judaism; and an illustration which plainly discourages the fanciful and arbitrary principles of some typical commentators.

II.

In the ninth and tenth verses, the writer speaks of the inefficacy of the old ritual to "*perfect*" the spiritual consciousness of the worshipper; to inspire, that is, a full and satisfactory sense of fellowship with God. It consisted in the offering of meats and drinks, and in external baptisms, and ordinances altogether of a material and physical kind. No spiritual man could acknowledge in them any real and intrinsic power to remove the stain of sin or to exalt him into communion with God;* the closing of the Holy of Holies against all the burnt-offerings in which was expressed the

---

* The "perfecting" of the spiritual consciousness of man is effected only by open and habitual communion with God.

devotion of individuals or of the nation to God's service, and against the daily incense which represented the praises and thanksgivings and worship of all devout hearts, confirmed this instinctive distrust of the moral efficacy of the whole ceremonial system. It was "*imposed*" on the people till the time when the new and better covenant should be established, of which the later prophets spoke distinctly, the time when—through the coming of the Messiah, for whom the whole nation, from the very earliest period of its history, had been taught to wait—the true kingdom of God should be established among men.

But Christ having appeared as "*High Priest* of those *good things*" which had been the object of Jewish hope through all generations, "*entered once for all*" the very home of God; He entered it, not as the High Priest entered the Holy of Holies, by passing through the Holy Place of a material sanctuary, but "*through a greater and more perfect tabernacle, one not made with hands, that is, not belonging to this visible creation;*" He entered it, not as the High Priest entered the Holy of Holies, by means of "*the blood of goats and calves, but by His own blood,*" and so He "*obtained eternal redemption for us.*"

What was that "*greater and more perfect tabernacle, not made with hands, that is, not belonging to this visible creation,*" through which the writer says that Christ "*passed*" in order to enter the immediate presence of God? His entering the presence of God, is plainly His ascension into Heaven after His atonement for the sins of mankind had been completed. And the vestibule, the ante-chamber, through which He passed, was surely that lower region of Divine communion in which He lived during the years of His humiliation. He dwelt in the Father, while He was here. He breathed a Divine air. His devotion had higher aids than the temple, with all its venerable and sacred ordinances, could afford. He served God in another sanctuary—a sanctuary not made with hands, and not constructed of the materials belonging to this visible creation. The incense of His reverential worship, the offerings of His perfect obedience, were not presented in the Holy Place of the Jewish tabernacle, and when He entered with His own blood into the more immediate presence of God, He did not stand in the sacred chamber assigned to the ark and the cherubim, but in the heaven of heavens, the true and eternal abode of the Most High.

Yes! He has *"obtained eternal redemption for us; for if the blood of bulls and goats, and the ashes of an heifer sprinkling the unclean, sanctifieth to the purity of the flesh, how much more shall the blood of Christ who through the Eternal Spirit offered* HIMSELF *without spot to God, purify your conscience,* or rather, your spiritual consciousness, *from dead works that you may be free to serve the living God?"*

The first thing requiring notice in these verses, is the efficacy conceded to certain ritual observances.

I need hardly remind you that the Levitical Law excluded from the public worship of God persons who had contracted ceremonial uncleanness. The leper, the man who had touched a dead person, either accidentally or in rendering to the dead any necessary services, was "unclean;" and uncleanness was the result of many other circumstances which it is unnecessary to describe in detail. The design of these regulations is not obscure: they appeal, for the most part, to instincts and convictions natural to the heart of man. The body is not only associated most intimately with the soul, but physical diseases and physical infirmities have in all ages provided the very language in which men have described spiritual evil. Disease itself is the penalty of sin, and though not in all cases a manifestation of the Divine anger against the particular individual on whom it may rest, it is a visible sign that he belongs to a sinful race; every material instrument of punishing human crime against human laws is regarded with disgust because of the use to which it is applied—we shrink from the touch of the gallows—and it has been justly observed that "every form of disease might have been held to be polluting, and to have required separate purifications. This, however, would have rendered the ceremonial observances an intolerable burden. One disease, therefore, was chosen in particular, and that such an one as might be fitly regarded as the head of all

P

diseases, the most affecting symbol of sin."* The repulsive and loathsome effects of leprosy on the physical life of man constituted, no doubt, the reason of the choice; while the disease lasted the unhappy sufferer was obliged to live apart from the community, and was denied access to the service of the tabernacle. When it had disappeared certain rites were performed, and the separation ceased.

Death is a still more emphatic and impressive sign of the presence of sin in the world. It was the express penalty of the original transgression. All contact with it, however justifiable, however necessary, recalls our sad condition, and reminds us that we too belong to a sinful race. We can perceive that the temporary isolation which the Levitical Law attached to those who had touched the dead, was obviously and intimately associated with the profoundest moral ideas. There could be no real sin in the physical contact, but the ceremonial uncleanness which it entailed would naturally suggest to all thoughtful Jews that sin itself, which was the original cause of human death, must be a grievous offence against God, and must exclude the soul from communion with Him, since even accidental and external contact with its great penalty, separated the most holy from the sanctuary seven days, and imposed the necessity of undergoing ceremonial cleansing. To remove uncleanness of this kind, a red heifer was slain, and burnt with most remarkable ceremonies, the significance of which, I think, we are now in no position to interpret; and the rite of purification was effected by sprinkling the unclean person, on the third and seventh day, with a bunch of hyssop dipped in water, in which the ashes of the heifer had been preserved.

Other ceremonies were appointed to remove uncleanness resulting from other causes. It is conceded that these external rites could cleanse the body from external impurities. The typical uncleanness could be removed by typical observances.

But "the blood of bulls and goats" is mentioned in addition to the blood of the heifer, and it is plain that the writer was still thinking of the great annual expiation, and not merely

* Fairbairn ii, 410.

of the ritual for the removal of occasional ceremonial defilements. Hence, some theologians have inferred that he means to teach that the whole design, even of those annual solemnities, was to purify the nation from external and ceremonial uncleanness. You will have learnt from the discourse of last Sunday morning that I cannot yield to this opinion. The ritual of the great day of atonement cannot be fairly limited to such a purpose as this. It had a wider and a deeper range, and pointed to results which it had no power to accomplish. It was a symbolic atonement for all the sins, transgressions and iniquities of the people; and all its circumstances indicated that it was only symbolical. The proof of this was given last Sunday and need not be repeated.

What the writer meant I think was this: by the old law provision was made for the removal of the external impurities, which excluded men from access to God in the tabernacle, and from uniting with the rest of the nation in His service. Those who had been defiled by contact with the dead, regained their external purity when they were sprinkled with water with which the ashes of the heifer were mixed; nay, it may be conceded, that the great annual ceremonies of expiation, though powerless to remove interior and spiritual uncleanness, and though securing by themselves no actual pardon for any solitary offence, had this effect, that when they were accomplished, every man was free to enter the tabernacle and to appeal to the Divine mercy; they actually renewed the access of the whole people to the visible sanctuary; they removed whatever external hindrances might have otherwise excluded the sinful nation from the external service of God; they sanctified "*to the purity of the flesh.*"

But there are impurities of another kind from which these ceremonial observances could not cleanse. The touch of a dead body might render the flesh unclean, but there are "*works*" which are the sign of death in the soul;—thoughts, passions, volitions, which reveal the mortal corruption of our spiritual nature. By these, not the flesh, but the spiritual consciousness of man is made unclean; and he shrinks from the presence of the living God. How are we to be purified from the interior and real defilement? It is answered that if the external ritual could remove external uncleanness, "*much more shall the blood of Christ, who offered Himself without spot to God*," whose offering was not the act of a mere man, but of "*the Eternal Spirit,—purify your consciousness from dead works, to serve the living God.*"

There are two points in this verse which we shall do well to consider.

(1) The voluntary sacrifice of the Lord Jesus Christ was a Divine act. He assumed the nature of man, but even in His humiliation He was God still. When He laid aside His eternal glory, it was God who made Himself of no reputation and took upon Him the form of a servant, and assumed the likeness of men; and throughout the whole history of His sorrow and shame, although the majesty and splendour of His heavenly estate were obscured, it was still the everlasting Son of the Father,—the Divine Word dwelling upon earth,—that was the object of the malignity of Satan and the cruelty of man. The sufferings of the sacrifices of the ancient law were not to be ascribed to any voluntary submission on their part; but it was "through the Eternal Spirit,"—the Divine personality and will which constituted the very centre and root of the life of the Lord Jesus Christ,—that He endured the cross, despising the shame. The mystery of the union between the Divinity and the humanity of our Lord cannot be penetrated; but the difficulties are metaphysical, not moral. They defy the power of the intellect, but do not trouble the conscience. On the other hand, if this union is forgotten, and if the sufferings of the Lord Jesus for human salvation are regarded as the sufferings of a third person intervening between God and man, to allay the wrath of the One and to secure the escape of the other, moral difficulties arise of the most portentous kind; and the conscience, instead of finding rest in the sacrifice, is tortured and discouraged. When God determined to have mercy upon man, He did not command or permit holy angels to endure the sufferings which men had deserved; nor did He command or permit an innocent man to sink under the awful burden of the iniquities of the race; but, since it be-

longed to Himself to maintain the eternal distinction between right and wrong, and He had resolved not to maintain it in this case by inflicting just penalties on those who had sinned, He came into the world Himself, in the person of the Son, assuming our nature that He might become capable of suffering, and the suffering of Christ was the act of the Eternal Spirit.

(2) The design of this sacrifice is that sinful men may now be free to serve the living God. The consciousness of evil filled Isaiah with dread, when he saw the divine glory in vision, and heard the ceaseless cry of the seraphim—" Holy, holy, holy, Lord God of Hosts ;" and when we come into the presence of the living God,—know that He is near to us,—that His very eye is upon us,—that His thoughts are occupied with us,—that we are face to face with the High and Lofty One, whose name is Holy,—the consciousness of sin oppresses and paralyses our spiritual powers, and we sink terror-stricken into the dust at His feet. We dare not praise His glorious perfections, nor thank Him for His goodness, nor even implore His mercy. Our strength is dried up ; heart and flesh fail. It is then that the remembrance of His own humiliation for our sakes, and of the blood which was shed upon Calvary, restores our fainting spirits. We are unclean in our very souls ; but the great sacrifice was offered that we might be able to worship God, and the remembrance of that, relieves our fear. If the intellect cannot explain the atonement, the heart and the conscience confess its power. Whatever other effects it may have, it has this,—we can now venture to worship God.

Grievously do they mistake the design of the death of Christ, who suppose that it was intended simply to deliver us from the penalty of sin and to leave us free to continue in transgression. The unclean were purified that they might enter the tabernacle and take part in its services ; and the blood of Christ has been shed for us that we may have access to God. It does not render worship and obedience unnecessary, it is the means by which we are delivered from that which hindered both. Hence it is that whether we offer adoration and praise, or invoke the Divine blessing on ourselves or intercede for others, or venture to contemplate the Divine glory, and endeavour to enter into communion with the Divine blessedness, we do all in the name of the Lord Jesus. His sacrifice is the foundation on which our religious life is built; by His blood we are cleansed from impurity that we may serve the living God.

THE TESTAMENT.

"And for this cause He is the Mediator of the New Testament, that by means of death for the redemption of the transgressions that were under the first testament, they which are called might receive the promise of eternal inheritance. For where a testament is," &c.—HEBREWS ix, 15-23.

THE great argument of this Epistle is now moving rapidly towards its close. All that has been said about the Divine glory of the Lord Jesus Christ, the dignity to which human nature has been exalted in Him, His superiority as Son of God to Moses, who was only God's servant, and the superiority of His priesthood to that of Aaron, culminates in the proof that He has established a new Covenant between God and man.

The Jewish Christians had not apprehended the magnitude of the change produced by the mission of Christ in the religious condition of man. They had clung to the old ritual, and the development of their Christian life had been checked. They had not understood that Christ had introduced new relations between God and man.

They were in a condition not unlike that through which our own country passed during the early years of the Reformation. New thoughts were in the hearts of men, but the outward forms of the decaying faith were still celebrated. Our fathers did not at once perceive all the inevitable consequences of renouncing the authority of the Roman pontiff, and appealing to holy Scripture on all questions of religious belief. For a time there was a chaotic struggle between two hostile and irreconcileable forces for the control of the English people. It seemed at last that, by the cruelties of the Marian persecutions and the intercourse between the English and Swiss reformers, God had "divided the light from the darkness;" but even then the traditions of the old faith continued to exert a disastrous influence on the new.

The Jewish believers, at the time this Epistle was written, were passing through a similar transition. They acknowledged that the Lord Jesus was the Messiah, but they retained the institutions of Moses; and there were "many thousands of Jews that believed" who were "all zealous of the law." (Acts xxi, 20.)

This was, no doubt, partly the cause of the serious perils which threatened their faith when times of storm and trouble came. They had not learned to "walk by faith." They still relied on the external supports to holiness and the visible aids to devotion, which belonged to the ancient system. They had not completely broken with the national worship, and when they were required to make a final choice between the Church and the temple, their resolution was enfeebled not merely by fear of persecution, but by love of the ancient customs and ceremonies. They would have been saved from this, though exposed, no doubt, to other dangers, had they seen from the first, that the use and authority of the Mosaic institutions had passed away.

In the seventh chapter, the writer has intimated that since the priesthood has been changed,—the order of Melchizedek having succeeded to the order of Aaron,—the whole law is necessarily changed. In the eighth, he has recalled to them the prophecy in their own Scriptures of a new and better covenant established upon better promises. Instead of external laws and an imperfect revelation of the Divine character and will, there were to be laws written in the heart and a universal knowledge of God. In the first half of the ninth chapter, he has shown that the Levitical sacrifices which could not perfect the spiritual consciousness of man by elevating it into direct communion with God, have given place to the sacrifice of the Lord Jesus Christ, whose blood purifies us from dead works to serve the living God.

That sacrifice, absolutely unique, marks the close of the old dispensation and the beginning of the new. The external purifications and symbolic atonements had given place to an offering which cleanses the soul from all the stains that excluded it from the immediate presence of God.

The sacrifice of Christ, therefore, introduces a new covenant; this is the thought which constitutes the foundation of all the remaining argument. Everything now rests on His death.

Keep this in mind, and the perplexities of the rest of the chapter will, I think, disappear. His death is to the new covenant between God and man, what the death of a testator is to the arrangements he has made in his will (vv. 16, 17). His blood is to the new covenant what the blood of the sacrifices, sprinkled on the people and on the Book of the Law when the nation solemnly accepted the Mosaic institutions, and sprinkled on the tabernacle and its holy vessels when the sanctuary was erected,—was to the old covenant (vv. 18-23).

They were to see in Christ's death what they saw in the death of one who had made a testament—the event which secured the inheritance to his heirs. They were to see in Christ's blood what they saw in the blood that was sprinkled on the book and on the people at Sinai, and afterwards on the tabernacle—the establishment of a covenant between God and man, and the establishment of a new method and order of worship. Christ, therefore, does not stand in the line of the prophets and priests of Judaism. He is not a defender, or even a reformer of the ancient system; He is not only personally greater than Moses and all the supporters and interpreters of the Mosaic institutions; He is "*the Mediator of a New Covenant*," a covenant under which they who are called are to receive the eternal inheritance; and the same sacrifice on which the new dispensation rests expiates all the transgressions committed under the old, for a new system could not be founded until a real and effective atonement was made for former iniquities.

I have given a bare outline of the contents of this passage; it will now be necessary to examine it more closely.

Verses 16 and 17 have been the occasion of great perplexity to all commentators on this Epistle. The question in dispute is, whether we ought to interpret these verses as referring to a *testament, a will;* or whether we ought to retain the idea of a *covenant* between two consenting parties. The same Greek word denotes both. Up to this point in the argument of the Epistle it hardly admits of dispute, that it ought to be translated, not "testament," but "covenant." Indeed, I believe that in every other passage in the New Testament Scriptures it stands not for "testament" but for "covenant." The language has therefore been strained and stretched to make it bear the same meaning in these two verses. The "death of the testator" is explained to be the death of the sacrifices slain at the ratification of a covenant; and the testament being "of force after men are dead" is explained to mean, that not until the sacrifices are slain is the covenant firmly established. I cannot enter into the critical discussions which seem to me to render this interpretation altogether untenable, but can only say that I think no Greek scholar would resort to it, unless absolutely compelled by the context.

To my own mind, it seems certain that, although the word bears the sense of "covenant" everywhere else in the Epistle, and everywhere else in the New Testament, it means here, what it means most frequently in ordinary Greek writers,—the disposition or arrangement of property by a testament. With this meaning of the word the Jewish Christians would be familiar; for although there seems to have been no power under the Mosaic law for a man to distribute his property by will, the customs of other nations, and especially the Roman law, must have made them acquainted with the practice, and it had no doubt become common by this time among themselves.

But how was it that the inspired writer of this Epistle dropped for a moment the meaning in which he had been using the word up till now, and adopted the other meaning? I think the answer is not difficult. The ruling idea in his mind at this point in the Epistle is that a new dispensation rests on the sacrifice of Christ. The persons to whom he is writing had probably been humiliated, as I have shown in previous sermons, by the shameful circumstances of Christ's death. He wants to make them feel that that death, instead of being forgotten or evaded, is to be regarded as a transcendently sublime and significant fact. The argument of the early part of the chapter has that effect. He wants to fix the truth firmly in the conviction of the Jewish Christians, and having said that under the new covenant which rests on Christ's death, we are "*to receive the eternal inheritance,*" the idea at once occurs to him that ordinary inheritances rest also upon the death of those from whom they are derived. He, therefore, employs the word he has been using, in its most common secular meaning;—it is as if he had said, This death of Christ, of which you are ashamed, from the thought of which you shrink, is as indispensable to the establishment of the covenant under which you are to possess the everlasting inheritance, as the death of the testator is, to the efficacy of the will under which his heirs possess their secular property—"*Where a testament is, there must also of necessity be—brought in* or adduced—*the death of the testator. For a testament is of force after men are dead, otherwise it is of no strength while the testator liveth.*"

And there is a profound truth hinted at in the sudden transition to this meaning of the term. It is not a mere play on words. The new relations between God and man may be justly regarded as resting rather on a will than on a covenant. In a covenant there are conditions to be fulfilled on both sides. The terms require fidelity from both parties. But the inheritance we hope for, hardly seems to depend on our fulfilling the conditions of a proper covenant. There is no proportion between what God requires of us, and what He intends to bestow. The inheritance is a free gift; it has to be received with gratitude rather than purchased by obedience. It is like what comes to us by the terms of a will, rather than what we secure by fulfilling the provisions of a bond.

And now, in the eighteenth verse, he returns to the idea of a covenant. He has still in his mind the truth which originated the reference to a will,—that Christ's death is the foundation of the new spiritual order; and he says that in harmony with this "*the first covenant was not dedicated or inaugurated without blood.*" For the same reason that a real atonement was necessary to introduce the new dispensation, symbolic atonements were necessary to introduce the old.

The account given in these verses of the ceremonies which accompanied the solemn ratification of the Mosaic covenant is much fuller than that given in Exodus xxiv, in which nothing is said about the sprinkling of the book with blood; and the account of the ceremonies at the consecration of the tabernacle is much fuller than that in Exodus xl, in which an anointing with oil is spoken of, but not a sprinkling with blood. We know, however, from Leviticus viii, 30, that when Aaron and his sons were consecrated to the priesthood, blood was sprinkled both on them and their garments. No doubt the description given in these verses of the ritual on the two occasions referred to had come down by tradition, and it is confirmed by the spirit and provisions of the whole Levitical system. "*Almost all things were by the law purified with blood, and without blood there was no remission.*"

When the covenant was ratified, and when the tabernacle was consecrated, the blood of bulls and goats reminded the Jewish people that there could be no friendly relations established between them and God,—that they could have no access to Him,—without the acknowledgment of sin on *their* part, and a merciful provision for pardoning it on His.

Their transgressions would defile the very sanctuary in which they worshipped. It was necessary to sprinkle it with blood in anticipation of their entrance; and, year after year, blood was shed again and solemnly applied to the altar of incense, from which the symbol of their prayer and adoration ascended continually; and blood was sprinkled on the very Holy of Holies itself. As the condition of our spiritual access to God a better sacrifice must be slain; nobler blood must be shed. We should defile the invisible tabernacle in which we worship, the city of the saints needing "no temple, for the Lord God Almighty and the Lamb is the temple of it"—"the heavenly places in which we are blessed with all spiritual blessings in Christ"—if atonement had not been made before we were suffered to draw near to God. The death of Christ has effected this atonement. It signalises the founding of a new covenant—the consecration of a new sanctuary. The heavenly world is free to us now, and we can offer, without fear, spiritual worship.

ATONEMENT.

" For Christ is not entered into the holy places made with hands, which are the figures of the true; but into heaven itself, now to appear in the presence of God for us. . . . Now, where remission of these is, there is no more offering for sin."—HEBEWS ix, 24-x, 18.

THIS passage is most intimately connected with that which we considered last Sunday morning. In the fifteenth verse of the ninth chapter, the writer has declared that since by the death of Christ the soul is cleansed from the impurity of dead works to serve the living God, " *Christ is the Mediator of a New Covenant.*" This is the root of the whole series of thoughts with which the argumentative part of the Epistle closes.

The sacred writer is evidently most anxious to fix in the heart and judgment of the Jewish Christians this great truth,— that the system of Moses, with its laws and promises, with its visible sanctuary and symbolic ritual, passed away when Christ died. The crucifixion, which seemed the last disgrace of the Church, was the foundation of all its glory and of its very existence. By the death of Christ new relations were established between God and man. His death, instead of being a thing to be forgotten or ashamed of, was like the death of a testator, which is necessary to give force to all the arrangements of his will. The blood of Christ was like the blood of the sacrifices slain at the solemn ratification of the Mosaic covenant, and at the consecration of the tabernacle to God's service; it signalised and confirmed a new covenant between God and man, and has given us access, not to a material sanctuary, but to the immediate presence of God. The sacrifice of Christ is final and complete; there is no need that it should ever be repeated.

As men have to die but once and then to be judged, so Christ had to be offered but once; and to them that wait for Him, He will appear a second time, not with the sins of mankind upon him, but unto salvation. The constant repetition of the ancient sacrifices, which were but shadows of heavenly things, indicated that they could not perfect the soul by restoring it to complete and abiding fellowship with God. Sins were recalled to mind every year; "*for it is not possible that the blood of bulls and of goats should take away sins.*' And then, two passages from the Old Testament Scriptures are quoted to show that even from the inspired books of Judaism proof might be adduced that the Jewish sacrifices gave no real satisfaction to God, and that when the New Covenant was established a complete remission of sins was to be granted, a remission implying that sacrifices were no longer necessary.

In previous discourses I have had occasion to develope at considerable length the principal truths which are essential to a right understanding of this line of thought; a verbal exposition of the whole passage is therefore unnecessary. I wish, however, to call your attention to the two passages from the Old Testament.

The first is taken from the fortieth Psalm: the verses quoted are the sixth, seventh, and eighth. The sacred writer is not careful to reproduce the exact words: he takes the Septuagint translation as it stands, although in one place, at least, that translation does not accurately represent the Hebrew original. If you turn to our own version of the Psalms, you will find that the sixth verse reads, "Sacrifice and offering Thou didst not desire; *mine ears hast Thou opened:*" in this Epistle it reads as it stands in the lxx., "Sacrifice and offering Thou wouldst not, *but a body hast Thou prepared for me.*" We need not inquire how it was that this singular change in the form of the expression found its way into the lxx; whether it was a mistake of the translators, or whether the change in the image was intentional, or whether in the Hebrew text which they used there was a different reading. What is interesting to us is, that here is a text from the Old Testament, quoted inaccurately, so far as the mere words are concerned, by an inspired writer in the New. But is the substantial accuracy of the quotation affected? Not in the least. The writer quotes the passage in its true meaning, though he does not take the trouble to change the Greek translation of the Old Testament which was in the hands of the Jews at that time, into more exact agreement with the Hebrew text. Now, if he had believed himself, if he had been anxious that others should believe, that the mere words of the Psalm were dictated by the Spirit of God, do you not think he would have been careful to rectify the translation and bring it into stricter harmony with the original text? Does not his mode of quotation show that he cared for the thought, not for the exact form in which the thought was expressed?

That the principal thought of the passage is preserved, notwithstanding the difference of the form, will be apparent on a moment's consideration. In the Psalm it is said that sacrifices and offerings were not what God desired, but "*mine ears hast Thou opened,*"—Thou hast made me understand the true spirit and meaning of thy law;—"*Lo, I come to do Thy will, O God.*" In other words—Obedience is more acceptable than sacrifice. In the Epistle it is said, Sacrifices and offerings are not what God requires, but "*a body hast Thou prepared for me,*"—Thou hast given me the nature of a man, of a creature,—that is, that I may keep Thy holy law,—"*Lo, I come to do Thy will, O God.*" In other words—Obedience is more acceptable than sacrifice.

There is nothing in the Psalm to indicate that it was anything more than an inspired utterance of David's personal gratitude and devotion to God. It does not contain, in the proper sense of the word, a Messianic prophecy. The words, "*in the volume of the Book it is written of me,*" which give the impression that the speaker is a person of whom prophecy had spoken, do not exactly represent the idea of the psalmist. He means, I think, to say, that his doing the will of God was what was prescribed to him in the inspired Scriptures. The force of the quotation lies in this, the writer of the Epistle virtually says to the Jewish Christians—You need not be alarmed or shocked when I tell you that the death of Christ has abolished and superseded the ancient sacrifices of your law. Venerable as are the institutions of Moses, and sacred as are the associations which cluster round the altar and the priest,—when Christ came into the world to establish a new covenant with a nobler and more spiritual worship, His purpose is exactly expressed in one of your own Psalms. He proclaims no heresy in affirming that your ancient ceremonial is morally valueless. He says nothing more than had been said by David himself, writing under Divine inspiration. The germ, the principle, of this doctrine, which some of you are ready to think a blasphemous insult to Moses and to God Himself from whom the Mosaic system derived its sanction, is to be found in your own Scriptures. David declared that God had no pleasure in burnt-offerings and sin-offerings, and that what God cared for was obedience. This is the exact expression of Christ's own doctrine. "*He taketh away the first, that He may establish the second.*"

It is of great importance that we should understand the manner in which the writers of the New Testament appeal to the Old. They find in the ancient Scriptures germs of truth, undeveloped principles, glimpses of something more glorious than the psalmists and prophets themselves perceived, elementary illustrations of the deepest laws of God's government; and they quote these passages to illustrate the work and confirm the doctrine of Christ. David saw that holiness was better than burnt-offerings, that if his own life were regulated by the Divine will, *that* would be more acceptable to God than the blood of the appointed sacrifices; and though it cannot be affirmed that he anticipated the sublime illustration of this principle in the obedience and submission to God's will of the Lord Jesus Christ, the principle itself had been asserted by him, and to this the New Testament writer appeals.

It is not merely in the direct prophecies of the Old Testament that the thoughtful Christian will recognise "the shadow of heavenly things;" he will find simple lessons on the highest spiritual truths in the history of the patriarchs, and the sorrows and hopes of the psalmists; just as Sir Isaac Newton is said to have first recognised in the fall of an apple the law which guides the motion of the planets, and sustains the harmonies of the universe; just as the student of the most difficult questions of philosophy will recall some of the experiences of his childhood, as affording the earliest illustrations of the most remarkable and subtle laws of man's intellectual activity.

Christ has abolished the ancient sacrifices, and established in their place His own obedience to the Divine will. And by the Divine will we are sanctified—cleansed—all hindrances to our access to God are removed "*through the offering of the body of Jesus Christ, once for all.*" Every priest stands ministering to God day by day, and repeating continually the same ineffectual sacrifices; but this Priest, "*having offered one sacrifice for sins, sat down for ever on the right hand of God;*" the completion of His atoning work is suggested by the very contrast between his own attitude and that of the merely human and symbolic priesthood: and henceforth He is "*waiting till His enemies be made His footstool.*" "*For by one offering He hath perfected for ever them that are sanctified,*" has given them an everlasting access to God.

The second passage from the Old Testament occurs in the sixteenth and seventeenth verses; it is taken from Jeremiah xxxi, 33-34, and has already been appealed to for another purpose, in the eighth chapter of this Epistle. There the writer quoted it to show that a new covenant had been foretold by the Jewish prophets. Here, the emphasis of the quotation is on the closing words: after that it had been said before, "*This is the covenant that I will make with them after those days, saith the Lord, I will put my laws into their hearts, and on their minds will I write them;*" it also said, "*their sins and their iniquities will I remember no more.*" The prophecy had intimated that in connection with the New Covenant there was to be a complete forgiveness of transgressions; and this implied that sacrifices were to cease; the calling of sins to remembrance every year, as on the day of atonement, would be no longer necessary: "*Where remission of these is there is no longer offering for sin.*"

Strangely enough, some of those who deny the expiatory

character of the sufferings of the Lord Jesus Christ have ventured to appeal to the quotation from the fortieth Psalm on behalf of their theory of the nature and purpose of His work. One of the most distinguished representatives of this school of theology has maintained that according to the teaching of this part of the Epistle Christ did not come to offer "figurative ceremonial sacrifices," which may be readily granted, "but to perform solid substantial obedience in all acts of usefulness and beneficence to mankind, by which He became a High Priest after the order of Melchizedek;"—that "the blood of Christ, or that by which he has bought us, is His love and goodness to men and obedience to God, exercised, indeed, throughout the whole of His humiliation on earth, but most eminently exhibited in His death." And it is alleged that God, on account of Christ's "goodness or perfect obedience so highly pleasing to Him, thought fit to grant unto mankind, whom he might in strict justice have destroyed for their sin and wickedness, the forgiveness of sin," etc. And it is further maintained that God delivers us from guilt by the blood of Christ, because it is the most powerful means of freeing us from the pollution and power of sin; and that it is the ground of redemption as being the means of sanctification.

This theory, while conceding that it is because of Christ that God pardons the iniquity of mankind, eliminates the atoning element altogether from the agonies of Gethsemane and the death on the cross; represents the immediate object of Christ's earthly mission as simple obedience to the precepts of the Divine law, and excludes all recognition of His voluntary submission for our sake to its penalty; maintains that God forgives the sins of mankind through Christ, not because Christ made expiation for our sins by submitting to undeserved suffering, but to demonstrate the Divine approval of Christ's holy life and patient death; it contends that we have redemption through the blood of Christ, not because His sufferings were the foundation of a new moral constitution under which the just and holy God can freely pardon our most grievous offences, but because the transforming power of Christ's bright example and the pathetic argument of His love, cleanse, renew, and ennoble our character and life.

It was a daring policy for any defender of a theory like this to attempt to sustain it on a passage taken from this Epistle; no great acuteness is necessary to demonstrate that the appeal is as presumptuous as it is bold.

The quotation from the Psalm is plainly made for the purpose of shewing that in the Jewish Scriptures themselves, there was proof that the Levitical sacrifices and offerings had no real value in God's sight; that the Christian doctrine that the blood of bulls and of goats cannot take away sins, is in harmony with the teaching of the ancient .books; that Christ in abolishing the symbolical ritual might have used David's words,—that to do God's will is better than to offer bulls and goats. In using this language, as Christ virtually did, He pronounced the abolition of the ancient service, and the introduction of something nobler in its place. But, as if to prevent the very mistake into which the advocates of this theory have fallen, the writer of the Epistle does not pause when he has said this; it might then have been inferred that the holy life of Christ, His doing God's will, had really accomplished all that to which the symbolic sacrifices had pointed; and therefore he adds, that by the will of God, we are purified, cleansed from sin, obtain the removal of whatever hindered our worship and devout service, "*by the offering of the body of Christ, once for all.*"

He rises from that general obedience to the Divine will, which is better than all the Levitical offerings, to the special and supreme proof of Christ's submission to the Father. Not to the general obedience, but to the "offering" of Himself as a sacrifice, does the writer ascribe that freedom of the soul to worship God which had been provided for symbolically by the rites of the ancient system.

But, even apart from this direct and unambiguous protection of the meaning of the passage from mistake, the whole Epistle is an answer to the theory.

Throughout this great argument, which we have examined together, there is no attempt to weaken the power of the institutions of Moses over the heart and imagination of the Jewish believers, by representing the sacrificial system as a mischievous superstition. The ancient ritual is honoured as a Divine ordinance. Shadows of heavenly things are recognised in the temple, the altar, the atonement, and the priest. If Christ came to establish the second covenant, it is admitted that Moses was divinely commissioned to establish the first. The Christian faith is exhibited throughout, as the clear and substantial revelation of what Judaism had revealed only imperfectly. The language of the old faith is employed to teach the doctrines of the new.

What ideas, then, did the Jews connect with the sin-offerings which were presented every year on the great day of atonement? Was there no laying of the sins of the people on the head of the sacrifices? Was it imagined that the benefit, whatever that may have been, derived from the service, was a kind of reward for the symbolic purity of the offerings? Was the infliction of death, was the sprinkling of blood, a subordinate part of the ritual? I had occasion, in a previous sermon, to explain the probable significance of that great day to a devout Jew, and so have anticipated the answer to these enquiries.

And is there any hint in this Epistle that we obtain forgiveness simply because God is well pleased with the obedience of His beloved Son? Does not all the doctrine, all the imagery, compel us to believe that it was not the holiness of Christ alone, but His death, which opened the way of access to God? He is a High Priest whose intercession is mighty, not merely because of the purity of His robes, but because of the blood of His sacrifice. He is a Sacrifice; and although the ancient offerings had to be without blemish, or they could not be slain in God's tabernacle and presented on God's altar, it was not their symbolic perfection, but their blood, which effected symbolic atonement for sin; and although Christ could not have made expiation for us without personal holiness, it was not His holiness, but His sufferings, which made the expiation. It is His death which gives validity to the "testament" and ratifies the "covenant;" His blood, which cleanses the heavenly sanctuary, and purifies us to serve the living God. If it can be proved that the writer who used this language and these metaphors meant to say that God's approbation of Christ's moral perfection is the ground on which God pardons our sin, I decline to attach to his teaching the authority of inspiration, I decline to acknowledge in him any claim to my intellectual respect; he is utterly destitute of the power to convey his own thoughts, and can have no right to govern mine.

But perhaps he is humouring the theological error of the Jewish believers, and talks of sacrifice and priesthood, not because there is anything in Christianity really corresponding to what the Jews meant by these words, but because the words themselves, though used by him in a different meaning, would be very pleasant to his readers, especially to those who might not happen to discover that the ideas they had always represented had altogether vanished. If it be so, then I have only to say that a writer who intentionally uses sacred words in a "non-natural sense" is a cheat and an impostor, whether he belongs to the first century or to the nineteenth. In the world of thought he occupies the same position as the man who passes bad sovereigns or a forged cheque in the world of commerce. He deserves contempt, not confidence. Instead of honouring him as a great teacher, I must despise him as a dishonest man.

But there is no excuse for this insulting slander on the writer of the Epistle to the Hebrews. It is plain he does not use the old words as a blind; he uses them in their old sense. Every link in his argument gives way, if you deprive these words of their ordinary meaning; and the whole structure of his thought, instead of being most consistent, harmonious, and intelligible, becomes a confused and irrational chaos.

Nor is it in this Epistle alone, or when the apostles are arguing with their own countrymen, that they insist on the expiatory character of the death of Christ.

To the Church at Rome Paul wrote that "God hath set forth Christ to be a propitiation (through faith) in His blood, for the remission of sins;" to the Corinthians, that "God hath made Him to be sin for us who knew no sin, that we might be made the righteousness of God through Him;" to the Ephesians, that "we have redemption through His blood, even the forgiveness of sins;" to the Thessalonians, that "Christ died for us;" to Timothy, that "Christ gave Himself a ransom for all." Peter declares that Christ "bare our sins in His own body on the tree;" suffered "the just for the unjust." John gives glory to Him who has "washed us from our sins in His own blood."

In heaven itself, where, I suppose, there can be no longer any need to humour the prejudices of the Jews, they sing a new song, saying, "Thou wast slain and hast redeemed us to God by Thy blood out of every kindred, and tongue, and people, and nation."

Speculate on it how we may, the death of the Lord Jesus Christ is presented to us in the new Testament as the everlasting reason of every happy relation between sinful man and the moral government of God.

The conscience bows before the cross and is at peace, even when the intellect is baffled and defeated in the attempt to construct a theory of the atonement. "When we were yet sinners, Christ died for us," is the answer to the deepest and most agonizing distress of the heart; and the theology which ignores or evades this truth can claim neither to be in harmony with the faith of the apostles nor to interpret the grandest and most awful facts of the spiritual universe.

THE GREAT APPEAL.

"Having therefore, brethren, boldness to enter into the holiest, by the blood of Jesus," &c.—HEBREWS x, 19-39.

AT the commencement of this series of discourses, I reminded you, that although the temptations and difficulties of our Christian life are very different from those which imperilled the fidelity and constancy of the Jewish believers, we, like them, may be in danger of falling away from Christ after we have been "once enlightened, and have tasted of the heavenly gift," and have been "made partakers of the Holy Ghost." At this very moment some of us may be drifting back into worldliness, as they were drifting back into Judaism. Like them we may be "neglecting the great salvation." The same arguments, though in a different form,—the same appeals,—the same warnings,—may be necessary to renew and strengthen our faith in Christ, to quicken our spiritual affections, to awaken our alarm.

And now that the great demonstration is closed, of the inferiority and inefficacy of the Mosaic law, and the glory and permanence of the new covenant, we have arrived at a succession of practical exhortations and an impassioned appeal, having as great a value for ourselves, as for the Churches of Palestine in the primitive age.

In the passage on which I have to speak this morning, we have the judgment of an inspired writer on the solemn questions which some of us have had occasion to consider ;—How can I renew and recover the intensity of my earlier Christian life ? How can I arrest the progress of spiritual decay ? How can I escape from the miserable, and guilty, and perilous indifference into which I have permitted myself to sink ? How can I make way against the strong tide which is drifting me to destruction?

There are three distinct duties to be at once discharged, and there are startling and affecting motives to sustain us in the endeavour to return to a better life.

I.

(1) The persons to whom the Epistle is addressed are directed, first of all, to "*draw near*" to God. It has been shown that sinful men have free access—not to a mere material temple—but to the immediate presence of God, through the Lord Jesus Christ. The Holy of Holies was but the symbol of the heavenly sanctuary, which is now open to all mankind. The blood of Christ has really atoned for the sins which excluded man from the Divine presence. There is "*a new and living way*" to the Father. The courts of the visible sanctuary were constructed of inanimate material things, of costly wood, and richly embroidered curtains; but it is through Christ Himself that we draw near to God. The death of His body was like the rending of the veil which secluded the Holy of Holies from all approach (v. 20); external baptism (v. 22) is the sign that we are members of a race whose iniquities need no longer separate them from God; and the blood of Christ, if its power and virtue are inwardly acknowledged, delivers us from the fear and dread connected with the consciousness of sin; and we ought to "*draw near with a true heart,*"—a heart free from all insincerity, willing neither to deceive itself, nor to deceive God,—and "*with full assurance of faith,*"—trusting confidently in the Divine mercy and love.

It is not enough that the judgment should be convinced of the reality and transcendent greatness of the blessings conferred upon man by the Lord Jesus Christ. An intellectual belief, however intelligent, however firm, will not have sufficient strength to stand severe and protracted trials such as threatened the Jewish Church; the soul must enter into the actual possession of the prerogatives and joys which are the inheritance of all who believe. The abstract creed must be rooted in the experience of the heart as well as in the logic of the intellect, if it is to remain firm and strong.

This is the general truth which seems implied in this exhortation. It would be useless to prove that men have access to God through Christ, unless those who were convinced of the truth drew near to God. Unless the intellectual conviction were translated into a spiritual act, the mere belief would soon pass away. The impression of the argument would be lost, if not deepened and perpetuated by the consciousness of the soul.

A truth this, of infinite importance. We ourselves are passing through times of speculative unbelief as well as of spiritual indifference. Learned argument is necessary to convince the understanding of the Divine mission and nature of Christ, but the faith of Christendom will perish unless the truth is sustained by the testimony of the inner spiritual life. You may prove that this book contains a Divine revelation, but it is very possible that the proof may go for nothing and the belief it produces perish, unless by the devout study of these sacred pages the conscience and the heart come to discover that a voice of mighty and mysterious power speaks through the writings of prophets, psalmists, evangelists, and apostles. You may prove that by the Lord Jesus Christ atonement was made for human sin, but nothing can infallibly perpetuate a full assurance of this great doctrine, except the consciousness that through Christ's death the soul is enabled to speak to God without fear. If the creed, no matter how orthodox, is separated from a vigorous and healthy spiritual life, no logic, no learning, can prevent it from perishing: unless it brings forth fruit it is cast forth as a branch, it withers, it is burned. Having demonstrated that by the death of Christ we have access to God, the inspired writer endeavours to rivet and secure the conviction he has produced, by saying, "*Let us draw near.*"

This exhortation should be most gratefully received by all who are conscious that they have permitted their religious life to sink into feebleness. To "*draw near*" to God is not only possible to them still—it is their immediate duty. The blood of Christ will deliver them from terror. When they stand in the Divine presence they will see by their side "*the great Priest*" who has atoned for their sins and ever liveth to make intercession for them. Remember that these words were expressly addressed to those who had been sharply rebuked and sternly warned. They are especially for you, who have just discovered that, though you once believed, you have now an evil heart of unbelief, and that you have begun to depart from the living God. Their direct appeal is not to those who have served God faithfully, but to those who are in danger of apostatising from Christ altogether.

And if it be still possible for you to approach God, how strong are the reasons that should induce you to do it! You greatly need His pardon. Your sins are more grievous than the sins you confessed when you came to him first, and if they remain unforgiven, they will involve you in a more appalling destruction than that which you first sought to escape. You greatly need the power of His Spirit to invigorate your religious life: it is not yet impossible to renew you to repentance; but where love to Christ has been overborne by the love of pleasure, where thirst for communion with God has been deadened by the passion for wealth, where zeal for the Divine glory has been quenched by sluggishness and sin, the difficulty of delivering the soul from its shameful and guilty relapse is manifestly great, and it increases every day.

"*Draw near to God*," then; though you find it almost impossible to pray. "*Draw near to God*," though all the joy of communion with Him has gone, and your only feeling is that of almost intolerable shame and self-contempt. "*Draw near to God*," though you feel as though even He could not recover you from the entanglements of sin and give you the spiritual freedom which you once possessed. Even for you, the blood of the great Sacrifice has atoned; and the intercession of the great Priest will be effectual for you.

(2) These vacillating Jewish believers are directed to "*hold fast the profession of*" their "*hope without wavering.*"

Prayer would not be enough, without the firm and energetic resolve "to hold fast" that which they professed. They had once exulted in the anticipation of a glorious future. They had confessed that the Lord Jesus Christ had come to confer on men, not a mere earthly inheritance, but everlasting blessedness and splendour.

But their hope had been slipping from their grasp. No longer were they eagerly waiting for the hour when Christ should appear with glittering armies of angels and with the sainted dead in robes of white. No longer did they anticipate with rapture their entrance through the gates of pearl and their abode in the mansions which Christ had gone to prepare for all that love Him. The clear vision of the ever brightening splendours of immortality no longer made them forget shame and suffering and danger. Dense clouds had settled on their future, and without the inspiration it had once afforded, the struggles and persecutions of their Christian life had become intolerable.

Their former hope must be grasped again, and the confession of it boldly maintained. In happy song, in exulting hallelujahs, they must declare once more that they cling still to the promises of God.

"*For He is faithful that promised.*" One is tempted to turn aside from the main current of the thought to linger on these pleasant words, just as in travelling through some strange country one is sometimes induced to interrupt a journey for a day or two, attracted by the peace and beauty of some quiet valley, and tempted to explore all its loveliness.

In a very obvious and legitimate sense the whole of Divine revelation is a promise. That God should have manifested Himself by supernatural methods to man at all, is an indication that he has not cast us off because of our transgressions, and that all hope is not yet destroyed. He spoke to man as soon as man had sinned, to prevent despair; and all that He has revealed of Himself encourages our confidence. "They that know Thy name will put their trust in Thee."

The doctrine of the Incarnation is a promise; it assures us that God has become man to save us from sin. The doctrine of the Atonement is a promise; it explains the grounds on which God grants the pardon of sin. The doctrine of Justification is a promise that the penalty of sin may be cancelled;

the doctrine of Sanctification, that the power of sin may be destroyed.

The very narratives of the Old Testament and the New are promises; the past is recalled to fill the future with peace and joy. God's fidelity to Abraham, His providence over Joseph, His mercy to David, His amazing forbearance with the Jewish race,—are all reasons and arguments for trusting in Him.

The very laws of Gods are promises. Laws are not given to the lost, but only to those who can either obey them, or who are to be led by a sense of their sinfulness to appeal to the Divine mercy for pardon and salvation. That God tells us how to live, proves that he still cares for our obedience; nay, His precepts indicate, not so much the measure of the strength to obey Him that we naturally possess, as the measure of the help which he intends to afford to our obedience. "Thy statutes have been my songs in the house of my pilgrimage."

But look at those passages in Holy Scripture which are properly called Promises. They are so numerous that when collected they make a volume. Read every one of them, remembering that "*He is faithful that promised.*"

Read them, remembering that *they are meant to be fulfilled.* Of course this is implied in the very form of a promise; but if I am not greatly mistaken, this is not always heartily believed, even by very good people; and with many of us, the moments are comparatively infrequent, when we really expect God to be "*faithful.*" Is it not true that, sometimes, even in great trouble, we read the most precious promises in Holy Scripture, just as we read pleasant poems, to tranquillize and soothe our agitated hearts by their mere music and sweetness?

The very idea of rest is a refreshment to the weary, the mere dream of conquest over sin is a solace to those who are wretched under defeat, the bare conception of perfect holiness, and of abiding for ever in God, has a purifying and elevating influence on the sinful soul. "Cast thy burden upon the Lord, and He shall sustain thee;" there is strength in the thought of that—quite apart from the expectation of receiving actual support. "The Lord God is a sun and shield; the Lord will give grace and glory; no good thing will he withhold from them that walk uprightly ;"—words like these make the heart leap and sing, even when there is no definite and firm confidence that they will be actually fulfilled. But it is shameful unbelief to think that God will not keep His promises. He was not obliged to give them at all. When he gave them, He meant they should be kept.

Aye, and we may take the promises of God in their fullest and broadest meaning. Fidelity includes not exciting groundless expectations as well as standing true to the bare letter of what we have said. We are responsible for all that we consciously lead men to hope for, and not merely for the close and legal interpretation of our word. But we are too apt to treat God as though we thought Him in the habit of talking beyond His meaning,—as though we thought that He had sometimes been hurried away by excitement into promises so magnificent that we could not reasonably expect Him to fulfil them. We forget that " the word of the Lord is *tried*,"—refined, purified, like silver and gold, in which there is no alloy ; and that " He is able to do exceeding abundantly above all that we ask or think."

Nor are the promises of God to be thought of as though they were the formal terms of a treaty. There may be times when the soul may need all the strength derived from the knowledge that He has given His pledge never to forsake any that put their trust in Him; but it is nobler to go to Him with an unstinted confidence, to be willing that the papers which bear His signature should be cast into the fire, and to think of all the assurances of His mercy and grace rather as appeals to our faith than as bonds of His fidelity. If he had never promised anything, He would bless us just as bountifully.

But, though we do not need God's promises to make Him unchangeably good to us, how desolate the world would have been, had He never spoken them ! I like to remember how they have been the strength and consolation of a long line of saints. When a river is flowing at our feet, we often, in imagination, trace it along its course from the remote and silent hills where the melting snows and the perennial springs give birth to its waters,—and on through the dark glens where it wanders as a brook among the green grass and the wild flowers and the graceful ferns,—and through plains which are yellow in harvest-time with the golden corn, and between frowning cliffs, and by quiet villages, and under the crumbling walls of ancient cities; and so these promises of God have been flowing on through age after age, cherishing a thousand forms of spiritual life and beauty. They gave rapture to David's praise; they kindled the fire of apostolic zeal in the heart of Paul, and Peter, and John; confessors in their prisons, martyrs at the stake,—"a multitude that no man can number,"—saintly men and women who are now among the angels of God, found in these promises courage to confront all danger, patience to endure all suffering, peace and triumph in the hour of death. You may not be able to visit the spots which the memories of these holy men have consecrated; but you are on the very brink of the living waters at which they drank immortal strength; and you are surrounded by the mountainous outlines of the glorious hopes on which they delighted to gaze. "*He is faithful that promised.*"

(3) These Jewish Christians are directed to "*consider one another to provoke unto love and good works,*" and not to "*forsake the assembling*" of themselves together.

The aids to be derived from Christian fellowship are especially needed by those who have become spiritually feeble and are drifting back to sin. The Jewish believers had been grievously injured by their negligence in maintaining religious intercourse with each other, and attending the meetings of the Church. The turbid torrent of patriotic fanaticism was rushing fiercely past them, and a firm and hearty union of affection and sympathy with their fellow-Christians would have confirmed their fidelity to Christ.

And it is to me a matter of astonishment that in these days, when the excitements of business are plainly working such disastrous effects on the religious earnestness of the Church, Christian men do not more clearly see that their only safety lies in drawing more closely the bonds of Christian fellowship. You are often too weary and anxious to pray alone, with any concentration of thought or any fervour of feeling, but you would find that among your brethren, the pulses of a genial and healthy excitement would begin to throb in your souls. Listening at first with sluggish unconcern to their songs of adoration, you would soon begin to glow with sympathetic gratitude and joy. Unmoved at first by their earnest supplications, you would soon be conscious that the fires of devotion were kindling in your hearts. You will find yourself breathing a calmer air, surrounded by a purer light, and would go home, not to say that you had discharged your duty, and that private worship was now unnecessary, but thirsting for still more intimate communion with God.

II.

I can only refer very briefly to the motives with which these exhortations are enforced.

(1) "*Ye see the day approaching*"—the final catastrophe, in which the polity of the Jewish church and state was to be broken up, was at hand. The signs of its approach were thickening and multiplying; and the Hebrew Christians had been taught to look forward to it as "the bloody and fiery dawn" of the Great Day itself. To relapse into Judaism at the very time that the appalling judgments of God were hanging over the Jewish nation,—to apostatise from Christ in the very presence of that dread event, which, in its spiritual significance and temporal horrors, would be no faint anticipation of the more awful hour when the Lord Jesus would "be revealed from heaven in flaming fire, taking vengeance on them that know not God and that obey not the Gospel of our Lord Jesus Christ," would be the insanity of wickedness.

(2) For those that abandon their Christian profession—"*sin wilfully after*" that they "*have received the knowledge of the truth, there remaineth no more sacrifice for sins.*" They could not return to the temple, and plead with God for mercy over the offerings which their fathers had presented to Him. The old covenant had passed away. Its priests had lost their con-

secration. Its altars had lost their sanctity. Its sacrifices had lost their power with God. There was now only one atonement for sin which God would regard; and if they turned away from that, there was nothing for them "*but a certain fearful looking for of judgment and fiery indignation, which shall devour the adversaries.*" For a Jew to be left with all his sins upon him, and no sin-offering by which to invoke the Divine pardon, was for him to be condemned to intolerable despair.

(3) Nor would apostates be merely left with their common transgressions unexpiated; the guilt of their apostacy would bring a dreadful penalty: "*He that despised Moses' law died without mercy, under two or three witnesses; of how much sorer punishment, suppose ye, shall he be thought worthy who hath trodden under foot the Son of God, and hath counted the blood of the covenant, wherewith He was sanctified, an unholy thing, and hath done despite to the Spirit of Grace? For we know Him that hath said, Vengeance belongeth unto me, I will recompense, saith the Lord. And again, The Lord shall judge His people. It is a fearful thing to fall into the hands of the living God.*"

(4) They are exhorted to "*call to remembrance the former days*" the days of their early Christian life—in which they "*endured a great fight of afflictions.*" They had begun well, and their boldness and courage, if only sustained to the end, would bring a "*great recompense of reward:*" "*cast not away therefore your confidence.*"

(5) There is an appeal to Hope. They had "*need of endurance,*" that they might continue to "*do the will of God, and receive the promise.*" Only let them wait, and God would fulfil His word; only let them wait, and their troubles would all pass away. "*For yet a little while, and He that is to come will come, and will not tarry.*" But for them, as for the saints in the old time, unfaltering trust in God is necessary; "*the just,*" Habbakuk had said, "*shall live by faith.*" This was the law under the old covenant; it is the law still under the new; and "*if any man draw back*"—weary of trusting in My word—"*My soul shall have no pleasure in him.*" "*But we,*" concludes the writer, "*are not of them that draw back unto perdition; but*

of them who believe to the saving of the soul." After his ordinary manner, he cannot leave his readers agitated and alarmed by words of terror and threatening; he asserts, indeed, the imperative necessity of preserving faith, if salvation is to be secured, but lovingly and hopefully expresses his confidence that his brethren, though sorely tried and weakly vacillating, will, after all, stand true to their Lord.

THE CLOUD OF WITNESSES.

"Now faith is the substance of things hoped for," &c
HEBREWS xi, 1;—xii, 3.

IN Christ's last discourse to His disciples, He had distinctly foretold the great trouble which was now impending over the Jewish believers—"They shall put you out of their synagogues." Hitherto the Jewish Christians had continued to celebrate the ancient ritual, and their presence in the temple and the synagogues had been tolerated by their unbelieving countrymen: but now, they were in danger of excommunication, and it is hardly possible for us to conceive their distress and dismay. Their veneration for the institutions of Moses had not been diminished by their acknowledgment of the Messiahship of the Lord Jesus; for them, as well as for the rest of their race, an awful sanctity rested on the ceremonies from which they were threatened with exclusion. Nor was this all.

The intensity of national feeling among the Jews at this time has never been paralleled in any age or in any country, and the ties which united the Jewish Christians to each other had not yet become strong enough to compensate for the loss of all fellowship with their countrymen. The Nation was more to them than the Church.

When threatened with separation from the solemnities of the ancient worship,—from the priesthood, the altars, the sacrifices, the festivals,—it must have seemed to them that they were threatened with the loss of all those venerable and sacred recollections which were the most cherished possession of their race. Their connection with the past would be broken as well as with the present. When banished from the temple, they would no longer be able to claim any part in Abraham, Moses, David, and the prophets. Excommunication was more terrible than the loss of property, or the loss of life itself.

Therefore, the writer of this Epistle calls up the most glorious names of Jewish history to confirm his vacillating brethren in their fidelity to the Lord Jesus Christ. He demonstrates that all the saints of former generations had been conspicuous for their invincible faith in the Divine word; that this was their common characteristic, whether they were warriors, prophets, martyrs, or kings; that by faith they had won God's approbation, and wrought deliverance for their country; and the spirit and meaning of the whole chapter is this—that the Jewish Christians had only to imitate the example of their most illustrious ancestors.

It was not by offering sacrifices, nor by attending festivals, nor by the pomp and exactness with which they had celebrated any external rites and ceremonies, that the noblest of their forefathers had won their greatness, but by their firm and stedfast trust in God. The inspired writer had been exhorting them to "hold fast" the confession of their faith without wavering,— not to "cast away" their " confidence,"—to "wait patiently" for the fulfilment of the Divine promise; and now he shows that a *conviction of the reality of things unseen*, triumphing over all visible difficulties and outward calamities, a *confident persuasion of the certainty of things hoped for*, making the heart strong to bear present suffering, and to endure the sickening weariness of disappointment and delay, had been the life of the Jewish people from the beginning,—the great characteristic of their religion,—the supreme glory of their saints. From the very first, what God had asked for, what He had chiefly honoured, was that very reliance on His word, from which, in this moment of peril and perplexity, the Jewish Christians were shrinking. Let us see how he illustrates and developes this truth.

He begins at the very opening of their sacred books, and reminds them that the first article of their religious creed rested on faith. It was because of the Divine word, and the Divine word alone, that they believed that "in the beginning God created the heavens and the earth,"—that "*the worlds were framed by the word of God.*"

He turns the page, and reads the story of Cain and Abel. The two brothers bring their sacrifices to God : the one a lamb, for he was a shepherd ; the other, fruits of the earth, for he was a tiller of the ground. Both these sacrifices were in themselves acceptable to God, for under the Levitical institutions, wheat and barley were offered by the Divine command, as well as lambs, and bullocks, and goats. But the "*faith*" of Abel made his sacrifice "*more excellent*" than that of Cain ; and "*by his faith,*" not by his sacrifice, "*he obtained witness that he was righteous,—God,*" in some way, "*bearing testimony*" to him when he was presenting "*his gifts.*" The narrative in Genesis tells us nothing about the reason why " He had respect unto Abel and his offering," or why " to Cain and to his offering he had not respect." I suppose that the explanation given here of the difference between the religious acts of the two brothers was commonly received among the Jews to whom this Epistle was addressed, and there was no need for the writer to fortify the explanation by any proof ;—by adopting it he has given it the sanction of his own authority.*

A little further on in the book of Genesis, the writer finds a genealogical table, and he reads that Adam died, Seth died, Enos died, Cainan died ; but presently comes an interruption to the dreary monotony of the record—" Enoch walked with God, and he was not, for God took him." " He walked with God." Nothing is said about the building of a temple, or the consecration of priests, or the slaying of sacrifices. "*He pleased God ; but without faith it is impossible to please Him : for he that cometh to God, must believe that He is, and that He is a rewarder of them that diligently seek Him.*" Enoch's acceptable service and holy life rested on his faith.

As the details of the sacred history become more numerous,

---

* " God is not taken with the cabinet, but with the jewel ; He first respected Abel's faith and sincerity, and then his sacrifice ; He disrespected Cain's infidelity and hypocrisy, and then his offering."—*Charnock,* i, 300 (Nichol's edition).

the writer finds more striking and obvious proofs of his principle. But for faith, the whole race would have perished, and the history of mankind would have come to a miserable end in the waters of the flood. It was not by sacrifices and ceremonies that Noah saved himself and his children, but "*being warned of God of things not seen as yet,*" he believed, in the Divine word, "*was moved with fear, and prepared an ark to the saving of his house.*"

And as the world would have perished but for the faith of Noah, the national distinctions of the Jewish race would never have been theirs,—the Jewish race would never have existed at all,—but for the faith of Abraham. His faith was his great title to human veneration, as it was the great reason which obtained for him the Divine favour. Nor was it by one act of confidence in God that the promises inherited from him by his descendants were secured; crisis after crisis occurred in his history when all would have been lost, had his trust in God failed. When he was called to leave the land of his fathers, he might have distrusted God and refused to go; but through faith "*he obeyed, and he went out, not knowing whither he went.*" For years he wandered in the land of promise, having no property there, moving about from place to place among tribes who were constantly increasing in numbers, wealth, and power; and he might naturally enough have lost all hope that the land would ever become his; but his confidence in the Divine word was unshaken. The time came when, according to the course of nature, he and Sarah could no longer expect a child, and, but for their faith, Isaac would never have been born, and the history of the Jewish race never have begun; but through faith "*there sprang even of one, and him as good as dead, so many as the stars of the sky in multitude, and as the sand of the sea shore innumerable.*" When that child was rising to man's estate, Abraham was called to offer him as a sacrifice; and had he shrunk from the trial, the great promises he had received would surely have been cancelled; but by faith "*he offered up Isaac * * * his only begotten son, of whom it was said, In Isaac shall thy seed be called, accounting that God is able even to raise from the dead.*" Throughout Abraham's history there is nothing to indicate that it is by observing the external rites of a ceremonial religion that the Divine favour is won; everything rests on a high and unconquerable trust in the word of God,—a trust defying all adverse appearances, unsubdued by present sorrows, and resting immoveably in "things unseen" and "things hoped for."

It was the same with Isaac; the same with Jacob; the same with Joseph; they all died with the promises unfulfilled, but "blessed" their descendants and "gave commandments concerning their bones," in the sure confidence that God would be faithful to His word. They died in faith, and inasmuch as the earthly inheritance had not become theirs, they set their hearts upon "*a better country, that is a heavenly; wherefore God is not ashamed to be called their God.*"

The history of Moses is as full of illustrations of the significance and power of faith as that of Abraham himself. He would have perished in infancy but for the faith of his parents. But for his own faith he would have abandoned the fortunes of his countrymen and become "*the son of Pharaoh's daughter*" It was faith which inspired him with courage and boldness to lead the people out of Egypt; faith which prompted him to arrange for the celebration of "*the passover;*" faith which divided the waters of "*the Red Sea,*" for the armies of Israel to pass through on dry ground. Trust in God,—this was the law of his life, and this was the power which wrought out the deliverance of the nation.

"*The walls of Jericho fell down*" because Joshua had faith in the Divine command; "*the harlot Rahab*" saved her life by her faith in the Divine power. "*Gideon,*" "*Barak,*" "*Samson,*" "*Jephthæ,*" "*David,*" "*Samuel;*" all the illustrious names in the Jewish annals, the memory of whose valour, sufferings, and triumphs, was even now adding fire to patriotic passion, and giving courage to despair, had all been strong in the strength of faith. They had trusted God, when cruel calamities had broken the spirit of their countrymen: they had trusted Him, when His providence had seemed to forsake them, and when torture and death were their only reward. In the strength of their faith they had won glorious victories; in the strength of their faith they had made suffering and disaster sublime. Through faith they had "*subdued kingdoms, wrought righteousness, obtained promises, stopped the mouths of lions, quenched the violence of fire, escaped the edge of the sword, out of weakness were made strong, waxed valiant in fight, turned to flight the armies of aliens. Women received their dead raised to life again; and others were tortured, not accepting deliverance; that they might obtain a better resurrection; and others had trials of cruel mockings and scourgings, yea moreover, of bonds and imprisonments; they were stoned, they were sawn asunder, they were slain with the sword: they wandered about in sheepskins and goatskins; being destitute, afflicted, tormented; (of whom the world was not worthy): they wandered in deserts and in mountains, and in dens and caves of the earth.*"

And now the followers of Christ were called to emulate the heroic confidence of their ancestors. The virtue which had been most conspicuous in the history of their fathers was the very virtue demanded by the perils and sufferings which at this moment encompassed them. They might be driven from the communion of their contemporaries; but if their faith was unbroken, they would enter into fellowship with the noblest saints of former generations. In their isolation from the Jewish church and state of their own days they would become the brethren of Abel, and Enoch, and Noah, and Abraham, and Moses, and Joshua, and David, and Samuel, and all the prophets. It was for them to add a new and shining chapter to the history of their race; to prove that still the Jew could hold fast his confidence in things hoped for, in spite of present miseries, and could sacrifice all visible blessings,—comfort, ease, honour, the outward solemnities of an ancient religious life,—for the sake of things unseen. They are "*surrounded by a great cloud of witnesses.*" They have to choose between communion with their countrymen who have rejected the true Messiah, and fellowship in faith, in suffering, in endurance, in final glory with all the good of past generations. They have to choose between bearing the contempt and the hatred and the cruelty of living men, and disappointing the hopes of the illustrious dead. It is impossible to hesitate · they must "*lay aside every weight,"*—their innocent, their honourable devotion to their country, their sympathy with the struggle for national independence, their traditional veneration for the temple and its services : "*and the sin*" which, like a loose garment clinging to the limbs of a runner, impeded all their energy,—the sin of unbelief, of impatience, of being ashamed of Christ; "*and run with patience,*" or endurance, "*the race set before*" them.

This is the general spirit and drift of the writer's appeal to the great names which all Jews regarded with love and pride; and it is inconceivable that this thrilling passage could have been read to any church in Palestine without tears of wonder, penitence, and delight. And after the first shock of its fervid eloquence had passed away, it would be seen that every separate link in the impassioned argument was flashing with electric inspiration; and I can imagine one man after another rising in the church and drawing courage and hope and entreaty and warning from every separate sentence. By faith "*the elders obtained a good report,*"—and we, by trusting in God, and defying present shame, may also win the honour of coming generations. "*Through faith we understand that the worlds were framed by the word of God,*" and for that truth we should be ready to suffer the most cruel tortures and the most horrible death; we have the same ground for confidence in the glory promised to all that are true to Christ, and for that too should be prepared to endure all that the hatred of our enemies can inflict. What though we perish like Abel?—our blood, like his, shall cry aloud to God, and our death shall be eloquent to all generations : or it may be that God in His mercy will deliver us from the power of our foes and translate us, like Enoch, to heaven. We are alone in the world; like Noah, we are surrounded by a wicked and impious generation,—but as God threatened to destroy the old world with a flood, so hath Christ warned us that frightful calamities are coming upon our country and our race; and if we only trust in the Divine word, spite of mockery and contempt, we may be saved ourselves from the judgments of heaven, and may become the fathers of a new and more godly race.

Like Abraham, we may have to leave the house of our ancestors; may be driven from the temple to which our hearts cling with an imperishable affection; like him, we may be unable to penetrate into the future, and may not know whither God is leading us; but if we obey, God will surely give us a better inheritance than that which for His sake we forsake. To us there may seem no reasonable hope of success in the enterprise to which we have put our hand; but Abraham also, to whom God had promised a numerous seed, remained childless till old age, and yet at last God gave him a son.

In Isaac were treasured the blessed hopes which were Abraham's recompense for a life-time of endurance, and yet Isaac was to be slain; in the institutions of Moses are treasured the strength and joy of our religious life, and yet the institutions of Moses must be abandoned; let us believe that God is able to restore to us what we are losing, and to "raise the dead" body of our ancient faith in a nobler and more glorious form, and that we may henceforth find in the CHURCH more than the holiest of our fathers have ever found in the TEMPLE.

The whole chapter is intended to carry to the Churches of Palestine the conviction that the true representatives of the ancient saints are henceforth to be found among those, who for Christ's sake are excluded from participation in the national acts of worship. They are to be sustained under the contempt and hatred of their contemporaries, by their veneration for their ancestors.

Nor was this the whole effect of the appeal. It is a law of human nature that the motives to discharge any duty are multiplied and stengthened when we see it illustrated in the acts and sufferings of good men. The consciences of these Jewish believers had told them that they ought to stand firm against persecution. Their fears had been alarmed by the penalties denounced against apostasy. Their intellect had begun to discover that, in losing the temple and sacrifices of their fathers, they lost only the visible symbols of the true atonement for sin and of spiritual access to God; but every passion of their souls is stirred when they are challenged to imitate the example, and to win the rewards. of the very noblest men of the old time. The abstract law becomes a thing of flesh and blood. The imagination and the affections sustain the authority of conscience. A holy ambition is awakened. The heart burns for fellowship with the illustrious dead. They too, in their day, had been compassed about with infirmity, and what through God's help had been achieved once, might be achieved again. And thus it is that the memory of conspicuous goodness fires the zeal and invigorates the courage of remote generations.

We know the power of any appeal to the great names of our secular history. There is no scholar, however humble or obscure, whose exhausted energy is not renewed when he is reminded of the famous students of former times. The honours which cluster and thicken, as the ages roll by, round the names of great poets, artists, philosophers, statesmen, stimulate the enthusiasm and sustain the energy of those who, in distant times and countries, strive for the same glory. When nations are struggling for freedom, it is not living patriotism alone which gives strength to their arms and daring to their hopes,—the memory of the patriots of other lands and of other centuries kindles enthusiasm and inspires heroic endurance. Defeated, while living, in their conflicts with tyranny, they triumph gloriously after death.

It is no doubt the prerogative of men who have been endowed with great powers, or held great positions, thus to act permanently on the imaginations and the passions of mankind; but, without learning, without genius, without official rank, without social distinction, it is yet possible for every Christian man to illustrate to the hearts of some, the beauty of holiness, and to vindicate by his personal obedience, the authority of God. Every holy life is a visible republication of the Divine law, a solemn appeal to the consciences of men, an unanswerable proof that in this world of temptation and sin, it is possible to recover the image of God and to live so as to please Him. Your life may not become famous. Orators, in coming ages, may not recall your names amidst the plaudits of crowded assemblies. But the craving for an immortal reputation, natural, I suppose, to the heart of man, may yet be satisfied; for if the soul of the humblest, poorest, most ignorant among your friends and acquaintances, is prompted or encouraged to live a holy life by your example, the memory of your deeds will endure as long as the blessedness of the glorified.

In the verses with which the eleventh chapter closes, the writer reminds the Jewish Christians that, severe as was the trial of their own faith, it was, in one particular, less severe than that to which their fathers had been subjected. "*These all, having obtained a good report through faith*, received not the promise, *God having provided some better thing for us, that they without us should not be made perfect.*"

Through one weary century after another, the patriarchs and prophets had waited for the kingdom of God, and their faith had been equal to the prolonged strain. For them there was no real sacrifice for sin. Their access to the Divine presence was imperfect. The spiritual powers by which their holiness was sustained were comparatively feeble. Their knowledge of God was very limited. The great promise on which their hearts rested, began to be fulfilled only at the coming of the Lord Jesus. We might almost say that they had nothing in actual possession; that for them everything lay in an indefinite future. It was not so with those to whom this Epistle was written: it is not so with us.

The Messiah, for whom former ages hoped, has come. The kingdom of heaven has been established. The atonement for sin has been effected. In the person of Christ our nature has been united for ever with the nature of God. We ourselves are made one with Him, and have become the temples of the Holy Ghost. Instead of having to rely on an unfulfilled promise, we have to thank God that the mystery and wealth of the Divine Word have begun to be unfolded. The process of fulfilment has commenced, and is moving forward day by day. What was a matter of simple faith in other ages, is a matter of knowledge and of consciousness to ourselves.

This however is only a part of the meaning of these remarkable words. They seem to teach that there is a unity between the spirits of the just who have departed this life, and the Church remaining upon earth, far more intimate than we commonly suppose. Not merely while the saints of ancient times lived, were they waiting for the coming of Christ; even after their decease their bliss was imperfect. They rested in God; but the fulness of their spiritual bliss was not attained, until God became man, died for human sin, and established the kingdom of heaven.

There was an intimate connection between the ascension of the Lord Jesus Christ to the Father, and the coming of the Holy Ghost—a connection which I think the profoundest theologians have been able only most inadequately to understand. Why, we know not, but the Spirit could not come until Christ was glorified. And it seems that the saints above were waiting for the fuller communication of the Divine life, as well as the saints below. For them, as well as for us, a closer union with God became possible when humanity was made one with God, in the complex nature of the Lord Jesus. They were not to reach the consummation of their spiritual strength and joy and the fulness of their blessedness, "*without us.*" The promise fulfilled to us, brought to them what they had long been waiting for.

It is altogether probable, that among the Jewish Christians there would be great anxiety to know what had been the condition, in the unseen world, of their saintly forefathers who had died before the coming of the Messiah. It is probable, too, that on this subject revelations may have been made by the apostles which were not recorded in Holy Scripture, because their chief interest and practical importance would cease before the true tradition of their teaching had been corrupted and passed away. An incidental sentence of this kind seems to imply a knowledge, in primitive times, of the state of good men who had died before Christ came, which has disappeared from the memory of the Church.

But it is clear that the truths here alluded to, not fully expressed, gave great additional force to the argument and appeal of the writer. Your fathers, he says, the greatest of them, while they lived, and after they entered Paradise, were waiting and hoping, for the coming of Christ. Neither on earth nor in Heaven could they be "*made perfect*" until He came. Till His birth, till His death, till His ascension to glory, *their* life was a life of faith; and yet *you* are ready—though the Divine promise is already in part fulfilled—to surrender your confidence in God, because the complete fulfilment is still delayed.*

It is implied that "the spirits of the just" were longing for the fulfilment on earth, of the promise God had given in the old time. Their attention was fixed on the movements of Divine Providence, which prepared for the coming of our Lord Jesus Christ. They gazed with awe and wonder and unutterable solicitude on His birth and childhood, and the acts of His public ministry; they watched, and not afar off, the agony in the garden and the mystery of the cross; they waited, not with doubt and fear, but with eager, confident hope, for His resurrection from the dead; they filled Heaven with an ocean of exulting, rapturous song when He ascended to His throne. Nor would they cease to bend their eyes towards the earth when He was no longer there. Those to whom the great struggle with the powers of evil was entrusted were their brethren; and their own ultimate perfection would not be attained until the fight on earth was over and the victory won. They formed a great "*cloud of witnesses*," testifying from their thrones to the fidelity of God to His promises, for the encouragement of those whose faith was sorely tried, and whose hearts were failing in the strife.

Finally. It is not merely to mortal men that these Jewish believers are exhorted to look, in order that their trust in God may be sustained to the end. Christ Himself is the most

---

* However obscure and mysterious this may be, it is certain from other parts of Holy Scripture that even now, those who are with Christ have not entered into the full inheritance of everlasting glory; and it is still true, though in a different sense, that "without us" they are not to be "made perfect." The resurrection of the body is everywhere referred to, as necessary to the perfection of the heavenly state. The "*spirits* of the just" are made perfect by the coming of Christ; but there is a perfection still before them which they will not know until the whole Church is ready to enter into everlasting bliss.

illustrious Example of the Faith they are now called to exercise. Patriarchs, prophets, martyrs, saints, are but the shining hosts of which He is the great "Leader."

Throughout His earthly history, He was sustained by the vision of things unseen, and by the expectation of things hoped for. It was in the strength of His Faith in God that He overcame the temptations of the devil in the wilderness, relying on the Divine word against all the falsehoods of the wicked one. It was in the strength of His Faith, that He laboured for three years and a half among the fishermen and peasants of Galilee, and the harlots and publicans of Jerusalem, believing that by His obscure, and, as it would seem to human eyes, inglorious success among the poor, the ignorant, and the sinful, He was laying the foundations of an eternal kingdom. It was in the strength of His Faith, that He endured the agony of Gethsemane, expecting and receiving the Divine support when His mortal weakness was failing. It was in the strength of His Faith, that by His patient endurance of the tortures and shame of the cross, He would atone for the sins of the world, that He permitted His enemies to scourge Him, bind Him, and put Him to death; and in the very crisis of His sufferings, He demonstrated His Faith, by promising to the repentant thief an immediate entrance into Paradise. Crucified by His enemies, forsaken by His friends, denied for a time the consciousness of the Divine presence and favour, He did not "draw back." He held fast to His confidence in the Father. He clung to the hope of "*the joy set before Him,*" the joy of forgiving and saving all that should come to God through Him. He is the "*Leader*" of all who live by Faith; and in His own life Faith was "*perfected.*"

The history of His followers was to be a repetition of His own; and if they were conformed to His image in suffering, in endurance, in Faith, they might confidently expect to rise with Him to the right hand of God. "*Consider Him, therefore, who endured such contradiction of sinners against Himself, lest ye be wearied and faint in your minds.*"

CHASTISEMENT.

"Ye have not yet resisted unto blood," &c.—HEBREWS xii, 4-11.

IN the first verse of this chapter, the strenuous resistance of temptation and the patient endurance of suffering, are represented as the running of a race. In the fourth verse, the figure is changed; the Christian is a wrestler, a pugilist, struggling, fighting against sin; and the Jewish believers are told that up till now no "*blood*" had been drawn; that is, the fierce severity of the conflict had yet to come. They had no right, therefore, to give way, and no excuse for exhaustion.

But the ruling thought of the passage we have to consider this morning is, that all they were suffering was to be regarded as the wise and loving chastisement of God, who was overruling and employing the malice of their enemies, for the correction of their sins and the discipline of their holiness.

I think I am not mistaken in saying that we are very unwilling to regard our troubles as *chastisements*. It is rather our habit to think of sickness, of losses, of troubles in our families, of estrangement from friends, as affording us the opportunity of manifesting our faith and our patience, and proving the reality and strength of our religious life. This would be all very well, if we were quite sure that there were no unknown sins for which we needed correction, or even if we were free from the actual reproaches of conscience. But we are constantly confessing our transgressions, constantly imploring the Divine mercy, constantly lamenting over broken purposes and violated vows, and entreating God to give us more strength in the time to come. We must not refuse, therefore, to think of our sorrows as "*the chastening of the Lord*," nor think it impossible that we should be "*rebuked of Him.*"

Sometimes we can trace easily enough the connection between the sin and the chastisement. Friends may talk of the mystery of Divine Providence, and wonder why we should be so afflicted; but, if we liked, we could soon remove their difficulty. We know that we are reaping what we have sowed. There has been neglect of duty, there has been positive transgression, and we can recognise in our suffering, the direct and natural consequence of our offences.

At other times, there is no visible link between present troubles and past wrong doing. I imagine that this was partly the case with the Jewish Christians. The persecutions under which they were sinking were not, so far as we can see, the natural result of their sin.* And yet they are told that they are being chastened and rebuked of the Lord. There is always reason, therefore, for us to apprehend that our sorrows may be of this nature. Whether or not we can connect them with particular sinful acts or habits, it is surely, in the case of most of us, more likely than not, that they are intended to correct us for some folly or fault. And it is a curious instance of want of simplicity of heart, that we should be so ready to confess that we have disobeyed God, and so unwilling to believe that we are ever chastened for our disobedience.

I.

The general object of chastisement is fully stated in the tenth verse; God chastens us that we may "*be partakers of His holiness;*" but, speaking more in detail, we may say that sometimes the chastening comes, *to awaken repentance for sin not yet repented of.* If the suffering is the plain and unmistakeable consequence of our wrong doing, our attention is fixed upon

---

* No doubt they would have suffered less from being excluded from religious fellowship with their unbelieving countrymen, had their Christian life been more vigorous: and, perhaps, they would not at this time have provoked so much hostility had they, from the very beginning, renounced their old Jewish habits, and committed themselves body, soul, and spirit, to Christ and His Church. But yet the immediate causes of their trouble are to be sought in the malicious hatred with which the unbelieving Jews regarded the followers of Him who had been crucified, and in their fanatical enthusiasm for national independence.

the indolence, the presumption, the carelessness, of which, perhaps, we had not thought much at the time; or we are stung to the heart by a sense of the sinfulness of actions or habits which conscience had been bribed, or drugged, or violently forced, not to condemn. The connection between the sin and the trouble is sometimes too plain to be overlooked. There was a definite offence of which we did not heartily repent, a particular habit of sin which we did not firmly resist, and now we see the result of it. There can be no mistake. The shadow is the precise counterpart of the substance; the sorrow is the natural fruit of the offence. I will not give illustrations, for these might divert you from the facts in your own history which exactly answer to what I am saying. If you are conscious that at this moment you are suffering from the omission or careless discharge of duty in past years, from self-indulgence, from self-will, from indolence, from violence of temper, from pride,—"*despise not thou the chastening of the Lord;*" acknowledge the sin, seek God's pardon for it; "*be in subjection unto the Father of spirits and live.*"

But very often, as I have already said, there may be no obvious connection between our suffering and any acts of our own. It may seem to come direct from the hand of God, or may be the result of the sins of others, instead of being bitter fruit growing naturally out of our own transgressions. An accident may overtake us while we are engaged in honest work, or while we are taking lawful pleasure. We may lose half our property by the dishonesty of men whom we were perfectly justified in trusting. A bad harvest, a foreign war, the failure of a bank, the invention of a new manufacturing process, an unexpected change of fashion, might suddenly plunge some of you into serious difficulties. The sin of a relative with whose education and actions we have never had anything to do, may harrass and annoy us. We may fall ill ourselves, or sickness may attack a child or a parent, from causes altogether beyond our control. There may be no link at all, so far as we can see, between anything we have done or anything we have omitted to do, and some of our greatest troubles. However we had acted, it would have been all the same.

And yet even these troubles may be "*chastisements,*" and may be intended to awaken us to repentance. I suppose many of us are conscious that when we are in full health and strength, and have no anxieties, we are indisposed to think seriously about sin. We take things lightly; nothing weighs on the heart long. We may be keenly interested in religious truth, and very zealous and laborious in religious work; we may like to sing God's praise, and may rejoice in the bright hopes and present honours of the Christian life; but, perhaps, are hardly in the mood to think gravely enough about sin and God's displeasure. And so it happens that we become careless; some foolish and wrong acts we never notice at all; others trouble us, but not enough. Then the "*chastisement*" comes. The brightness fades away and the excitement sinks, the sober evening gathers round us with its grey clouds and its solemn stillness; we become different men altogether.

There are very few good men, I imagine, who have not discovered in times of trouble, sins of which they had never thought before; fewer still, who have not felt the exceeding sinfulness of sin, as they had never felt it before. Sorrow disposes us to deeper and more earnest thought about our own acts; creates a certain "mood"—I know not how else to call it—in which the heart becomes unusually susceptible to right impressions about offences against the Divine Law, subdues self-sufficiency, and encourages a lowly estimate of ourselves.

If, therefore, we are not sure,—and who can be sure?—that our trouble has not come upon us as a chastisement, it becomes us to examine seriously our past lives, our present habits, and to cry to God to search us and try us, and to show us if there be any wicked way in us, and to lead us in the way everlasting.

The *chastisement may last even after repentance has been awakened;* and that for many reasons.

We may need it, to assist us in mastering the failures which it has revealed to us. Perhaps we have learnt by sorrowful experience, that we are very apt to grow careless and forgetful about the sins which at times have caused us great self reproach, and which we have confessed with bitter sorrow and prostrate humiliation. While the chastisement lasts the offence can hardly be forgotten, and to be kept in remembrance of it, is a great help to overcoming it.

Or, our natural temperament may be so joyous, that we may need to have it checked and saddened. Light-heartedness may expose us to certain forms of temptation, and we may be safer in sickness than in health, safer in anxiety than when free from care, safer with straitened resources than with the means of gratifying all our tastes. The chastisement may remove the temptations to which we are most exposed, or may induce that temper of mind in which we are most likely to overcome them.

Or, the chastisement may be continued for the sake of others. They have known our sin, and if we did not suffer for it they might think too lightly of it. It is not enough that we have repented; they cannot see the depth of our sorrow; they have not heard our cries to God for mercy; they know nothing of the stings which our conscience has inflicted, nothing of our loss of Divine joy, of courage, of hopefulness, of rest; and the continuance of the visible chastisement may be necessary to warn them against the evils into which we have fallen; and if, even after our repentance, we submit with uncomplaining patience and undiminished trust in God,—while they are warned by our suffering,—we ourselves shall be rapidly growing in all the elements of true holiness.

But certain difficulties may be felt by some of you about this subject. It has been a favourite phrase among a particular class of religionists that God sees no sin in His children: if this be true, of course it is altogether wrong to speak of His chastising them. I confess myself unable to understand what a rational, thoughtful man can mean by such a phrase as that. If there *is* sin in the children of God, He must see it. If He did not see it, He would not forgive it. If He did not see it, He would not give them the strength they need to overcome it. It destroys the reality of our religious life, if we suppose that God does not regard us exactly as we are; as weak, if we are weak, strong if we are strong, holy if we are holy, sinful if we are sinful. He has "searched us and known" us; He is "acquainted with all our ways." He "knows" our "labour" and our "patience." He "knows," too, if we have "left our first love," if our "works are not perfect before Him," if we are "wretched, miserable, poor, blind, naked," while we "think we have need of nothing." He sees us as we are; if in any of His children He sees no sin, it is because there is no sin to see.

And yet it may be asked, Has not God laid all our sins on Christ? If He has, why are we chastised for them? Does He not forgive the sins of all believers? If He does, why have they to suffer for them?

These difficulties are very similar to those which are felt in relation to the future judgment. Those who cannot understand why Christians are chastised for their transgressions, cannot understand why Christians should have to give account of their deeds before the bar of God, whether they be good or whether they be evil. I have often had occasion to deal at length with this subject; and to enter fully into the wide and deep discussion which it involves, would lead me far away from the practical truths taught in the passage we are now considering. A few sentences must indicate what the truth really is.

It is the clear teaching of Scripture that Christ has atoned for the sins of all mankind; and that in consequence of His atonement God is released from the moral necessity of condemning us to eternal death because of our transgressions.

To every one that trusts in the Lord Jesus Christ, God has promised eternal life. Faith secures immortal salvation; the curse is revoked, and the soul is regenerated and "made meet for the inheritance of the saints in light." Unbelief is the only sin which now dooms any soul that hears of Christ, to eternal destruction.

But there is a displeasure in the Divine heart when the believer sins, although that displeasure may not rise into the wrath which would inflict the last penalty of transgression. There is estrangement between the soul of the believer and God while any sin remains unrepented of, although that estrangement may not issue in complete and hopeless alienation,

So long as faith continues, the heart is looking to Christ not merely for escape from final ruin, but for the aid of the Holy Ghost to live a good life, and evil does not triumph over good; and yet if there is sin for which no adequate sorrow is felt, and against which no firm resistance is maintained, the power of the Spirit is resisted, and God is displeased. For such sins as do not separate the soul from Christ altogether, there is chastisement, that the soul may be brought to repentance, and that the displeasure of God may pass away. For the exclusion of Christ and the Spirit from the soul altogether, there is not chastisement, but condemnation.

II.

In what spirit chastisement should be borne, has already been partly indicated. We must not "*despise*" it. This is intended to forbid that hardened defiance of suffering which arises from self-will, and from a proud reluctance either to acknowledge that we have deserved chastisement, or to be made better by it.

We must not "*faint*" when we are rebuked of God. This is intended to condemn that moral weakness which is altogether crushed by pain. The soul that can bear to sin, is often unable to bear any adequate punishment for sin. It faints. There is no care for any duty, no courage to meet any difficulty, no hope that things will ever become better, no strength to remember the cause of the suffering, no disposition to do anything except to lie and moan under it.

We must "*be in subjection unto the Father of spirits.*" There must be no unwillingness to think of our sorrow as being intended for chastisement, no resentment against God as though He had no right to punish. Your children do not take punishment rightly, if they ignore the fact that it *is* punishment, or if they resist and revolt against your authority. And, as I have already said, we are sometimes very unwilling to think that God is really chastening us, and are even disposed to believe that, since He has forgiven us for Christ's sake, He has surrendered the right to chasten. We seem to imagine that He is simply trying experiments with us—seeing how many strokes we can bear without crying out, what pleasures we can sacrifice without tears. That is not being in subjection.

Nor must there be impatience or distrust. We must accept the chastisement without charging it with excessive severity, without distrusting the love of Him from whom it comes.

III.

The reasons, alleged or implied in this passage, for bearing chastisement in a right spirit, may be summed up in a few closing sentences.

It is "*chastisement,*" the result of our own sin, not of God's caprice, and should, therefore, be received humbly and uncomplainingly.

It is *God's* chastisement; He has a right to correct us for our faults. "*If we gave reverence to the fathers of our flesh, much rather should we be in subjection*" to Him. All the authority they had over us in our childhood, He has over us, as spiritual and immortal creatures.

It is inseparable from Divine sonship. If we are in God's household, we must come under His discipline. We are "*not sons*" at all, if nothing is done to rebuke our sins and to discipline us to holiness. It is a Father who is troubled by our imperfections who chastises us, not an enemy who is thirsting for revenge.

The chastisement is as wise as it is loving. It originates in no mistake,—it is of the right kind,—and is neither excessive nor too prolonged. Our earthly "*fathers chastened us*" at their discretion, as it "seemed" good to them, sometimes, perhaps, when we were not guilty at all; sometimes, beyond our desert; and sometimes injudiciously; so that sometimes we were injured rather than benefited by their chastening. Their authority was but "*for a few days,*" and the results of their discipline were doubtful; but God makes no blunders, when He chastens it is "*for our holiness.*"

Finally, it is well that we should contrast the present suffering with its ultimate effect. It brings pain, anxiety, restlessness; discomposes our minds; destroys our peace; desolates our outward happiness. From its nature it neither is, nor "*seems to be, joyous, but grievous.*" As the ground is first ruthlessly broken up and disturbed by the plough, and its depths laid open to the wind and the rain and the cold, and is then tormented by the harrow; so are our hearts bruised and wounded by chastisement, and we think that nothing can compensate for the suffering; but, by and bye, there come calm autumn days, and the golden corn waves peacefully in the sun.

Or, at present we are like vines in the spring, and the sharp knife comes upon us, cutting off our branches, and making our souls bleed; we quiver under the pain; through every bough, and down into the very roots of our nature, the keen anguish is throbbing, and we think no quietness and ease can ever return to us. But in a few months it will be all forgotten. The wounds will have healed. A richer, fuller life will flow through every fibre of our being; and, amidst the luxuriant foliage, will hang the beautiful clusters,—no rude winds disturbing them,—no sharp frosts nipping them,—all danger past,—all need of pruning over,—"*peaceable fruits of righteousness.*" The need of chastening will have ceased; we shall be "*made partakers of God's holiness,*" and have fellowship with His tranquil and everlasting bliss.

MOUNT SINAI AND MOUNT SION.

"Wherefore lift up the hands that hang down, and the feeble knees; and make straight paths for your feet, lest that which is lamed be turned out of the way;" &c.—HEBREWS xii, 12-29.

THE Hebrews who had become faint and weary under the Divine correction, and were ready to abandon their faith in Christ, are now exhorted to show greater manliness, courage, and vigour. "*Lift up the hands which hang down, and the feeble knees.*" Their troubles are not a reason for despair They are only enduring the chastisement by which all the sons of God are corrected for sin and disciplined to holiness. If they bear it well, it will yield the "peaceable fruits of righteousness."

They are charged to be more resolute and simple-hearted in their obedience to Christ. It is implied that their difficulties had been increased by their indecision. A definite and immoveable purpose to be true to their Christian profession at all costs, would cause new strength and hope to rise up throughout the Church; the feeble and irresolute would find inspiration and vigour in the firmness of their brethren. Without that, many would fall away altogether. "*Make straight paths for your feet,*"—let there be an unhesitating and irrevocable choice of the perfectly right course; "*lest that which is lame be turned out of the way,*"—any other conduct will be full of danger and temptation to those whose faith is weak; "*but let it rather be healed*"—by a stern fidelity to Christ on the part of the church generally, its feebler members will not only be kept from apostasy but will become strong.

There are two principles here, which are of the greatest practical importance :—

(1) The difficulties of a religious life are felt the most, by those who shrink from complete and unreserved devotion to God ; "*the straight paths*" of perfect loyalty to Christ are, for many reasons, easier to walk in, than the crooked paths of compromise; and this is especially true for those who are deficient in moral and religious strength.

(2) There are many men who will serve God well, or drift away from Him altogether, according to the spirit and temper of the particular church to which they belong. They will stand fast if the church is resolute in its fidelity; if not, they will fall away. The communion of saints is the strength and defence of their religious life.

The inspired writer goes on to say, that at such a time of peril, all personal estrangements among Christian men must cease ; that they must strive after " *holiness;*" that there must be vigilance "*lest any fail*" to obtain the favour of God, which can be won only by patient continuance in well doing ; lest any iniquity rise up among them unchecked, like a bitter poisonous plant, and thereby the " many" in the Church be betrayed into sin ; lest there be among them "*any sensual person,*" or any " *like Esau,*" who profanely despised the promises of God, and yielded himself to the instincts and appetites of the flesh, uncontrolled by the fear of losing his birthright. " *Follow peace with all, and holiness, without which no man shall see the Lord. Looking diligently lest any fail of the grace or favour of God; lest any root of bitterness springing up trouble you, and thereby many be defiled; lest there be any fornicator or profane person as Esau, who for one morsel of meat sold his birthright.*"

It is clearly the writer's intention to warn the Christian Jews against repeating the folly and guilt of Esau's sin. As the eldest son of Jacob had a birthright and sold it, so they who were God's firstborn, the " heirs of God and joint heirs with Christ," might cast away and lose for ever, their diviner honours and nobler inheritance. Their decision *for* Christ or *against* Him would be final ; it would not admit of being revoked ; its consequences would be irreversible. In the unavailing sorrow of Esau, they might see foreshadowed their own miserable doom: "*ye know that afterwards when he wished to inherit the blessing he found no place of repentance, though he sought it carefully with tears.*" Then follows the closing warning against apostasy.

The awful grandeur of the revelation of God in the wilderness had left a profound and imperishable impression on the Jewish race. It suggested to psalmists and prophets their sublimest imagery. "The earth shook and trembled: the foundations also of the hills moved and were shaken, because He was wroth. * * He bowed the Heavens also and came down; and darkness was under His feet. And He rode upon a cherub and did fly; yea, He did fly upon the wings of the wind. He made darkness His secret place; His pavilion round about Him were dark waters and thick clouds of the skies. * * * The Lord also thundered in the heavens, and the Highest gave His voice; hailstones and stones of fire." (Psalm xviii, 7-13.) "O, that Thou wouldest rend the heavens and come down, that the mountains might flow down at Thy presence." (Isaiah lxiv, 1.) Many other passages might be quoted from the Old Testament to show that when poets and prophets longed for the manifestation of the Divine power and glory, or celebrated deliverances wrought by the Divine hand for individuals or the whole nation, their thoughts clothed themselves in the imagery afforded by the Sinaitic revelation. Let us try to recall what that revelation was.

For several centuries the Jewish people had been feeding their flocks, or building vast cities, in the flat, luxuriant pastures which formed the north-eastern province of the land of Egypt. Their ancestors had lived in a bolder and wilder country, but the generation which left Egypt had seen the hills only afar off. No sooner, however, had they left the shores of the Red Sea, than they found themselves surrounded by scenery which must have powerfully affected their imagination, and prepared them for the sublimity and terrors of Sinai. Slowly and painfully they marched upwards, day after day, through the rugged passes and winding valleys of a desert mountain region, until they reached the plain lying in front of the perpendicular cliffs of Horeb. There, they were shut in, on nearly every side, by mighty walls of rock,—stern, naked, and desolate. The silence of the desert rested on the camp; and in a dreadful solitude they were to meet God.

They were told that on the morning of the third day the Lord would come down in the sight of all the people, upon Mount Sinai; and they were to make ready for the vision of His glory. A new element of terror was added, by the command that the cliffs of Horeb were to be fenced round against all approach, and that "*if so much as a beast touch the mountain it shall be stoned.*" This they "*could not endure;*" (v. 20) it made them feel in what mysterious and fearful proximity they stood to the invisible presence of God.

The morning of the third day came; and we can imagine the agitation and wondering awe which filled every heart, while waiting for the manifestation of GOD; at last they saw dense black clouds sinking on the mountain; then came flashing lightnings; presently the earth shook under the shock of pealing thunders; then came the sound of a trumpet, long and loud, streaming through the camp, and echoing from the surrounding hills; and "the Lord descended in fire," and it seemed that the mountain itself was burning, and "the smoke went up like the smoke of a furnace, and the mountain trembled greatly." And "out of the midst of the fire, of the cloud, and of the thick darkness" came "a great voice;" God began to speak to the people, and to declare His law. But when ten commandments had been given, they could bear no more; they removed and stood afar off. And the heads of the tribes came to Moses and said, "We have seen this day that God doth talk with man, and he liveth. Now, therefore, why should we die? for this great fire will consume us: if we hear the voice of the Lord any more, then shall we die," (Deut, v, 24-25); and they "*entreated that the word should not be spoken to them any more;*" (v. 19).

To recall the splendours and portents which accompanied

the giving of the law, at the very close of a protracted argument against the permanence of the Mosaic institutions, and on behalf of the Christian faith, was a bold and perilous thing; but the inspired writer knew the strength of his position, and could rely on the impressions, far more awful and glorious than the visible terrors of Sinai had produced, which the new revelation had made upon all believers. He knew that by the preaching of the Gospel and the power of the Holy Ghost, these Jewish Christians had been emancipated from the dominion of the senses, and had entered into the spiritual world; that to their purified and invigorated vision " things seen and temporal" had vanished away, and they had stood face to face with things "unseen and eternal." They, themselves, had not forgotten the time when they were " enlightened," and " were made partakers of the Holy Ghost," and felt the "powers" of the new and spiritual kingdom to which all believers belong. Even now, though their faith had become weak, and their hearts treacherous, and the glories which once encompassed them were dim and ready to fade utterly away, this lofty appeal to what they had " seen " with their "eyes" and " looked upon," would rekindle the glow of almost extinguished fires, and recall the joy and fear of their early religious life.

Sixteen centuries ago, Moses had " brought forth the people out of the camp to meet with God" before Mount Sinai (Exod. xix, 17); "*but ye have drawn near to Mount Sion, and to the city of the living God, the heavenly Jerusalem, and to innumerable hosts, to the festal assembly of angels, and the church of the first-born which are written in heaven, and to God the Judge of all, and to the spirits of the just made perfect, and to Jesus the mediator of the new covenant, and to the blood of sprinkling, which speaketh better things than the blood of Abel.*"

We might examine in detail this vivid contrast between the new revelation and the old. God revealed Himself to your fathers on the wild and rugged heights of Horeb; but "ye *have drawn near to Mount Sion,*" and seen the towers and pinnacles of the glorious temple of the Most High. God came to them in the dreary solitudes of the desert; but ye have drawn near "*to the city of the living God, the heavenly Jerusalem,*" in which the nations of the saved walk in white raiment, and dwell in palaces of blessedness and splendour. At Sinai the angels were in chariots of fire, and increased the awfulness of the scene; but for you they are gathered as on a day of triumph, with songs of joy and golden harps, and their faces bright with love and bliss. Your fathers were a chosen nation, blest with lofty privileges; but you have drawn near to "*the church of the first-born, whose names are written in heaven,*"—a spiritual community, scattered over many lands, poor, persecuted, despised, but enrolled on high, invested with the dignity, and heirs of the glory, which belong to the first-born of God.

Your fathers stood in the Divine presence to receive a law which, if they kept, would bring them, at some remote and unknown day, the rewards of obedience; but you have drawn near "*to God the Judge of all,*"—you knew that the hour of your salvation was come, and you waited without dread to hear from His lips the sentence which would determine your everlasting condition. And "*the spirits*" of the ancient saints "*made perfect*" at last by the death and resurrection of Christ, were there. And instead of Moses, "*Jesus,*"—"*the new covenant*" in the place of the old;—and "*the blood*" which appeals to God for mercy, not for vengeance, and which cleansed you from the infirmity which would have hindered your approach to God.

But the great interest of this passage lies in this,—that it strikingly illustrates the spiritual life of the early Church. It is not to be regarded as a mere burst of impassioned and imaginative eloquence, although it assumes a highly-wrought rhetorical form. It is the expression, though perhaps the fullest and most remarkable, of what we know from other parts of the New Testament, was the actual experience of apostolic times. It explains the strength, the joy, the spiritual triumph, of the first Christians.

There is a singular omission, I think, in most modern preaching, of certain truths which occupy a very large space in the pages of the four Gospels, and which appear in a somewhat different form in the Apostolical Epistles.

John the Baptist preached that "the kingdom of heaven was at hand;" Christ Himself preached "the gospel of the kingdom." The twelve were commissioned to preach the same. When the seventy were sent out, the solitary testimony they were to bear wherever they came, was this,—"the kingdom of God is come nigh unto you." A remarkable series of parables illustrates the nature and laws of "the kingdom." To the disciples it was given to know the "mystery of the kingdom of God." If a man's heart was drawn to Christ, Christ said to him, "Thou art not far from the kingdom of God." The blessing pronounced on the poor in spirit is that "the kingdom of heaven" is theirs. The authority of the apostles is represented under the figure of the keys of the "kingdom of heaven." This subject was so prominent in the preaching of Christ and His followers, that at one time the people thought that "the kingdom of God would immediately appear;" and when Christ was hanging on the cross,—all His hopes apparently defeated, and His mission ended in miserable defeat and shame—the repenting thief cried to Him, "Lord, remember me when Thou comest into Thy kingdom." After His resurrection He talked with the apostles "of the things pertaining to the kingdom of God." Immediately before his ascension He asserted that all power "had been given to Him in heaven and on earth," and this was the basis of the apostolic commission to baptize and to teach all nations. On the day of Pentecost, Peter proclaimed that Christ was "Prince," as well as "Saviour;" and John, in the Apocalypse, spoke of himself as the companion of the saints "in tribulation, and in the *kingdom* and patience of Jesus Christ."

In a most important sense, every member of the human race is a subject of the Lord Jesus. When He ascended to the Father, "the heathen" were made His "inheritance," and "the uttermost parts of the earth" "His possession." Prophecy had declared that He should have "dominion from sea to sea, and from the river to the ends of the earth"—and the promise has been fulfilled. But under His rule there are "oppressors" whom

He has "to break in pieces," "enemies" who have to "lick the dust." As the disciples of Christ are "in the world" but not "of the world," belong to the human race by birth, and place, and external relationships, but are exalted above it by the power of a new life; so the irreligious are in the kingdom of Christ, but not of it; they are His subjects by God's appointment,—by the moral constitution under which they are born; but they sink beneath their high estate by wilful sin and unbelief.

To them pertain the "adoption and the glory," and the new "covenant," and the "grace of the Gospel," and "the service of God," and the "promises;" but "they are not all Israel which are of Israel." They "cannot see the kingdom of God." It *may* even be said that they do not belong to it; as dead branches do not belong to a living tree; as rebels against royal authority do not belong to the state, although they were born of its best blood, live on its soil, speak its language, have been disciplined by its customs and laws, and might, through the mercy of their prince, obtain on their submission, not only the protection afforded to the meanest loyal subjects, but the splendour and rank which were theirs by their birth. "Except a man be born again, he cannot enter the kingdom of God."

But the spiritual birth, with the forgiveness of all past sin, was offered by the apostles to all mankind; and their epistles imply that, as the result of it, Christians had passed into new regions of life,—had received, so to speak, new senses,—so that they saw and heard what other men could not see or hear,—had discovered that they were surrounded on every side by the institutions and powers of an eternal kingdom, of which they were the subjects, and Christ the king.

The full extent and perfect glory of this kingdom they did not know; but they never thought of it as limited to believers living in their own times. They knew that angels and men, the living and the dead, have a common Lord, and do homage before the same throne. The thin walls of their mortal flesh did not separate them from their brethren who had departed to be with Christ. "That which is born of the Spirit is Spirit." God had already "delivered them from the power of darkness," and "translated them into the kingdom of His dear Son." In Christ, this world and the next, things seen and things unseen were no longer divided by strong and firm lines of distinction. "The middle wall of partition"* was broken down. God had "gathered together in one all things in Christ, both which are in heaven and which are on earth, even in Him." They, too, were "of the household of God." Their "conversation" was "in heaven." They "sat together in heavenly places in Christ Jesus." One kingdom included all the saints on earth, and "all principality, power, and dominion, and every name that is named not only in this world but also in that which is to come." Already they had "*come to Mount Sion, to the city of the living God, the heavenly Jerusalem.*"

That many of us have failed to enter the high and lofty life which such declarations as these represent, must not induce us to impoverish and degrade the plain language of inspired men. In striving to recover the habits of thought characteristic of apostolic times, we may, perhaps, be assisted to recover the fervour of their devotion and the energy of their labours.

The recognition of the undivided unity of the kingdom of Christ will be an aid to *holiness*. If it is a difference of outward circumstance rather than of true relationship to God, which distinguishes the living from the dead, we are bound to love Him with an affection as ardent, trust in Him with a faith as firm, and serve Him with an obedience as cheerful, as the spirits of the just themselves. We are under the same sceptre and the same laws; it is only a narrow brook which runs between the bright and pleasant land where they live and ours! We must speak their language, and like them walk in light. They must not be troubled with the noise of our discordant passions, or by the sight of our unseemly acts. We may hear, even now, the music of their songs, as the dwellers in the valley may hear the Sabbath bells of village churches on the neighbouring hills; we may join their worship and share their joy.

---

* I need hardly say that the true reference of this passage is to the breaking down of the distinctions between Jew and Gentile.

Courage and *strength* in Christ's service will receive inspiration and stimulus from the same source. We are no longer maintaining a doubtful conflict with unequal forces against the world, the flesh, and the devil. The saints of every generation and all the thrones of heaven are on our side. The great leaders of the church in past ages are not lost to us ; they seem to be lying dead at our feet, but they are living still, and near at hand, mightier and nobler than ever before. When disheartened and dismayed, we can turn our eyes, and look upon the goodly fellowship of the prophets, the glorious company of the apostles, the noble army of martyrs. We, who are on earth, are but a single division of Christ's mighty army ; it is only against *our* ranks that the storm of the battle is raging ; we may hear already the shouts of victory from every other part of the field.

It is surely an error to suppose that the life of faith in things unseen, includes no remembrance of the holy angels and glorified saints who dwell in the immediate presence of the Most High. Our vision is not strong enough as yet to endure a fixed and uninterrupted gaze on the Divine glory. We shall sink exhausted under the too ambitious effort. But, when the eye of the soul is too weak to bear the direct splendours of the Godhead, we may still look on the bright forms of His servants, and, in fellowship with them, may catch the spirit and learn the service of the skies.

The remaining verses of the chapter contain an earnest exhortation to listen to the voice of God who now speaks, not as of old from the summit of an earthly mountain to the outward sense, but from Heaven itself to man's very soul. The unwillingness of the Jewish people to hear the law from God's own lips is treated as representing the rebellion and disobedience of their subsequent history ; and it is urged "*if they escaped not who refused Him that spake on earth, much more shall we not escape if we turn away from Him that speaketh from heaven.*" This, indeed, is the burden of the whole Epistle—the certain and irretrievable ruin which must come upon Christian men who apostatise from Christ. This dark and terrible truth breaks through the course of the argument again and again; it returns and returns like the echoes of thunder among the hills. "*How shall we escape if we neglect so great salvation?*" "Your fathers tempted me—I was grieved with that generation—I sware in my wrath they shall not enter into my rest; *let us therefore fear.*" "If we sin wilfully after that we have received the knowledge of the truth, *there remaineth no more sacrifice for sins, but a certain fearful looking for of judgment and fiery indignation.*" "*Esau found no place of repentance.*" And now "*if they escaped not, much more shall not we escape.*" To us, God has come nearer than to them. He has revealed to us the glory of His kingdom; He has exhausted all motives to love, to trust, to fidelity, to obedience. He has told us all that is in His heart. He has made His last effort. "*If we turn away*" our doom is finally sealed. It is as if His angels should revolt in heaven—as if the spirits of the just should abjure their allegiance to His throne.

"The end of all things is at hand." "*His voice then shook the earth, but now hath He promised, saying, yet once more I shake not the earth only but also heaven.*" In His last revelation to mankind, God's purposes are reaching their perfect accomplishment. Empires which had overshadowed the whole earth had decayed and perished. The institutions and laws which God Himself had originally established, the temple He had consecrated, the priests He had anointed, were now ready to vanish away.

The heart of man was sick and weary of perpetual change. But at last there is set up "an everlasting dominion which shall not pass away," "a kingdom which shall not be destroyed." All human civilizations, and philosophies, and religious beliefs, —all forms of political power, however venerable, however mighty, which withstand its progress, are destined to destruction. Ancient prophecy had foretold a final overthrow of whatever could "*be shaken,*"—that only the eternal and unchangeable might remain. That overthrow had already begun. Centuries might roll by, before it was consummated, but the "*voice which shook the earth*" in the old time, would continue to "*shake*" all things visible and invisible, until the "kingdom which cannot be moved" reached its complete development and perfect glory.

That kingdom "*we have received.*" Let our hearts be filled with thankfulness, "*whereby we may serve God acceptably with reverence and godly fear.*" For us eternity has begun. The order of things to which we belong is not doomed to perish or change. Our King is enthroned for ever. The laws we obey, the promises in which we trust, are the final revelation of the will and love of God. Here our souls may rest. And if we reject the grace of God and judge ourselves unworthy of eternal life, there is but one alternative,—"*our God is a consuming fire.*" This is the terrible close of the argument, the climax of the protracted appeal. For every Christian man there is the kingdom of God with its eternal glory, or "indignation and wrath, tribulation and anguish." This is the last and most terrible form in which the question is put which stands on the first page of the Epistle :—" How shall we escape if we neglect so great salvation ?"

PRECEPTS.

"Let brotherly love continue," &c.—HEBREWS xiii, 1-19.

THE great argument against apostasy is now complete; but the writer, before concluding his Epistle, exhorts the Hebrew Christians to cultivate certain virtues and graces necessary to the perfection of their personal character and to the peace and vigour of their Church life.

He exhorts them to cherish "*brotherly love*" (v. 1), and to manifest it by showing hospitality to "*strangers*" (v. 2), and sympathy to those who were suffering for Christ (v. 3).

He charges them to maintain the purity of marriage, warning them that "*whoremongers and adulterers God will judge.*" (v. 4.)

After the manner of other New Testament writers, he passes at once from sensual sins to "*covetousness.*" In 1 Cor. v, 10-11, "*covetous*" persons and "extortioners" are classed by St. Paul with "fornicators and idolaters." In 1 Cor. vi, 9-10, it is declared that "neither fornicators, nor idolaters, nor adulterers, nor effeminate, nor abusers of themselves with mankind, nor thieves, nor '*covetous*,' shall inherit the kingdom of God." In Ephesians v, 3, it is written, "But fornication and all uncleanness, or *covetousness* let it not be once named among you." In the enumeration of the sinful passions to be mortified, in Col. iii, 5, "Fornication, uncleanness, inordinate affection, evil concupiscence, and *covetousness*, which is idolatry," are placed together.

Nor, as I have intimated, is this a peculiarity of St. Paul's

St. Peter, in his first Epistle (chap. ii, 14), describes the wicked who would defile the Church, and provoke the fierce vengeance of God as "Having eyes full of adultery, and a heart exercised with *covetous* practices." Christ Himself said (Mark vii, 21-22) that "out of the heart of man proceed adulteries, fornications, murders, thefts, *covetousness*." It is not our habit to class the excessive love of money, with sins of sensuality and violence. The profligate is the object of scorn, of loathing and disgust; the close-fisted, hard-hearted man, whose intellect and energy and passions are all concentrated on the miserable endeavour to create a vast fortune, receives the respectful courtesies of good men, and is welcomed into every house. If he is successful, he may command, during his life, public honours; and if he distributes his wealth with tact and ostentation when he can no longer retain it, he may become famous, after his death, as a great public benefactor.

In primitive times "whoremongers and adulterers" were left to the judgment of God; now, happily, they are branded with the burning condemnation of society, and are made to pay in many forms the heaviest penalties for their sins. Perhaps, the day will come when the vengeance of the community will also flash upon the "*covetous;*" but in order to this, the public opinion of the Church must be brought into nearer harmony with the spirit and teaching of the New Testament, and a noble superiority to the common passion for wealth must be regarded as an indispensable element of Christian holiness.

"*Be content with such things as ye have.*" Why? "*For He hath said I will never leave thee nor forsake thee.*" To Jacob (Gen. xxviii, 15), in his dream of the ladder with the ascending and descending angels—to Joshua and the Jewish nation (Deut. xxxi, 6-8) through the lips of Moses—to Solomon (1 Chron. xxxviii, 20), through the lips of David,—God had spoken words almost identical with these; and it is an interesting illustration of the manner in which the inspired writers thought themselves justified in appropriating Divine promises, that the words are quoted here, as if they were the property, as indeed they are, of all good men. For a Divine promise, no matter to whom it may have been originally given, is a revelation of the Divine character; and in its substantial meaning may be claimed by the universal Church. Stripped of the accidents which it derived from the circumstances of those to whom it was first spoken, it is a manifestation of the Divine bounty, or mercy, or stedfastness, and is of universal interest. It was to Paul personally that God said, "My grace is sufficient for thee;" but we all feel that we may lay our hand upon the words and plead them in God's presence, as though they had been spoken to us; for they show to us, as they showed to Paul, the love and faithfulness and power of God, and so confirm our faith in Him.

Then follows a precept, to which we will return presently, requiring a remembrance of former leaders and rulers of the Church, who to the end of their days had continued faithful to Christ (v. 7), and a declaration that Christ, whom they served, changes not, but is "*the same yesterday, to-day, and for ever.*" (v. 8.)

The mention of the unchangeableness of Christ, forms a natural transition to an exhortation against being "*carried about with divers and strange doctrines*" (v. 9). What the particular doctrines were, of which the writer was thinking, is shown in the same verse, "*For it is a good thing that the heart be established with grace*"—the merciful and mighty help of God's Spirit—"*not with meats, which profited not them who were occupied therein.*" I imagine that under the influence of their fellow countrymen, who continued in the old faith, the Jewish Christians were attaching importance to fanciful distinctions between one kind of food and another, as though abstinence from the suspected meats would keep the heart pure, and indulgence in them defile and enfeeble.

Without apostatising from Christ, it was possible to listen to Jewish ascetic teaching; just as it is possible without forsaking Protestantism, to indulge in certain Romish practices which, whether they are wise or foolish as parts of that great religious institution to which they properly belong, are childish and grotesque when observed by the adherents of a spiritual system of an altogether different type and genius. There was a reason why a Jew should honour the sanctity of certain times and places and things; and it was in harmony with some of the characteristics of his religion that he should even speculate on the religiousness of abstaining from certain kinds of food which might be eaten without transgressing any definite precept of his law; but all this was contrary to the spirit of the Christian faith. And the pretty, artistic crosses to which some Protestants attach a sentimental sanctity, not very remote from the reverence of a Catholic for his crucifix,—the taste for luscious books of devotion,—and the playing at "mortification" in secret, are not less inconsistent with the distinctive elements of Protestantism. "*It is good that the heart be established with grace*," not with such things as these; if the mighty power of the Spirit of God,—regenerating, sanctifying, illuminating the soul, uniting you with God in Jesus Christ—cannot make you strong to resist temptation, these sentimental follies are not likely to help you; harmless as they seem, they may divert your confidence from the only foundation on which it ought to rest.

The protest against a false method of cultivating religious perfection, suggests to the writer a very characteristic line of thought. He has just condemned the folly of perpetuating imaginary moral distinctions between different kinds of food; he proceeds to say, "*We have an altar, however, of which they have no right to eat who serve the tabernacle.*" Just as the sin-offerings, whose blood was brought into the Holy Place by the High Priest, were burned without the camp, as being too sacred to form, like other sacrifices, the food even of the consecrated priesthood, so Christ, who "*suffered without the gate*," cannot be the life and strength of those who continue faithful to Judaism. The Jewish priests are not suffered to eat the most sacred of their own sacrifices, nor have they any right to "*eat*" His flesh of whose atoning death those sacrifices were but the symbol.

When they crucified Christ outside the walls of the city that the sacred ground might not be defiled with His blood, they were unconsciously adding one more circumstance of external analogy between the ancient rites and the history of Him in whom their meaning was perfectly fulfilled. "*Let us go forth, therefore,*"—not waiting to be driven from Judaism by a sentence of excommunication, but leaving the nation and the church from which Christ was expelled, of our own free-will,—"*unto* HIM;"—we lose communion with our countrymen only to enter into closer fellowship with our Lord;—"*without the camp;*" our fathers dwelt in tents when they left Egypt,—and the venerable institutions of Moses and this ancient city, with its glorious temple and mighty walls, are not more lasting than the shifting encampment of the wilderness; they are destined soon to pass away. "*Here*"—in this visible world—"*have we no continuing city, but we seek one to come.*"

Excluded from the services of the TEMPLE, "*By* HIM *therefore, let us offer the sacrifices of praise to God continually, that is, the fruit of our lips, giving thanks to His name.*"

"*But*"—in order that there may be material sacrifices as well as acts of spiritual worship—"*to do good and to communicate*" of your earthly resources to those that are in need, "*forget not, for with such sacrifices God is well pleased.*"

As the duty of remembering their former church rulers had been inculcated—verse 7—the duty of obedience to those who were still living is inculcated—verse 17. The writer then requests the prayers of the Church for himself and his friends (v. 18);—they could claim the prayers of their brethren, for they were persuaded that they had "*a good conscience—desiring in all things to act honourably and becomingly.*" The request is urged with the more earnestness that the writer may be "*restored*" to his brethren "*the sooner*" (v. 19).

The precepts contained in this passage to "*obey*" the living rulers of the Church, and to "*remember*" those who were dead, remind us that the Churches of primitive times were organised communities, having their appointed officers, whose duty it was to govern as well as to teach, and whose official position their brethren were required to honour. Elsewhere the elders of the Church are called its "overseers" (Acts xx, 28), and its "presidents" (1 Thess. v, 12),—names implying the authority of their office.

The elders that "rule well" are to "*be counted worthy of double honour, especially they who labour in word and doctrine*" (1 Tim. v, 17). He who made some "apostles" made others "pastors and teachers." (Eph. iv, 11.) It was in the discharge of their apostolic commission that Paul and Barnabas " ordained elders in every church." (Acts xiv, 23.)

Although it may be thought that we Nonconformists, in our assertion of ecclesiastical freedom, and in our protest against every form of priestly assumption, are likely to forget that the strength and order and peace of Churches, as of all other societies of men, can only be maintained and protected by respect for Law and Government,—I am not disposed to admit that our people resent the wise, firm, and moderate exercise of the authority of their church officers. For yourselves, you have shown, during more than a hundred years, a manly, intelligent, and unfaltering loyalty to your successive pastors and elders. It is well, however, that we should sometimes consider what is the nature of the obedience and submission which the rulers of the Church have a right to claim.

(1) It is *not obedience to the will, or submission to the judgment, of one man.* It is a perilous thing for a church, as well as for a nation, to be under the authority of a single individual; and Christ never meant that it should be. Even in those rare cases, in which the sole ruler has a prudence and a weight of moral influence, which enable him to govern with uniform success,—firmly and yet not tyrannically,—the church suffers harm. Those of its members who have a faculty for rule, lose the moral and religious discipline which they would derive from sharing the responsibilities of government; and at the death of its solitary chief the church is likely to be thrown into confusion and disorder, because there are none left whose guidance it has been accustomed to follow.

In every one of the apostolic churches there seem to have been several bishops and several deacons: among ourselves, although the public instruction of the church is entrusted too much to a single pastor, we preserve, I think, the spirit of the apostolic constitution; we have substantially the same officers, though they are called by other names. In our diaconate we comprehend, under one title, functions which in apostolic times seem to have been separated. Some of our deacons are, in fact, "elders;" and most of them discharge the duties of both offices.

During the last year or two, novelists that know very little of the true life and habits of Congregational churches, and a few of our own ministers who must have been singularly unfortunate in their ministerial experience, have entertained the public, and found relief for their own dissatisfaction and disgust, by sketching clever caricatures of the follies and imperfections which cling to deacons as well as to most other men, and which, perhaps, might be found in other forms, even in the ordained clergy of every church in Christendom, bond or free. If Mrs Oliphant has shown that it is possible to make fun of dissenting deacons, Mr Anthony Trollope has shown that there are weak points in the people who live in the cathedral close, and that even a bishop may be made to look ludicrous. There is no harm in being amused at the vulgarity and self-importance of the arch-deacon of "Salem Chapel;" but if we are asked to accept him as a true representative of the whole order, we repel the insult. We could tell of deacons of a very different stamp; of shrewd merchants who, though under the pressure of large commercial transactions, devote many hours every week to the quiet and unostentatious discharge of the duties of the diaconate; of cultivated professional men, whose thought and energy are zealously and modestly devoted to the service of the church; of tradesmen and artizans, whose genial sympathy and sound judgment are the strength and pride of their minister, and whose devout and brotherly visits to the sick and the sorrowful never fail to leave the sad heart lighter, and to make the monotony of the sick-room more tolerable.

It is true, no doubt, that there are many of our deacons whose English is not faultlessly accurate, and that most of them, probably, are guilty of being tradesmen, which is a dire offence in the eyes of some of our critics. But, though it seems incredible to some people, there may be courtesy and intelligence, and humility, and self-sacrifice, and a sense of honour, where there is an utter incapacity to escape the perils of the letter H; a clear head and a generous heart may belong to men who earn their bread by the sweat of their brow; God sometimes confers on tradesmen intellectual and religious gifts which are sometimes unaccountably withheld from "scholars and gentlemen;" and, before now, fishermen have known more about Divine truth than rabbis, high priests, and statesmen.

The association of lay elders, with the minister, in the government of a church is an element of strength and stability, not of weakness.

(2) *The obedience is not claimed for self-constituted and self-chosen rulers.* The office was instituted by Christ; the men who fill it are elected by the church itself. You ought not to appoint to official authority those in whose judgment and spirit you cannot trust: when you have appointed them, they have a plain right to expect from you that consideration without which the duties of their office cannot be discharged.

(3) *The obedience, the submission, required does not involve any obligation to surrender the right which belongs to every Christian to listen for himself to Christ and to the apostles,* and to form his own convictions on the contents of the Christian revelation.

(4) *The obedience is to be enforced only by an appeal to the conscience and judgment.* The civil power never ought to have attempted to sustain the authority of the ministers of Christ; and the time is coming fast when it will be seen all through Christendom that the attempt is as useless as it is wicked. Nor are the ministers of Christ themselves invested with those awful spiritual prerogatives which have brought great kings and great nations to the feet of Christian bishops.

Nothing can be more generous or free than the submission of a Christian church, after the apostolic model, to its rulers. " They watch for your souls as they that must give account" is a motive of infinite pathos and unsuspected power. It is felt by many who would be provoked to resistance, by almost any other mode of urging the duty. It is sustained by the remembrance of religious anxieties and temporal sufferings in which the counsels and intercessions of the pastor and his official colleagues, brought blessed relief; and by the accumulated influence of a long succession of Sabbaths, in which the heart has been strengthened and made glad by the public services of the church.

There is hardly any relation on earth in which there are more opportunities for the display of generous and chivalrous qualities, than in the relation between the officers of a Nonconformist church and the people; and the mutual trustfulness, the willing co-operation, the surrender of personal preferences, the government of temper, the mutual tolerance of infirmities, and the cordial recognition of intellectual power and moral excellence wherever they exist, are too familiar to us, in the actual life of our churches, to awaken admiration or even attract attention.

It is not easy to define the limits of the submission which church members owe to their officers. It is not easy even to illustrate its nature at all adequately; but there are some particulars which are sufficiently obvious.

(1) It is plain, for instance, that the public teaching of the pastor ought to be listened to and spoken of with respect; and that there should be a careful abstinence from whatever would diminish its moral influence. On this point the ministers of our larger churches have generally no reason to complain; they have personal qualities and powers which usually secure all the consideration they can legitimately claim. But where the minister has not much culture and not much strength, churches are sometimes at fault. They forget that there is a respect due to him as their appointed teacher,—as one who, with whatever inadequate resources, occupies by their own consent an office which Christ instituted,—and that the authority of a minister rests, mainly, not on his natural or acquired gifts, but on the very relationship he sustains to his people.

(2) Sometimes, too, there is an indisposition to receive the honest and kindly remonstrances of church rulers in private, on questionable modes of doing business, on ostentatious living, on sins of temper, or of speech, or religious carelessness, and inconsistencies. The interference is resented as though it were unwarranted; when, in fact, all who enter a church, implicitly declare their readiness to receive with deference the

warnings and advice of those whom the church appoints to "*watch*" for the souls of its members.

(3) There should also be a willingness to act with the church cordially and earnestly in whatever plans for evangelistic usefulness or the culture of the religious life, may be recommended by its official representatives. If the pastor and elders request a man to engage in any particular Christian work, there should be very strong reasons to justify refusal; and if, in their judgment, another man is not qualified for work in which he is already engaged, the cases are very rare in which he should consider himself at liberty to continue in it.

In ordinary times, however, the restraints of government will be hardly felt; it is when the church is exposed to peril, that confidence in its rulers and loyalty to their authority, are most necessary.

While honouring the living we are called upon to remember the dead (v. 7).

Among the former leaders of the churches of Palestine, were men who had suffered grievous persecution and death itself in the service of Christ; and every church that has had a history at all, can look back upon examples of lofty saintliness among its pastors and elders. Their memory is a priceless inheritance —rebuking degeneracy, elevating the ideal of Christian holiness, encouraging the endeavour to please God perfectly. Their "patient continuance in well doing," their endurance to the end, their testimony when the shadows of death were upon them to the fidelity of Christ and the sufficiency of His grace, make the heart ashamed of its distrust in God, its weariness in religious work.

The honour paid to their memory will stimulate their successors to imitate their excellence, and will quicken and cherish in many hearts, a yearning for the labours and responsibilities in which their devoutness and zeal were illustrated; and thus the holy succession will be perpetuated.

CONCLUSION.

"Now the God of peace," &c.—HEBREWS xiii, 20-24.

THE warnings, entreaties, arguments, and precepts of this Epistle, are solemnly and devoutly closed, by the invocation of the Divine blessing on those to whom it is addressed. It is when we have striven most earnestly to warn men against dangerous error or grievous sin, that we feel most deeply that our persuasions and appeals will be ineffective unless our brethren are taught, and kept, and strengthened by the Holy Ghost; but the depth of our own solicitude for their salvation inspires us with a firm faith that God will not be indifferent to it. Hence, we never pray for others so fervently or so hopefully as when we have done our best to instruct and to impress them; unless indeed we see that they have already resisted and vanquished every truth and every motive we have urged upon them; in that case, though our failure may drive us to cry to God with more impassioned earnestness, our cry is too commonly the cry of despair.

But there is nothing like despair in the noble benediction we have to consider this morning; and, remembering the moral weakness of the Jewish believers against which the writer has been struggling all through the Epistle, and the thickening perils by which they were threatened, there is something wonderful in the breadth and fulness of his prayer for them. Their own fainting courage must have been re-animated when they discovered that one, who knew their sin so thoroughly, and had warned them so sternly, could pray that God would make them *"perfect in every good work to do His will."* Though they had almost drifted into apostasy, the highest holiness was still within their reach.

God is spoken of as the "*God of peace.*" No description could be more welcome. The Jewish Church was surrounded by an excited and disorganized nation. Wild hopes and fears were disturbing every heart. No one could tell how soon the hatred of the people for their Roman rulers would burst into revolt, and cover the land with flames and blood. Those who yielded to the current of sedition knew that they were committed to desperate courses, and that years of terror and tumult were before them; for those who resisted, there would be the hatred, contempt, and suspicion which always come upon men who, in times of revolution, are supposed to be faithless to the cause of their country. There was no peace for any soul in that unhappy nation and age, except the peace which the world cannot give. The "time of trouble" had come; but the God of the ancient saints was theirs; and like their great ancestor they might exclaim, "Oh how great is Thy goodness which Thou hast laid up for them that fear Thee; Thou shalt hide them in the secret of Thy presence from the pride of man; Thou shalt keep them secretly from the pride of tongues." God was still the "*God of peace.*"

Nor was it merely tranquillity in the midst of outward agitation that God might be expected to confer. The vacillating loyalty of the Jewish Christians to the Lord Jesus had brought interior trouble. They had been living, no doubt, a restless and unhappy life. Dissatisfaction and self-reproach are always the penalty of yielding to temptation: in God it was still possible for them to find "*peace.*"

There was another reason, perhaps, why God is thus described. The threatenings which occupy so large a space in this Epistle were necessary to startle and alarm, and to make the heart afraid to sin; but the duties and difficulties of God's service cannot be met, unless the love of God and trust in His mercy are blended with the fear of His anger. I may shrink from daring transgressions, because God is a "consuming fire;" but this awful truth will never enable me to obey Him lovingly and cheerfully. The assurance that there is no enmity in God towards me is indispensable, not only to my happiness, but to the success of my endeavours to please Him. It is when the storm has gone by and the happy sunlight of the Divine love rests on the soul, that holy affections blossom into beauty and ripen into fruit. And so, Paul, when writing to the Thessalonians, says, "The very *God of peace* sanctify you wholly," and the writer of this Epistle, "*The God of peace make you perfect.*"

The interpretation of the last clause of v. 20 is involved in considerable difficulty. Is it meant that God "*raised*" Christ "*from the dead*" because His resurrection was secured by "*the everlasting covenant,*" which His death had sealed and consummated?—or, that when Christ rose, "*the blood of the covenant*" was upon Him, as the blood of the sacrifices was on the hands of the High Priest when he entered into the Holy of Holies?—or, that Christ's voluntary submission to cruel sufferings and a shameful death for the salvation of mankind, distinguishes Him from all other pastors and teachers, and that it is by virtue of this, that He is the "*Great Shepherd of the sheep?*" There are many reasons which incline me to the last interpretation. Reference has been made to former church rulers, who were to be remembered with affectionate veneration, and whose fidelity to Christ was to be imitated; and to living church rulers who were to be obeyed, "for they watch for your souls;" and now, the writer turns to "*that great Shepherd,*"—great because He laid down His life for the sheep, and because His blood has sealed the everlasting covenant between God and man.

Having raised from the dead Him who "hath purchased" the church "with His own blood," God will listen to us, when we pray that the Church may be perfected in every good work.

"A glorious prayer it is," writes John Owen, "including the whole mystery of Divine grace in its original, and the way of its communication by Jesus Christ. He prays that the fruit and benefit of all that he had before instructed them in, might be applied to them. For the substance of the whole doctrinal part of the Epistle is included in it."[*]

It would, indeed, be easy to develope, from this passage, all

---

[*] Owen on the Epistle to the Hebrews *in loc.*

the characteristic truths and facts of the Christian system,—the mercy of God, the atonement of the Lord Jesus Christ, the sanctification and final glory of all who believe in Him. But the specific blessings sought in the prayer deserve our most serious and earnest consideration.

I.

The writer prays that God would "*make*" the Jewish Christians "*perfect in every good work to do His will.*" The word translated "*perfect*" in this and some other places in the New Testament, is sometimes, and, perhaps, most accurately, used to denote the repairing and putting in order of what has been injured or broken,—the mending of nets, for instance, and the re-setting of a fractured limb. It occurs in the Epistle to the Galatians, where it is said, " If a man be overtaken in a fault ye who are spiritual *restore* such an one in the spirit of meekness, considering thyself lest thou also be tempted."

From this Epistle we have seen reason to infer, that many of the Jewish Christians had sunk into a condition in which it was impossible for them, without passing through a great change, to do the will of God. Their thoughts about their ancient faith and about the Lord Jesus Christ needed re-adjustment. Human passions and spiritual affections were not rightly balanced. Their loyalty to Christ was overborne by their natural sympathy with the patriotic enthusiasm of their countrymen, and by their natural veneration for the institutions and traditions of their fathers. Their dread of present shame and suffering had greater influence than their faith in the Divine promises. The merciful and mighty interference of the Holy Ghost was needed to restore order and harmony, to suppress and subdue the passions which had usurped undue power, and to strengthen principles and convictions which had become too feeble.

Just as a machine which has got out of order must be set right, before it can work easily and well; just as a ship must be equipped and fitted up, before it can safely commence its voyage; so it was necessary that these Jewish Christians should have their whole nature re-organized before their Christian life could be vigorous or happy. The prayer is, that the re-organization should be such as would make them ready for "*every good work*,"—for the courageous confession of Christ, for the patient endurance of suffering, for worship, for all moral excellence, for brotherly love, for submission to their church rulers, for whatever duty the law of Christ, and the perilous times in which they lived, might impose on them.

This is a prayer which we should offer for ourselves, and offer with confidence in God's willingness to listen to us. If we are to be made ready, or perfectly equipped, for a holy life, we must receive from God a large and rich variety of blessings. Our habits of thought, perhaps, must be greatly modified. There is no necessity that we should receive clearer light on the transitory character of those ritualistic institutions which exerted a fatal power over the hearts of the Jewish Christians; but we may need clearer light on the transitory character of all earthly things, a brighter vision of the eternal world, a more vivid apprehension of the reality of the Divine anger and the Divine approbation, of the rapid approach of death and judgment, of the glory and terror which lie beyond.

It may not be necessary that love for our country should be subordinated to our love of Christ; but there may be great need that the love of money, of pleasure, of ease, should be diminished. It may be necessary that our feeling about the relative importance of different pursuits should be modified; that the distribution of our time should be changed; that our whole life should be reconstructed.

We may be ready for *some* good works; but what is required is that we should be ready for "*every good work;*" for personal service as well as generous giving, for generous giving as well as personal service; for devout worship as well as zealous activity, for zealous activity as well as devout worship; for spiritual earnestness as well as common human virtues, for common human virtues as well as spiritual earnestness.

You would not say that a child, deaf or dumb, was "perfected" for all the activities and exigencies of human life, whatever might be the clearness of its eyesight; or that its physical strength rendered intellectual imbecility no practical evil. Every limb must be vigorous, every organ of sense sound, every intellectual faculty active, or the child is more or less unprepared for the world into which it has come, and the life it has to live. And we ought to pray that God would "*perfect*" us "*for every good work.*"

II.

The prayer is completed by the clause "*working in you that which is well pleasing in His sight.*" This looks as much like Paul's handwriting as any phrase in the Epistle. Not only does the thought belong to that class of truths on which it was his habit to insist most strongly, but the *manner* is exactly his. The writer catches at the word he has just used, "*to do* His will," and adds, "*doing in you* that which is well pleasing in His sight." Your work, after all, is to be God's work. He must re-fit and re-organise your whole life, and then must continue to act in you and through you to the end of your days. This is very like, "Work out your own salvation—for it is God who worketh in you to will and to do of His good pleasure;" very like, "It is not I that live, but Christ that liveth in me;" very like, "Ye are God's workmanship, created in Christ Jesus unto good works."

Nor is there any real contradiction between those awful warnings against the consequences of apostasy from Christ which make this Epistle the most terrible, perhaps, of all the books of the New Testament, and the impassioned, triumphant, exulting testimonies to the steadfastness of the Divine love, and the power of the Divine grace, which are so prominent in St. Paul's writings. All these testimonies rest on the supposition that, as a matter of fact, Faith in God continues, not that it *must;* all these warnings, on the supposition that it has ceased. When St. Paul exclaims, "Who shall separate us from the love of Christ?" he defies tribulation to do it, and distress, and persecution, and famine, and nakedness, and peril, and sword; but he does not say that a man may not separate himself, by wilful and persevering apostasy. While I continue to rely on the mercy of Christ and endeavour to keep His commandments, every gracious promise the lips of God have spoken, is mine; every act of love His hands have wrought illustrates the greatness of the power and the wealth of the goodness on which I may rely. But if I am hesitating whether to remain a Christian or not, there is not a single sentence in Holy Scripture that tells me I have lost the power of choice, and am no longer able to resist the authority and reject the mercy of Christ. If I have already apostatised, there is not a solitary syllable which justifies the hope that because I once repented of my sin and once believed the Gospel, I may dismiss all fear of the judgment-seat and of eternal death. Paul kept his body under lest he should prove "a castaway." Peter declares that "the end" of the apostate "is worse than the beginning;" the writer of this Epistle asks, "How shall *we* escape—we Christian men—if we neglect so great salvation?"

But with those who are in Christ there is an "everlasting covenant"—a covenant which God will never desire to break.

His love is changeless. His power fainteth not, wearieth not, through all the ages of His eternal existence. Had He saved us reluctantly, we might fear that He would repent. Had He yielded to the impulses of His mercy without vindicating the honour of His moral government, we might fear lest in some appalling crisis of the history of the moral universe He might feel constrained to strip us of our splendours and drive us from our bliss. But it was His eternal purpose that we should "have redemption through the blood of Christ," and that purpose shall never be revoked. In saving the human race, He has revealed the riches of His wisdom, as well as the riches of His grace; His infinite pity for His sinful and suffering creatures, and His steadfast fidelity to the Moral Law. And "I am persuaded that neither death, nor life, nor angels, nor principalities, nor powers, nor things present, nor things to come, nor height, nor depth, nor any other creature, shall be able to separate us from the love of God which is in Christ Jesus our Lord."

Amen and Amen.

NOTES.

THE ARGUMENT OF THE EPISTLE. "*The comparison between evangelical Christianity and legal Judaism turns on two principal points—the relative dignity of the Persons who represent the two dispensations as Mediators between God and the world, and the nature of the results or benefits secured by the one and by the other.*" Reuss: *Histoire de la Théologie Chrétienne.*—Tom. II, 270.

NOTES.

Cap. I.

v. 1. *Sundry times—divers manners:* pp. 13-14.

By the prophets: the form of expression indicates that the Divine Spirit was "*in* the prophets;" they were more than mere messengers. The reference is to all who had received Divine revelations to communicate to the Jewish people—Moses among the rest. It was not the principal function of prophets to predict future events, but to make known the thought and will of God to men. In former times God revealed Himself through the teaching of prophets; now "*in these last days*" He has revealed Himself through the Son.

2. *In these last days;* rather "at the end of these days." The writer elsewhere (ix, 26,) speaks of Christ as having been manifested at the end of the world "to put away sin." The earthly life of Christ closed one great period in the history of the human race, and introduced another. When He ascended into heaven and was made "Prince and Saviour," the kingdom of God was established on earth—that kingdom for which devout men had been so long waiting, and which is, therefore, sometimes described as "the world to come." But there were vast numbers of men who did not enter into that kingdom, but remained in "that present world with all its evil," from which Christ came to deliver them; so that to the Christian of Apostolic times it seemed that he was living in two conflicting "ages;" the old "world" still lingered on undestroyed and its "last days" were not over; and yet that which had been spoken of as "the world to come" had actually come, and Christian men had risen with Christ and entered into the kingdom of heaven.

hath—spoken: The completeness of the revelation made by Christ is more emphatically marked by retaining the tense which the writer uses:—"God having spoken . . . . in times past to the fathers by the prophets, at the end of these days *spake* to us by [His] Son."

[His] Son. There is neither article nor pronoun before "Son." The absence of both, when taken with the emphatic position of the word, shows that the writer was thinking not so much of a person who stood in a certain relationship to God as of the relationship itself. The thought would be fairly represented if we translated "God spake to us by One who sustains to Him the relationship of Son."

hath appointed suggests that the appointment was made at a definite time, and perhaps after Christ's earthly history was over. The true rendering is "appointed" referring to an eternal determination.

heir of all things—pp. 10-17.

made the worlds—p. 15.

3. See a remarkable description of wisdom, contained in *Wisdom of Solomon*, cap. vii, 25, 26. "She is the breath of the power of God, and a pure influence flowing from the glory of the Almighty . . . . the brightness of the everlasting light, the unspotted mirror of the power of God, and the image of His goodness."

Brightness of His glory—p. 14.

Express image of His person: Christ is the visible form of the very Being of God.

by Himself: omit.

vv. 4—14. On the general interpretation of these verses and the quotations from the Old Testament, see pp. 25-29.

4. *being made:* having become.

by inheritance: p. 26.

5. *This day have I begotten thee:* The *I* is emphatic.

6. *And again, when He bringeth,* etc. Ebrard's translation seems best to meet the grammatical difficulties of this verse, without involving the grave difficulties of another kind suggested by the more obvious rendering ("When He again hath introduced the first-begotten, &c.") Ebrard, translating freely, reads, "But again He says of the time when He shall introduce the first-begotten into the sphere of the earth."

6. *Who maketh His angels:* etc. There is very much to be said for reading: "Who maketh His angels winds, and

His ministers a flame of fire," *i.e.*, He causes His messengers to act in or by means of the winds, and commissions them to assume the agency or form of flames for His purposes. That the angels are commissioned to use the forces of nature in God's service suggests how inferior they are to the Son, of whom it is said (v. 10.) that He *created* all things. The LXX which is quoted here is absolutely in favour of this rendering. The Hebrew may be fairly pleaded—though not with absolute confidence—for the view taken on pp. 27-28, which is also supported by the context of the passage as it stands in Ps. civ.

10. *hast laid*:—didst lay. In the Authorized Version the Greek aorist is very frequently represented by the English perfect. In some passages the idiom of our language makes this almost necessary; in very many it makes no difference in the sense; only where the more exact translation seems to bring out the author's meaning more accurately or more sharply, will attention be called to the true tense.

14. *who shall inherit*: who are about to inherit.

Cap. II.

1. *let them slip*: or, be floated past them.

2. *was steadfast:* became binding—as spoken by such authoritative Divine messengers.

3. *if we neglect:* having neglected : *i.e.*, How shall we escape God's judgment at last if we have neglected, &c.

was confirmed: recalls the adjective, translated "steadfast," v. 2, and suggests a ratification of the gospel somewhat corresponding to that there predicated of the law.

4. *God also bearing [them] witness:—i.e.* bearing witness to the great salvation. God Himself "by signs and wonders, &c.," bore witness with those who "heard."

gifts of the Holy Ghost: distributions of the Holy Ghost. The Holy Ghost was given or distributed in various measures and for various ends to those who received the great salvation.

5. *For unto the angels*, etc. : "For not unto angels did He put in subjection, &c.," *i.e.*, in His original idea and purpose.

the world to come: p. 46.

6. *One in a certain place testified*, etc: suggesting that the writer quoted from the Old Testament memoriter.

7. *Thou madest him*, etc. : p. 48.

8. *We see not yet*, etc. : p. 51.

9. *But we see Jesus*, etc. Alford translates " But Him that is made a little lower than the angels, even Jesus, we behold on account of His suffering of death, crowned with glory and honour, in order that He, by the grace of God, should taste death for every man:"—explaining the thought thus, " On the triumphant issue of His sufferings their efficacy depends."

10 *to make* .... *perfect:* pp. 58 and 62.

11. *all of one.* p. 61.

12. It is hard to see that the words quoted in this verse and the next had any prophetic reference : the writer uses them freely, as we use Shakespeare and Milton. Perhaps he shrank from putting his own words into the mouth of Christ, and yet felt that his argument would gain great force by being thrown into this dramatic form.

14. *through death*, etc. p. 72.

16. For *verily He took not on Him :* " For verily it is not angels that He helpeth."

Cap III.

1. *Holy brethren*, etc. p 74.

of our profession : Him whom we Christians confess to be the great Apostle of God and our High Priest. p 75.

2. *appointed.* I see no adequate reason for reading "made" or "created:" the introduction of the idea of creation violates the consistency of the metaphor. That "appointed" is a legitimate rendering of the word I hold to be shown by Mark iii, 13.

2. *His house: i.e.,* " *God's* household." p. 75.

3. *man* is supplied by the translators.
builded : "established" or "founded." So in v. 4.

5. *for testimony*, etc. : p. 76.

6. *rejoicing of the hope:* that object of hope in which we boast or glory.

unto the end: omit.

9. *when your fathers:* "where your fathers."

saw my works: meaning perhaps, God's penal judgments.

10. *that generation:* "this generation."

14. *For we are made partakers:* "for we have become partakers."

16. *For some, when they had heard,* etc.: "For who—having heard—perished? Was it not all that came out of Egypt by the help of Moses?" The whole nation rebelled against God: an awful warning.

18. *believed not:* "obeyed not."

Cap. IV.

1. p. 81.

2. *For unto us was the gospel preached,* etc.: "For unto us have good tidings been announced, etc."

the word preached: "the word heard."

not being mixed with faith: this is a clause of extraordinary difficulty. The Authorized Version represents a reading which is not supported by any adequate authority. The best reading seems to require a translation of this kind: "the word .... did not profit them, as they were not mingled by faith with those who heard it." The idea seems to be that the word of God is not really heard by those who do not receive it with faith, and that the people in the wilderness were not one with those whose hearts were really open to the Divine promises.

3. *enter into rest:* "are entering into the rest," *i.e.,* the rest already spoken of.

as He said: "as He hath said."

although the works, etc. p. 82.

4. *For He spake:* "For He hath spoken."

6. *those to whom it was first preached:* "those to whom the good tidings were formerly announced."

7. On the quotation and argument see p. 82.

after so long a time: the time between Joshua and David.

8. *Jesus:* "Joshua."

9. *There remaineth therefore:* "There still remains therefore a sabbath-keeping for the people of God."

10. *the rest: i.e.,* God's rest.

as God did from His: "as God did from His own." The meaning of the verse seems to be:—No one entered into the rest of God by entering into Canaan; he who has entered into God's rest has rested from his works as God rested from His own; and this could not be said of the ancient Jews.

vv. 12-13. p. 87.

vv. 14-16. pp. 88-96.

Cap. V.

vv. 1-3. p. 99.

4. *but he that is called*, etc: "but only when called of God."

5. p. 101.

7. pp. 104-106.

9. *being made perfect.* See cap. ii. 10.

10. *Called of God*, etc., *i.e.,* Christ is addressed by God as a High Priest after the order of Melchisedec. The word translated "called" here, is not the same as that in v. 4 ("*called* of God as was Aaron:") in that verse the writer is referring to the original appointment of any one to the priesthood: in this verse he represents God as recognizing Christ as being already a Priest, and addressing Him as such.

11. *hard to be uttered:* he had much to say about Melchisedec, and what he had to say it was difficult to make clear because those to whom he was writing had become "dull of hearing."

vv. 12-14. pp. 110-115.

Cap. VI.

vv. 1-6. pp. 116-123.

v. 3. *," God permit:* so far as it is possible to carry you with me into the higher regions of knowledge we will advance together; but it must be through the merciful help of God; He alone can help you.

v. 6. *if they shall fall away:* "and have fallen away."

7. *the earth:* the land.

herbs: specially referring to such crops as grass or corn.

by whom: for whom.

9, 10. pp. 124-129.

Ebrard has the following striking comment on v. 10 :—" The truth is, there is another righteousness besides that which *recompenses* or *rewards*. The righteousness of God spoken of in our passage is that which leads, guides, and governs every man according to the particular stage of development which he occupies. It is here affirmed of God that He does not give up to perdition a man *who can still in any way be saved*, in whom the new life is not yet entirely extinct, and who has not yet entirely fallen away; but that He seeks to draw every one as long as they will allow themselves to be drawn. This is not a judicial or recompensing righteousness towards man (for man has no right to *demand* the assisting grace of God as a thing deserved), but it is *the righteousness of the Father towards the Son Who has bought men with His blood, and to Whom we poor sinners still belong until we have fallen away from Him*. Not towards us, but towards Christ, would the Father be 'unjust' were He to withdraw His gracious assistance from a man ere he has ceased to belong to the *peculium* of Christ." Calvin, however, is nearer the thought of the writer when he says: "God is righteous in recompensing works because He is true and faithful: and He has made Himself a debtor to us, not by receiving anything from us, but as Augustine says, by freely promising all things."

vv. 11, 12. pp. 129, 130.

vv. 13-20. pp. 131, 132.

Cap. VII.

Having already affirmed (Cap. v. 6-10) that the Christ according to Old Testament prophecy is a Priest after the order of Melchisedec, he proceeds—not to prove this—but to show what is involved in it. The train of thought in this chapter is tolerably clear. First, it is shown in vv. 1-10, that Melchisedec's priesthood was of a higher order than the Levitical; then, in vv. 11—19, that since the Levitical priesthood was to give place to the Melchisedec priesthood in the person of the Messiah, the Levitical priests could not have fulfilled the idea of a priesthood; in vv. 20-28 the superiority of Christ's priesthood to the Levitical is developed in several particulars.

vv. 1-10.   pp. 138-143.

v. 4. *unto whom even the patriarch Abraham*, etc. It is difficult to represent the double emphasis in this sentence; Alford renders, " unto whom Abraham, even the *patriarch*, paid tithes from the best of the spoil ;" but this does not bring out the emphasis with which the writer reminds his readers that even Abraham paid *tithes* to Melchisedec—an act involving a recognition of Melchisedec's priesthood.

5. *They that are of the sons of Levi who receive the priesthood*, etc. The writer does not mean to suggest—what is alleged to have been the fact—that only the priests, and not the rest of the Levites, received tithes ; but as he is discussing the relative dignity of two contrasted priesthoods he naturally fixes attention on " those of the sons of Aaron " who became priests.

6. *He whose descent is not reckoned:* the " not " is very emphatic; it means that to reckon Melchisedec in the line of the Levitical priesthood is from the nature of the case impossible.

8. *Here indeed:* " in this case ;" *i.e.* in the case of the Levitical priests.

but there: " in that case ;" *i.e.* in the case of the ideal priest who is after the order of the Melchisedec.

9. *And as I may so say:* meaning that although Levi personally was not tithed, yet that he was involved in that inferiority of position which Abraham assumed in relation to

Melchisedec. Levi, "so to speak," or "as one might say," paid tithes, etc. The stream could not rise above the spring.

in Abraham: " through Abraham."

vv. 11-28. pp. 143-145.

v. 24. *hath an unchangeable priesthood:* "hath His priesthood unchangeable :" *i.e.* He holds it as an office which has not to pass from Him to successors.

v. 27. *daily:* "day after day"—not meaning " every day," but on one day of atonement after another.

CAP. VIII.

In this chapter and the two following chapters the writer shows that in the Jewish Scriptures, and in the very form of the institutions of Judaism, there were indications that the Mosaic Covenant and Ritual were imperfect and transitory, and that God always intended to establish a new and better covenant than that which had been established at Sinai.

(*a*) There were distinct *predictions of a new covenant;* the Law was to be written on the hearts of men instead of on tables of stone.   viii. 8—13.

(*b*) The *structure of the ancient Tabernacle* showed that man was not free to enter into the presence of God, ix. 1—8 ; but Christ, by a better sacrifice than could be offered by Jewish priests, has purged our consciences from dead works that we may enter into the very presence of the living God, ix. 9—28.

(*c*) The *constant repetition of the ancient sacrifices* suggested that they could not give the worshipper perfect freedom from his sin and perfect access to God ; and there was the definite prediction that the Messiah would come to " do the will of God," because God had no pleasure in " burnt offerings and sacrifices for sin."

The result is that we all have access to the holiest by the blood of Jesus.

vv. 1-4.   p. 153.

v. 1. *the sum:* " the principal thing." Ebrard says very felicitously that " key-stone " represents what the writer meant.

such a High Priest; i.e. such a one as is described in the words " who sat down on the right-hand, etc."

2. *true Tabernacle*, as contrasted with the mere shadow.

3. *this man;* "man" is supplied by the translators; perhaps it would have been better to supply "High-priest."

4. *For if He were, etc.* "If therefore He were on earth."

seeing that there are priests: "priests" is not found in the most ancient MSS.; *read* "seeing that there are those who offer the gifts according to the law."

5. *example:* "copy."

6. p. 164.

7. *For of that first covenant*, etc. "For if that first covenant were faultless, there would not place be sought for a second"—*Alford*.

8. p. 169.

9-13. p. 170.

11. *And they shall not teach, etc.* The negative is very strong; such teaching will be altogether out of the question because absolutely unnecessary.

Cap. IX.

vv. 1-5. pp. 172-185.

v. 1. *Then verily the first Covenant:* "The first [Covenant] therefore, had, etc.," referring back to Cap. viii. 5, in which it is said that Moses was directed to make all things according to the pattern shewed him in the mount.

a worldly sanctuary: "its sanctuary a worldly one," *i.e.* the sanctuary belonged to this world as contrasted with the heavenly sanctuary.

2. "*which is called the sanctuary:*" "which tabernacle is called the Holy Place."

3. *And after the second veil:* The conjunction has an adversative force "*but* after the second veil," the writer meaning to say—But the Holiest of all was not to be reached till after the second veil had been passed through.

4. *which had:* "having."

the golden censer: "a golden altar of incense."

the golden pot that had manna: "a golden pot containing the manna."

vv. 6-14.   pp. 186-214.

6. *Now when these things.* "Now these things being thus ordained"—the thought is renewed from v. 1. The first [covenant], therefore, had also ordinances of divine service and the worldly sanctuary . . . . "Now these things being thus ordained, etc."

went always: "enter always." Our translators have thrown into the past tense a series of verbs which the writer has given in the present tense. Ebrard, explaining the writer's transition from the historical tense in the first verse to the present tense in vv. 6, 7, says "in the description of the construction of the sanctuary, the author, for a very intelligible reason, has not had in view the Herodian temple, but has adhered to the description given in the Pentateuch of the original sanctuary, the tabernacle; here, however, when he speaks of the acts of worship, he describes them, with equal reason, *as still continuing;* for the acts had remained the same, and also the distinction between the Holy Place and the Holy of Holies, changed only in its outward form, had been maintained unaltered in the temples of Solomon, Zerubbabel, and Herod."
The temple worship was still in existence when the epistle was written, and, therefore, the writer described the acts of that worship in the present tense. The "very intelligible reason" for which the writer used the past tense in v. 1, it would have been well for Ebrard to explain. The most obvious explanation seems to be that the writer's line of argument required him to speak of the "first *covenant;*" but *that*, in his judgment, had passed away; he therefore says it "*had* . . . . the worldly sanctuary;" but as that sanctuary was still in existence when he wrote, and as the old rites were still maintained, he passed naturally enough into the present tense in v. 6.

7. *went:* "went" is supplied from the previous verse. If any word is necessary it should be "enters."

offered: "offers."

errors: i.e., sins of ignorance.

x

8. *was not yet made manifest, etc.*: "has not yet been made manifest while the first tabernacle [*i.e.*, the outer chamber, spoken of v. 2] is yet standing."

9. *Which was a figure*, etc.: the "was" is inaccurately supplied by the translators. The meaning is that for the time during which the tabernacle stands, the existence of the "first tabernacle," divided by the veil from the "holy of holies," remains a figure in parable teaching that the Levitical sacrifices have not been able to secure for man free access to God.

in which: "according to which;" the sacrifices were in harmony with the parabolical character of the sanctuary itself.

that could not make, etc.: having no power to perfect, in relation to the conscience, the person offering the service.

10. *Which stood*: "consisting."

vv. 11, 12.   p. 208.

vv. 13, 14.   pp. 209-212.

vv. 15-23.   pp. 216-220.

22. *And almost all, etc.*: "it is almost true that all things are by the law, etc."

23. *patterns of things*: "the copies *or* figures of things."

vv. 24-x. 18.   pp. 221-230.

24. *is not entered*: "entered not."

to appear: a forensic term.

25. *should offer*: "may offer."

26. *hath He appeared*: hath He been manifested.

27. *And as it is appointed, etc.*: "And inasmuch as it is appointed to men to die once."

28. *So Christ, etc.*: "So also the Christ having been offered once, to bear the sins of many, shall be seen a second time, without sin, of those who are waiting for Him, unto salvation."

without sin: in contrast to the time when He appeared "to bear the sins of many."

Cap. X.

v. 1. *The very image,* etc. "The very image" of the good things to come was shown to Moses in the Mount; the Law had only a representation of what was itself a representation of these things; it had nothing but a "shadow" of them.

can never, etc. The emphasis of this part of the sentence is thrown on the phrase translated "year by year." Alford translates, "can never year by year, with the same sacrifices which they offer continually, make perfect them that draw near."— "Year by year (the author here . . . . has evidently chiefly in his mind the yearly sacrifice of atonement) the *Law* remained incapable of making the comers thereunto perfect by its sacrifices."—Ebrard.

2. *conscience:* "consciousness."

vv. 5-9. On the quotation see pp. 222-225.

5. *hast Thou prepared:* "didst Thou prepare."

7. *I come:* "I am come."

8. *When He said:* "When He saith."

which are offered: "such as are offered."

10. *By which will,* etc. "In which will [*i.e.,* the will of God which Christ came to do] we have been sanctified once for all [*i.e.,* so purged from sin that we can draw near to God] through the offering of the body of Christ." The position of the word represented by "once for all" is peculiar; it almost seems to belong both to the "sanctification" and the "offering."

11. *which can never:* "such as can never."

12. *But this man,* etc. "But He, having offered one sacrifice for sins, sat down for ever on the right hand of God." The Jewish priests *stand* day after day offering sacrifices.

14. *them that are sanctified.* "Those who are from time to time the subjects of His consecrating (justifying) grace." —Webster and Wilkinson.

vv. 16, 17. On the quotations see pp. 225-227.

vv. 19-39. pp. 232-241.

20. *a new and living way:* a way which was new, not only as being a way now opened for the first time, but as being a way which would never become old, worn, and obsolete.

21. *a high priest:* "a great Priest."

23. *profession of our faith:* "profession of our hope."

25. *manner:* it had then become the "habit" of many to neglect the meetings of the Church.

26. *there remaineth,* etc.: "for sins there remaineth no longer a sacrifice:"—the emphasis is on "sacrifice;" the old sacrifices had lost their Divine sanction; if the sacrifice of Christ was rejected, no other sacrifice remained.

27. *"fiery indignation:"* "an indignation of fire;" *i.e.*, there remaineth a certain fearful looking for of judgment, and [there remaineth] an indignation of fire.

28. *He that despised,* etc. "For a man having despised Moses' law dieth without mercy," etc.

29. *Of how much sorer,* etc. "Of how much sorer punishment, suppose ye, shall he be found worthy, who trampled under foot the Son of God, and accounted common the blood of the covenant wherewith he was sanctified, and insulted the Spirit of grace."—Alford.

32. *in which after ye were illuminated:* "in which when [just] enlightened."

34. *For ye had compassion on me,* etc.: the reading on which this translation rests is rejected by all the principal modern editors of the Greek Text:—"For ye both had compassion on those who were in bonds, and the spoiling of your goods ye took joyfully,—knowing yourselves to have a better and an enduring substance."

35. *which hath great recompense:* "which" is something more than the ordinary relative; we might almost read, "Cast not away your confidence—a confidence which hath great recompense of reward."

36. *patience:* here as in so many other places in the New Testament, "endurance."

37. *For yet a little while,* etc. "For yet a very little time, and He that is coming will come, etc."

38. *Now the just shall live,* etc.   MSS. of very high authority read, "But my just man shall live by faith." Our translation obscures the warning contained in the latter half of the verse; instead of reading "but if *any man* draw back," it should read, and if he draw back—*i.e.,* if the just man already spoken of, instead of securing eternal life by enduring faith in God, loses his faith and apostatises—"my soul hath no pleasure in him."

39. *them that draw back :* the writer uses the abstract noun corresponding to the verb "draw back" in the previous verse. Alford translates, "we are not of back-sliding ;" but this is not very felicitous and conceals the verbal reference to the previous verse.   It is, perhaps, impossible to render the phrase except by some such periphrasis as that adopted in the Authorised Version.

Cap. XI.

xi. 1-xii. 3. pp. 242-254.

1. p. 243.

2. *By it the elders,* etc. "Faith was that element of their spiritual life *wherein* consisted the high character which they bore in the sight of God."—Webster and Wilkinson.

3. *We understand :* we apprehend.

4. p. 244.

5. *God had translated :* "God translated."

6. *is a rewarder :* "becomes [or 'proves to be'] a rewarder."

7. *moved with fear :* "taking wise forethought."

8. *By faith Abraham,* etc. "By faith Abraham when called. obeyed, in going out into a place which he was afterwards to receive for an inheritance ; and he went out not knowing whither he was going."—Alford.

10. *For he looked for a city,* etc. "For he was looking for

the city which hath the foundations, whose designer and builder is God."

13. *These all died in faith*, etc. : " In faith these all died, not having received the promises, but having seen them afar off, and hailed them with joy, and confessed that they were strangers and sojourners in the land :" *i.e.*, even in that land of promise which was to be theirs but which they died without possessing as their own. The words " were persuaded of them," are not in the best MSS.

14. *a country*—this hardly represents what is intended : it is not *any* country that the writer means, but a true home and fatherland.

16. *But now they desire*, etc   The " now " is, of course, not the adverb of time but the argumentative " now."

God is not ashamed, etc. He permits Himself to be called "the God of Abraham, Isaac, and Jacob."

17. *offered up :* " has offered up ;" the great act of Abraham's faith exerts to the present time its influence not only over the moral nature of all who are stimulated by it to manifest the same confidence in God, but over the course of the Divine administration of the world. Abraham's act had its place in the development of God's merciful purposes in relation to mankind.

received : the word means that Abraham had actively embraced the promises : they had not only been given to him, but by his faith he had appropriated them, and yet he offered up Isaac.

the only-begotten : the emphasis is thrown on this description of Isaac.

19. *Accounting that God was able*, etc. " Accounting that God is able to raise from the dead."

" *in a figure :*" " he received him back as a symbol." " The author shews that that remaining alive of Isaac, that deliverance from the danger of death, was a symbol or type of the resurrection of Christ."—Ebrard.

21. *worshipped, leaning upon the top of his staff.* In the Hebrew (Gen. xlvii. 31,) the words read as translated in the

Authorised Version. "And Israel bowed himself upon the bed's head." The LXX. reads, "upon the top of his staff;" and the writer quotes this reading, with which his readers would be familiar, and which would recall to them the whole passage. The grotesque idea that Jacob worshipped the top of his staff, is sanctioned neither by the Hebrew, the LXX., nor by the quotation in this Epistle; he leant on the top of his staff while he worshipped.

23. *they saw he was a proper child:* "they saw that the child was comely."—Alford.

26. *the reproach of Christ:* "the reproach of the Christ," who was always the great object of Jewish hope.

he had respect unto the recompense, etc.: "he was looking away [*i.e.* from the treasures of Egypt] unto the recompense," etc.

28. *He kept:* It is doubtful whether either here or in v. 17, it would be in harmony with our English idiom to adhere to the perfect tense, which is used in both places by the writer; but here, as well as there, something is lost by changing the perfect into the simple historical tense. What the writer says is that by faith Moses "*hath kept* the passover"; he is vividly conscious that the keeping of the passover was not an isolated event in a remote age; it had an enduring value and significance. Moses might have hesitated, and then the history of the Jewish race would have been different; but he *has kept* it; and from that act of his, results have come which are still affecting the condition not of the Jews alone, but of all mankind.

31. *with them that believed not:* "with the disobedient."

35. *a better resurrection:* *i.e.* than that spoken of in the first clause of the verse, in which women are said to have "received their dead raised to life again" in this world.

vv. 39, 40. pp 251-253.

Cap. XII.

1. *witnesses:* not merely spectators, p. 253.

the sin which doth so easily beset us: not a particular "besetting sin," but "sin which clings about us."

patience: "endurance."

2. *Looking unto Jesus:* the word denotes "the looking away from the nearest object upon which we unconsciously look, to an object upon which the eye is consciously fastened."—Ebrard.

Author and Finisher of our faith: "Leader and perfecter of faith." p. 245.

3. *lest ye be wearied and faint, etc.:* "that ye be not wearied, fainting in your souls."—Alford. The first word "denotes the state of being passively wearied and *unable* to do anything more;" the second denotes the being relaxed and careless as a culpable condition and the cause of the weariness.

vv. 4-11. See pp. 255-263.

4. See page 255.

5. *ye have forgotten:* "ye have quite forgotten."—Alford.
children: "sons."

7. *If ye endure chastening, etc.* There is a variation of reading here. Some of the modern editors of the Greek Text give a reading which may be freely translated, "it is for the purpose of chastisement that ye are enduring what you have to suffer."

8. *whereof all are partakers:* "of which all have become partakers."

9. *Furthermore we have had, etc.:* "Furthermore we once had the fathers of our flesh as chastisers."

10. *after their own pleasure: i.e.,* as it seemed good to them—at their discretion.

11. *which are exercised:* "which have been exercised."

vv. 12-29. See pp. 264-275.

13. *be turned out of the way.* There is considerable authority for interpreting this as meaning that unless straight or even paths are made, by the avoiding of everything that would cause others to stumble, feet already lame would become quite dislocated. Webster and Wilkinson have a very good note on the passage: "that the lame may not be turned quite away, but

may rather be healed; that the wavering may not be turned into other paths, but may be brought back and established in the faith. This is very condensed writing. It is not meant that making a path even would tend to heal the lame; or that bringing back is to be considered as healing; but, not only should even paths be made for the benefit of the lame, that they may not forsake them for others, but also, instead of such an unhappy result, the lame should be healed." Alford's note is also excellent: "If the whole congregation by their united and consistent walk, trod a plain and beaten path for men's feet, these lame ones though halting would be easily able to keep in it, . . . but if the tracks were errant and confused, their erratic steps would deviate more and more, till at length they fell away out of the right way altogether."

15. *Looking diligently, etc.*: "They are carefully to see (each one for himself, and also the one for the other . . .) that no one," etc. See p. 265.

17. *no place of repentance*. The fault was irrevocable; repentance could have no "place" or function; there is "place for repentance" when it is possible for repentance to avert the consequences of a crime.

vv. 22-24.   pp. 268-269.

vv. 25-29.   pp. 273-275.

Cap. XIII.

vv. 1-19.   pp. 276-288.

2. *have entertained:* "entertained."

4. *Marriage is honourable*, etc.   "Let marriage be honoured in all things; and let the bed be undefiled."

5. *He hath said*, etc.   "He" is emphatic—"He Himself hath said, etc."

7. *which have the rule over you:* rather "your rulers," for the exhortation indicates that the writer was thinking of the rulers of the Church who had passed away.

whose faith follow, etc.: "considering the end of their life*—

---

* "Life" in a moral sense, which is often represented in the Authorised Version by "conversation."

[*i.e.*, their faithful and glorious fidelity to Christ to the very last and, in some cases, their martyrdom]—imitate their faith."

8. *Jesus Christ the same*, etc. : " Jesus Christ is the same, etc."

9. *Be not carried about*, etc. " Be not carried away, etc." See pp. 278, 279.

12. p. 279.

13. p. 280.

14. *we seek one to come :* "we are seeking that which is to come."

18. p. 280.

20. p. 288.

21. p. 291

THE END.

www.ingramcontent.com/pod-product-compliance
Lightning Source LLC
Chambersburg PA
CBHW030755230426
43667CB00007B/978